Exercises in Instructional Design

Exercises in Instructional Design

Barbara Seels
University of Pittsburgh

Zita Glasgow

Merrill Publishing Company
A Bell & Howell Information Company
Columbus   Toronto   London   Melbourne

Published by Merrill Publishing Company
A Bell & Howell Information Company
Columbus, Ohio 43216

This book was set in Garamond

Administrative Editor: David Faherty
Production Editor: Ben Ko
Art Coordinator: Ruth A. Kimpel
Cover Designer: Russ Maselli

Library of Congress Catalog Card Number: 89–63047
International Standard Book Number: 0–675–20827–0
Printed in the United States of America
1 2 3 4 5 6 7 8 9—94 93 92 91 90

This book is dedicated to our mothers,
Reba Sleeth Billings
and
Frances Kochan Mussano

Preface

Instructional design is the process of solving instructional problems by systematic analysis of the conditions of learning. The competencies required for an instructional designer are a set of highly integrated behaviors involving extracting, analyzing, organizing, and synthesizing information. Because of the diversity of skills needed, instructional design usually involves team skills. Students of instructional design draw upon theory and knowledge from psychology, education, communications, and technology to develop their skills. The theoretical basis for instructional design is often abstract and confusing for the beginner. Our premise in writing this book is that the many theories and practices need to be integrated, or if in conflict, reconciled in a practical how-to book.

The development of qualified instructional designers is an evolutionary process that begins with formal education and continues for many years on the job. Graduates of instructional design courses enter a broad market. There are jobs for instructional designers in the training and development departments in health and industry settings, in faculty development or resource centers of educational institutions, and in instructional/training divisions in the civilian and military sectors of government. One purpose of *Exercises in Instructional Design* is to provide a set of exercises that requires students to apply design concepts and skills to job-related areas. However, this book is more than a series of exercises. It encompasses a philosophy of instructional design, research and practice, and theory on process.

The book is designed as a basic text for students entering the field. It is organized in a spiral fashion, moving from the general to the specific. Concepts are introduced at the most general level and refined and elaborated upon in subsequent chapters. The book may be used as a text or supplemental material in basic courses. Because it is organized in a logical sequence with exercises, it is suitable for independent study or external degree courses when used in conjunction with laboratory experiences. Also, it is suitable for short-term programs aimed at correcting or developing selective skills.

Exercises are of two types: (1) those that assess learning of the body of knowledge that constitutes instructional design at the verbal information level, and (2) those that assess the learning of intellectual skills required to apply instructional concepts and principles and solve instructional design problems. Exercises are embedded in the flow of the book, enabling students to do exercises as soon as they complete reading related conceptual material. Most of the exercises can be done by the individual student outside of class. Others are group exercises that can be assigned either as an outside project or a classroom exercise. The exercises provide opportunities to work on a much more realistic set of problems than most books offer. We made every attempt to develop exercises of sufficient complexity to challenge and motivate. It is anticipated that the instructor will provide feedback on exercises.

Students are expected to acquire the behaviors stated in the objective, but it is left to the instructor to specify the performance standard. Thus, the instructor has the flexibility to adjust to individual and group differences when evaluating performance.

Skills practice does not diminish the book's presentation of concepts. The book's 11 chapters are divided into two parts offering presentations of theory, research, and practice in the field. Part One presents an overview of roles in the field and competencies required for an accomplished instructional designer, the research and theoretical basis of the field, and instructional design models. Part Two progresses step-by-step through a systems approach. It contains extensive examples showing how each step is applied in a broad range of settings. The book can be used within the context of one course or over two or three courses. For example, in the first course students can complete Chapters 1 through 6, the profession and the analysis stage. In the second course students can complete Chapters 7 through 11, the design stage and the team approach. At the end of the first course, students can do an individual project; at the end of the second course, they can do a team project in the field.

In addition to the exercises, each chapter includes (1) study questions intended to orient students to concepts presented in the chapter, (2) a list of terms that students can define after reading the chapter, (3) questions to provoke discussions of controversial issues in the field or to help shed further light on complex concepts, and (4) references.

Part One contains five chapters. Chapter 1 introduces the student to instructional design as a profession. It defines instructional design as a process involving five basic steps: analysis, design, development, implementation, and evaluation. Several broad topics are covered, including how instructional design is defined, the types of jobs instructional designers occupy, and design competencies as defined by groups within the profession.

The goal of Chapter 2 is to teach that approaches to instructional design must be based on empirical evidence about learning rather than on personal preferences or intuition. Learning is defined, standards for evaluating research are set forth, and a framework is presented for examining research relevant to the design process. Theoretical positions are reviewed in light of how the positions influence the questions asked about learning and, in turn, of what the findings imply for prescribing instruction.

Chapter 3 introduces some of the best known instructional design models and demonstrates that they all incorporate the five steps introduced in Chapter 1. Different models are applicable to different situations; therefore, designers must usually adapt an existing model or develop one to suit their needs. This chapter introduces the model developed for this book. The chapter emphasizes the iterative nature of the design process and stresses that the analysis phase is critical to the success of subsequent steps.

Chapter 4 presents procedures for identifying a performance deficiency, determining whether instruction is the best solution, and writing a statement of the problem.

The basic skills and knowledge covered in Chapter 5 include the ability to define knowledge in terms of observable evidence of such knowledge, employ flowcharting and hierarchy construction techniques as tools for analyzing learning outcomes, and extract information about performance from a variety of sources.

Part Two contains six chapters. Chapter 6 presents a two-stage analysis: task analysis to define what the expert performer does, and instructional analysis to determine what the target audience already knows and what they must learn in order to achieve the desired outcomes.

Design activities are covered in Chapters 7 and 8. Both chapters elaborate and build upon the foundation established in earlier chapters. Chapter 7 continues the instruction on writing behavioral statements begun in Chapter 5. Chapter 8 emphasizes basing instructional decisions on empirical evidence and covers principles of learning derived from theory and research. Students are given the opportunity to devise strategies for learning that adhere to these principles.

Chapter 9 addresses both the design and development phases of a systems approach. On the design side, the chapter covers media options, including high-tech interactive media, and presents media selection models and procedures. On the development side, the chapter presents guidelines for maintaining the integrity of the design during production and packaging of the instructional materials.

Chapter 10 returns to the theme of collecting empirical evidence about what conditions lead to what learning outcomes. It covers formative evaluation and the use of tryout data to revise and refine instructional materials.

Chapter 11 introduces the team approach. It presents the skills necessary to achieve instructional design goals through teams and includes a section on how to summarize the team's work in a project report.

An epilogue offers an overview of the final steps in the Seels and Glasgow ID model. A reference for further reading supplements each step.

The first part of the epilogue describes activities essential for acceptance and implementation—that is, development of strategy to ensure the organization utilizes the finished product. The second part describes summative evaluation and how it differs from formative evaluation. Then the epilogue presents the stages of adoption and describes theory about diffusion of innovations. Project management, the first activity carried out on an instructional design effort, is presented last. In order to develop an effective project plan a person must have knowledge of the elements to be planned. The epilogue summarizes variables that affect how well a manager maintains professional standards within resource constraints.

In writing the book we assumed that the systematic approach is the theoretical force that allows findings from psychology and communications research to be applied to the design of instruction. Although this approach may be adjusted to reflect trends in research and practice, the basic approach remains an important tool for synthesizing guidelines from learning and communication theory. The order of steps may change and steps may be added or expanded, subtracted or reconceptualized, but a systematic approach to design remains vital.

ACKNOWLEDGMENTS

We are grateful to our editors at Merrill Publishing—Dave Faherty, who saw the project to completion, Ben Ko, our production editor, and Gail Burke, our copy editor.

Many colleagues have reviewed drafts and given valuable advice. We appreciate the suggestions and comments of the following reviewers: John Belland, Ohio State University; Barry Bratton, University of Iowa; Francis Dwyer, Pennsylvania State University; Barbara Grabowski, Syracuse University; Karen Medsker, Marymount University; Rita Richey, Wayne State University; and Mary Lou Routt, University of Kentucky.

Colleagues and students also contributed ideas to chapters. Don Ely helped place parts of Chapter 1 in perspective while Suzanne Lajoie and Maria Magone contributed examples for Chapter 1. Chantal Fourgeaud Cornuejols helped with the instructional analysis on French restaurant words. Tom Hillard, Vasiliki Vassilaros, Boo Ja Cox, and Jawaher Al-Shaheil assisted with the media selection model and resource guides in Chapter 9. Lou Berry made suggestions for Chapter 9, and Barbara Good wrote the script on NMR imaging.

Students in instructional design classes at the University of Pittsburgh patiently tried out the drafts of exercises. Sandi Behrens and Pam Brock helped correct them. In many instances, we drew on the models, procedures, and training developed for the U.S. Air Force and other government agencies by instructional designers at Applied Science Associates, Inc., Butler, PA.

We also appreciate the thoroughness of Marge Van Tassel, who did much of the word processing.

If we have overlooked a contribution, please be understanding. This textbook took several years to write. In fact, our families gave up vacations in support of the project. So to them, too, we are grateful.

Finally, the theory that is synthesized in the text was possible only because many professionals made contributions to the instructional design field over the past thirty years. We thank the researchers and practitioners who made this field and this text possible.

Barbara Seels

Zita Glasgow

Contents

Part One

Foundations of Instructional Design

Chapter One

The Instructional Design Profession

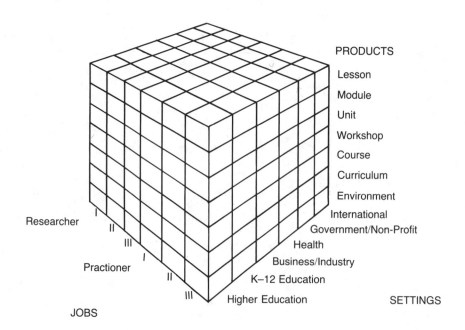

Objectives

- Given an essay question, compare the instructional design approach with the traditional approach to instruction.
- Given descriptions of job activities, match an instructional design role with each description.
- Given multiple-choice questions, identify the activities and outputs of the instructional design process.
- Given multiple-choice questions, match an activity with the associated step in the instructional design process.
- Given true/false questions, distinguish between instructional design research and practitioner activities.
- Given a matching question, identify which instructional design products are produced primarily by researchers and which primarily by practitioners.
- Given a worksheet, assess your strengths and weaknesses in competencies for instructional design.

Overview

Instructional design (ID) grew out of the systems approach to training developed by the military during World War II. It was based on the premise that learning should not occur in a haphazard manner but should be developed in accordance with orderly processes and have measurable outcomes.

Many disciplines contributed to the development of the ID field: psychology, communications, education, and computer science. As the field grew, roles for researchers and practitioners evolved. A generally accepted premise was that ID should have a research base.

Models for the systems approach evolved through practice as well as through research and theory. Techniques and methods were developed for carrying out steps in the process, such as methods for defining what is to be learned, for selecting the best media, for delivering instruction, and for measuring outcomes.

A generic instructional design approach includes the steps of analysis, design, development, implementation, and evaluation. The instructional design process thus encompasses defining what is to be learned, planning an intervention that will allow learning to occur, and refining instruction until objectives are met.

The instructional design approach has been formally adopted by large organizations such as the military, industries, and universities. It is used in a variety of settings from the banking industry to schools and hospitals. Instructional design can be used to develop a sophisticated curriculum for a large school system or on a micro level to improve a one-hour presentation.

Two organizations have proposed certification for instructional design practitioners: The National Society for Performance and Instruction (NSPI) and the Association for Educational Communications and Technology (AECT). The competencies proposed for this certification continually need updating; the field is changing rapidly because of computer-based instruction and telecommunications.

3

Study Questions

1. What is instructional design?
2. Why is instructional design needed?
3. What disciplines contributed to the field of ID?
4. What are the advantages of using an instructional design approach?
5. How does instructional design differ depending on the setting and product?
6. What competencies must an instructional designer master?

NEED FOR INSTRUCTIONAL DESIGN

Needed immediately: Twelve instructional designers to work in nuclear power plants in rural settings, must have degrees in instructional technology, will be responsible for ensuring the quality of instruction at all levels.

This position announcement was made by an educational contracting company after the Three Mile Island and Chernobyl nuclear accidents occurred; it illustrates the pressure for quality of instruction found in many settings. One way to prove commitment to quality of instruction is through the credentials of those developing and monitoring the instruction. Instructional design is a solution to quality of instruction problems in a variety of settings.

In the case of nuclear power plants, there is a desire to control as much of the instruction as possible, both for preventing accidents and for substantiating efforts to prevent accidents. The Institute of Nuclear Power Operations, an industry-established organization for self-policy, mandates standards for training programs. The standards include use of an instructional design process to develop instruction. The institute evaluates and accredits nuclear power operations, including their training components (Vandergrift, 1983).

The job of an instructional designer is to bring objectivity and orderliness to the process of planning instruction so that the quality of instruction is assured. The way this is done is to apply a systematic process and to use research and theoretical knowledge from instructional design and from other fields such as engineering, psychology, and art.

DEFINITION OF INSTRUCTIONAL DESIGN

In *The Theoretical and Conceptual Bases of Instructional Design*, Rita Ritchey defines instructional design as "the science of creating detailed specifications for the development, evaluation and maintenance of situations which facilitate the learning of both large and small units of subject matter" (Ritchey, 1986, p. 9). Ritchey's definition of design as a discipline clarifies the relationship of the researcher who is not involved with instructional design but who is contributing to the knowledge base.

In this text, instructional design is defined as both a process and a discipline. As a process it is the systematic development of instructional specifications using learning and instructional theory to ensure the quality of instruction. As an area of study it is that branch of knowledge concerned with research and theory about specifications for instruction and the processes for developing those specifications. ID encompasses creating specifications for instructional situations and for the development, evaluation, maintenance, and diffusion of those situations. An instructional situation can range in scope from a module, lesson, or experience on a micro level to a curriculum or environment on a macro level. Four important characteristics of instructional design are as follows:

1. Content selection based on data from the field
2. Instructional strategies based on research and theory

3. Test data based on absolute standards of performance

4. Technology used to optimize effectiveness, efficiency, and cost (Campbell, 1980)

Hannum and Briggs compare traditional and systematic instruction in seventeen areas. Their conclusions are given in Table 1.1.

THE GENERIC ID MODEL

An instructional designer takes knowledge from many fields and applies this knowledge to the steps in a systematic process for the development of instruction. Basically the systems approach requires defining what is to be learned, planning an intervention that will allow learning to occur, measuring learning to determine if objectives were met, and refining the intervention until objectives are met. From the features instructional design models have in common comes a generic ID model (Gibbons, 1981; Hannum & Hansen, 1989).

This generic ID model is so simplified it is unlikely to be used without modification or elaboration. Nevertheless, it provides a good introduction to the steps in the ID process. According to this generic model, instructional design is a systematic process involving these general stages: analysis, design, development, implementation, and evaluation. Analysis is the process of defining what is to be learned, design is the process of specifying how it is to be learned, development is the process of authoring and producing the materials, implementing is the process of installing the project in the real world context, and evaluation is the process of determining the adequacy of the instruction.

The steps of the generic model evolved over time; support for them comes from (1) surveys of procedures used in the field, (2) internal review, and (3) developmental testing (Burt & Geis, 1986; Kennedy, Esque & Novak, 1983; Weston, Burt & Geis, 1984; Wileman & Gambill, 1983). Surveys of procedures entail reviewing the literature in the field in order to determine the consensus and issues relating to a step. Internal review consists of an examination of how the steps were followed or adapted and an examination of the product. Developmental testing involves implementing a product and testing its effectiveness.

What is the status of knowledge about each step? The steps of analysis, development, and implementation derive their theoretical base largely from reports from the field and theoretical papers. These steps are also supported by logic. You cannot design a solution until you have correctly identified the problem. You must develop materials in order to implement and implement in order to evaluate.

The steps of design and evaluation developed from quasi-experimental and field studies. Knowledge about the design step is supported by research from the areas of learning and instructional theory. Some research questions, like "What are the most effective conditions for practice?," are thoroughly explored and guidelines have been generated (Jurgemeyer, 1982; Salisbury, Richards & Klein, 1985). Other research questions, like "What treatments are best for what learning styles?," are relatively untouched (Briggs, 1980).

The design step component is relatively well researched because the field of learning theory is older than other contributing fields. Findings from research on learning must be translated into prescriptions for instructional design. For this to happen, several stages of research must occur. Many studies must be conducted and synthesized before principles for design can be accepted.

There are many studies to support the use of specific evaluation strategies and techniques. Knowledge about evaluation is produced by experimental studies, methodological studies, and field studies (Burt & Geis, 1986; Weston, Burt & Geis, 1984). A review of literature indicates some areas of disagreement on aspects of design evaluation and few specific guidelines (Geis, Burt & Weston, 1984). Nevertheless, many areas related to evaluation, such as criterion- and norm-referenced testing, have been studied extensively.

Table 1.1   Comparison of Traditional and Systematic Instruction

Component of Instruction	Traditional Instruction	Systematic Instruction
Setting goals	Traditional curriculum Textbook Internal referent	Needs assessment Job analysis External referent
Objectives	Stated in terms of global outcomes or teacher performance Same for all students	From needs assessment/job analysis Stated in terms of student performance Chosen with consideration for students' entering competencies
Student's knowledge of objectives	Not informed; must intuit from lectures and textbooks	Specifically informed in advance of learning
Entering capability	Not attended to All students have same objectives and materials/activities	Taken into account Differential assignment of materials/activities
Expected achievement	Normal curve	Uniform high level
Mastery	Few students master most objectives Hit or miss pattern	Most students master most objectives
Grading and promotion	Based on comparison with other students	Based on mastery of objectives
Remediation	Often not planned No alteration of objectives or instructional means	Planned for students who need help Pursue other objectives Use alternate instructional means

In instructional design, the process is as important as the product because confidence in the product is based on the process. To be confident of the product, the steps in the generic ID model must be followed. For each step a series of tasks must be performed and specific output generated, as illustrated by Table 1.2.

An Exercise Designed to Compare Instructional Design with Other Approaches to Instruction

Directions: Choose a partner. Interview each other about a time when you had to teach. What did you do as an instructor? How did you decide what to teach? What steps did you follow? How did you conduct the lesson? How did you know if the student had learned from the lesson? Introduce your partner to the class by describing how he or she taught. Then your partner should do the same for you.

When everyone has been introduced, your instructor will introduce himself or herself as an instructional designer and tell why he or she is an instructional designer. The group should then discuss how other approaches to instruction compare with the instructional design approach. Discuss the attributes of traditional instruction and of instruction prepared by an instructional design process.

Table 1.1 (continued)

Component of Instruction	Traditional Instruction	Systematic Instruction
Use of tests	Assignment of grades	Monitor learner progress Determine mastery Diagnose difficulty Revise instruction
Study time vs. mastery	Time constant; degree of mastery varies	Mastery constant; time varies
Interpretation of failure to reach mastery	Poor student	Need to improve instruction
Course development	Materials selected first	Objectives stated first, then selection of materials
Sequence	Based on logic of content and outlines of topics	Based on necessary prerequisites and principles of learning
Instructional strategies	"Across the board" favorite Based on preference and familiarity	Selected to attain objectives Use of various strategies Based on theory and research
Evaluation	Often does not occur; rarely systematically planned Norm-referenced Data on inputs and processes	Systematically planned; routinely occurs Assesses student mastery of objectives Criterion-referenced Data on outcomes
Revision of instruction and materials	Based on guesswork or availability of new material Occurs intermittently	Based on evaluation data Routinely occurs

From "How Does Instructional Systems Design Differ from Traditional Instruction" by W.H. Hannum and Leslie J. Briggs, 1982, *Educational Technology, 22*, pp. 12–13. Copyright 1982 by *Educational Technology*. Reprinted by permission.

ROLES

An instructional designer's role can change depending on whether the subject to be presented is technical or non-technical and depending on the composition of the design team. If an area is highly technical the designer needs to instruct the content expert in design. If the subject is not overly technical, the designer can function more independently with the assistance of content expertise. Designers can work as external consultants who are responsible for all tasks, as in-house employees who are assisted by subject-matter experts, or as in-house employees who assist subject-matter experts. Three instances illustrate the variety of roles a designer can have, depending on the relation to content expertise.

1. A content expert adds instructional design and technology competencies and fulfills the role of designer without needing the assistance of content expertise.

2. An instructional designer is asked to work in a content area that may be familiar, but the designer still feels the need to work with a content expert.

3. A designer may be asked to manage development or research in an unfamiliar content area and therefore needs to select and work with several content experts.

Table 1.2   Tasks and Outputs of ID Process

Step and Definition	Sample Tasks	Sample Output
Analysis—the process of defining what is to be learned	Needs assessment Problem identification Task analysis	Learner profile Description of constraints Needs, Problem statement Task analysis
Design—the process of specifying how it is to be learned	Write objectives Develop test items Plan instruction Identify resources	Measurable objectives Instructional strategy Prototype specifications
Development—the process of authoring and producing the materials	Work with producers Develop workbook flowchart, program	Storyboard Script Exercises Computer-Assisted Instruction
Implementation—the process of installing the project in the real world context	Teacher training Tryout	Student comments, Data
Evaluation—the process of determining the adequacy of the instruction	Record time data Interpret test results Survey graduates Revise activities	Recommendations Project report Revised prototype

It is also important to distinguish between researcher and practitioner roles because the requirements for success in them differ. The researcher is interested in each of the steps in the generic model; so is the practitioner. Their interest and goals differ, though, as shown in Table 1.3.

Table 1.3   A Comparison of Interests and Goals of Researchers and Practitioners

Generic ISD Model	Researcher Role	Practitioner Role
Step 1 Analysis	Study of methods for problem identification Study of effect of learner characteristics Study of content area	Application of methods for problem identification Prescriptions for learner characteristics Using research on content area
Step 2 Design	Study of message design variables Develop instructional strategies	Use of prescriptions for design of instruction
Step 3 Development	Study of team processes	Working with producers developing scripts
Step 4 Implementation	Ethnographic studies of variables in environments Identification of variables affecting implementation	Design and management of environment and of variables in instruction
Step 5 Evaluation	Study of issues related to evaluation	Application of evaluation theory

Table 1.4   Role Profile: ID Researcher

Definition: An instructional design researcher's role is to systematically build knowledge about the steps for development of instruction. The role requires identifying questions that need study, planning a project that will yield information, conducting such projects, and reporting project results.

Critical Outputs: This role can produce the following:
Prescriptive theories
Instructional theories
Information on variables
Methodologies
Articles, reports, books
Research proposals

Critical Competencies: Questioning assumptions, reviewing literature, stating hypotheses, selecting methodology, designing research, analyzing data, writing proposals and reports, and investigating environments.

Comments: The ID researcher needs to be interested in parts of the ID process rather than the whole ID process. The researcher must have strong competencies in quantitative research and an interest in publication and specialization.

Depending on how the job is described, a practicing designer can perform each stage from analysis through tryout. If the designer's job is defined narrowly, then he or she may perform fewer steps, leaving the production, implementation, and evaluation steps to others.

An ID researcher is interested in studying variables and developing theories related to the delivery of instruction. An ID practitioner is interested in applying research and theory in the development of instructional methods and materials. One role leads to operating as a generalist (practitioner) and the other to operating as a specialist (researcher).

The field is broad enough to incorporate experimental research as well as product development research. There are areas, such as behavior modification, that have been explored all along the basic-to-applied-research continuum. There are other areas, such as affective learning, that need more research, basic as well as applied.

Table 1.5   Role Profile: ID Practitioner

Definition: An instructional design practitioner has the role of applying knowledge from many fields to the steps in a systematic process for the development of instruction. The role requires defining what is to be learned, planning an intervention that will allow learning to occur, measuring learning to determine whether objectives were met, and refining the intervention until objectives are met.

Critical Outputs: This role can produce the following:

Problem statement	Instructional strategy
Needs assessment	Tests
Performance requirements	Evaluation strategy
Learning requirements	Project proposals
Learning objectives	Publications

Critical Competencies: Gathering, analyzing, learning, synthesizing, evaluating, restructuring, and translating information; writing; creating environments, messages, and systems.

Comments: The ID practitioner needs a tolerance for ambiguity, an ability to move back and forth continually from the abstract to the concrete, and a high task orientation with effective interpersonal skills.

The discipline of instructional design is about thirty years old (Seels, 1989). It is the researcher's role to promote the growth of ID theory. Because this is an applied field, the researcher's role may seem isolated and less important. This is not true; without theoretical progress the field will stagnate. For your purposes you need to know that as a designer you can progress further in your career path if you are aware of research methods appropriate for each step. This book deals with instructional design theory relevant to product development research. Other research methodologies are not discussed.

Let's compare the role profiles on p. 9 for two different instructional designers—the first a researcher (Table 1.4), the second a practitioner (Table 1.5).

An Exercise Designed as a Test to Measure Your Knowledge and Understanding of the ID Function

Directions: Complete and correct the test. Use the chapter as a reference. Then check with the instructor about items that are confusing.

A. In two paragraphs compare the instructional design approach to instruction with traditional instruction.

B. Complete the sentence or give the definition.

1. Define "instructional design."

2. The words specialist and generalist are used to compare the roles of ID researcher and ID practitioner. The ID researcher is usually a _____. The ID practitioner is usually a _____.

C. Match the ID function with the job description.

a. Researcher

b. Practitioner

_____ 1. Manage the design and development of instructional materials for performance improvements within financial institutions. Duties: conduct content research, analyze needs, write instructional materials, communicate with division directly about project planning, complete reports, conduct project evaluations.

_____ 2. Manage research activities for establishing educational planning systems and methodologies. Use statistical or data-base software.

_____ 3. Analyze training materials; provide direction to course developers; conduct project review meetings; and apply knowledge of task analysis, design specification, media selection, and data processing.

_____ 4. Work on project to identify principles of message design, literature search, writing of proposals, and publication. Apply skills in experimental design, literature search, writing of proposals, and publication.

D. The correct answer to the following multiple-choice questions is one of these steps:

Step 1.   Analysis
Step 2.   Design
Step 3.   Development
Step 4.   Implementation
Step 5.   Evaluation

Write the name of the step in the space provided.

1. Instructional materials are tried out on a sample of the target audience. This activity takes place in

a. Step 1 _____

b. Step 2 _____

c. Step 3 _____

d. Step 4 _____

e. Step 5 _____

2. Job incumbents are surveyed to determine what tasks they perform and under what conditions they perform these tasks. This activity takes place in

   a. Step 1 _____

   b. Step 2 _____

   c. Step 3 _____

   d. Step 4 _____

   e. Step 5 _____

3. Necessary instructional resources are identified. This activity takes place in

   a. Step 1 _____

   b. Step 2 _____

   c. Step 3 _____

   d. Step 4 _____

   e. Step 5 _____

4. Instructional requirements are translated into measurable objectives. This activity takes place in

   a. Step 1 _____

   b. Step 2 _____

   c. Step 3 _____

   d. Step 4 _____

   e. Step 5 _____

5. Tasks and content to be included in the instruction are identified. This activity takes place in

   a. Step 1 _____

   b. Step 2 _____

   c. Step 3 _____

   d. Step 4 _____

   e. Step 5 _____

6. A plan of instruction is developed. Methods and media are selected. These activities take place in

   a. Step 1 _____

   b. Step 2 _____

   c. Step 3 _____

   d. Step 4 _____

   e. Step 5 _____

7. Tests are printed. This activity takes place in

   a. Step 1 _____

   b. Step 2 _____

   c. Step 3 _____

   d. Step 4 _____

   e. Step 5 _____

8. A student workbook is developed. This activity takes place in

   a. Step 1 _____
   b. Step 2 _____
   c. Step 3 _____
   d. Step 4 _____
   e. Step 5 _____

9. User groups are surveyed to determine whether the job performance of course graduates is satisfactory. This activity takes place in

   a. Step 1 _____
   b. Step 2 _____
   c. Step 3 _____
   d. Step 4 _____
   e. Step 5 _____

10. More practice exercises are added on the basis of tryout data. This activity takes place in

   a. Step 1 _____
   b. Step 2 _____
   c. Step 3 _____
   d. Step 4 _____
   e. Step 5 _____

E. Circle the correct answer. There can be more than one correct answer.

1. Which of the following outputs are produced in Step 1, Analysis?

   a. objectives
   b. assumptions about learners
   c. characteristics of the process
   d. student measurement procedures
   e. assumptions about needs

2. Which of the following outputs are produced in Step 2, Design?

   a. objectives
   b. instructional strategy
   c. student comments
   d. criterion-referenced tests
   e. project report

3. Which of the following outputs are produced in Step 3, Development?

   a. task requirements
   b. storyboards
   c. characteristics of learners
   d. slide-tape presentations
   e. prototype

4. Which of the following outputs are produced in Step 4, Implementation?

   a. data from tryout
   b. principles of learning
   c. sequence of objectives

      d.   description of constraints

      e.   problem statement

  5. Which of the following outputs are produced in Step 5, Evaluation?

      a.   instructional strategy

      b.   project report

      c.   interpretation of test results

      d.   revised prototype

      e.   media prescription

F. Match the step with the activity done at that step in the ID model.

  1. Analysis

  2. Design

  3. Development

  4. Implementation

  5. Evaluation

     _____ **a.** interpret and report test results

     _____ **b.** work with producers

     _____ **c.** conduct a needs assessment

     _____ **d.** teacher training

     _____ **e.** write objectives

     _____ **f.** sequence instruction

     _____ **g.** write a problem statement

G. Label each question as true or false.

  1. The ID practitioner is more interested in experimental research on learning principles than in the application of such principles. _____

  2. The ID researcher is more interested in studying a step in the process than in developing an instructional system. _____

  3. Neither the ID researcher nor the practitioner is interested in prescriptive theories of instruction. _____

H. Identify which of the following are produced primarily by

R–ID researchers

P–ID practitioners

_____ experimental study

_____ ethnographic study

_____ unit

_____ module

_____ curriculum

_____ small group discussion task

_____ message design principles

_____ course

_____ ID models or constructs

JOBS, PRODUCTS, AND SETTINGS

An instructional design practitioner's job may vary in the expertise required, the product produced, and the job setting. The ID practitioner may do a task analysis under a project manager's supervision in a research and development organization, or he or she may lead a team that develops a three-day workshop for industry. Design is not always a team effort. In a smaller organization, a single person may do the instructional design tasks and more. You must prepare yourself to adjust to different goals by understanding how jobs, products, and settings vary in the field of ID.

Jobs

There is a range of jobs available across settings and at different levels of expertise. Sometimes the instructional designer acts as a specialist in one of the steps in the process. Other jobs call for the designer to be a generalist competent to carry through a project from start to finish. Not only is there a range of jobs due to specialized functions, but some jobs require different levels of expertise. Table 1.6 illustrates three levels of expertise in ID jobs.

Typical advertisements for jobs in instructional design are shown in Table 1.7.

Jobs in public schools usually incorporate instructional design functions as part of other positions, e.g., curriculum supervisor, media specialist, instructional technologist, and director of instruction. Compared to other settings the impact of instructional design in schools has been low.

Some of the reasons for this low impact are the teacher-intensive nature of traditional schooling, the rigidity of the daily schedule, and the low amount of discretionary funding available to schools. For instructional design to become more prominent in school settings three changes would have to take place: (1) a reduction of amount of time spent by teachers and students in traditional classes, (2) more individualization within the curriculum, and (3) implementation of low cost delivery systems (Melmed, 1986).

The prospects for instructional design positions are excellent because of the statistics on retraining needs and the increasing level of sophistication required for jobs. Over forty percent of employers are having trouble finding qualified people for jobs.

Thirty-six percent of 322 Fortune 1500 companies reported consistently moving existing employees into positions requiring additional training. There are shortages of key personnel in many fields, and placing the unemployed is impossible without retraining ("Employers Still Balk at Retraining," Aug. 1984).

Products

Whatever job you assume, you may be responsible for any of a variety of products. The products of ID can vary in scope and sophistication. Scope can include variation in size or content. Sophistication can include variations in curriculum or media. At the smallest level of scope are lesson plans and modules. The next level includes courses, programs, workshops, and units. Courses, curriculum, and environments would be examples of large-scope products. At the highest level of sophistication are interactive learning media, such as interactive video. The lowest level of sophistication would be paper and pencil, with audiovisual materials in the middle. As Table 1.8 shows (p. 16), products can fall on any coordinates of the scope and sophistication dimensions. Examples of products are given in the project profiles in Tables 1.9 and 1.10 (pp. 16–17).

Table 1.6   Sample Levels of Expertise in ID Practitioner Jobs

Basic: The instructional designer works on parts of a project under the direction of another designer. She works with others to improve existing instruction. She works on small projects or parts of projects.

Intermediate: The instructional designer takes responsibility for developing an entire course or for major redesigning projects. He can be a team leader on small or medium-sized projects.

Advanced: The instructional designer is heavily involved in project management and proposal writing. She may direct needs assessment or evaluation studies which determine project directions. She supervises team leaders. She can oversee large projects.

Table 1.7 Job Ads for ID Positions

Assistant Professor (Higher Education)

Teach in graduate instructional technology program. Conduct an active program of research. Engage in scholarly work, publish regularly, and seek research funding. Special areas of expertise should include one or more of the following: video applications, computing applications, instructional media, instructional design, instructional evaluation, instructional management.

Assistant/Associate Professor (Higher Education)

Experience in public education at K–12 level. Proven professional growth as evidenced by publication, grant acquisition, conference presentation, and consulting. Experience in successful application of instructional technologies to schools. Possession of a research agenda of significance to public education. Teach courses in computing, media production and use, instructional design, integration of technologies into K–12 education curriculum, and program development.

Educational Specialist (Government)

Primary function is to provide instructional technology expertise in the design, development, production, and maintenance of aircrew training. The position requires a background and past experience in instructional systems development and technical training.

Materials Development Specialist (Health)

In a hospital setting, analyze, design, develop, and evaluate instructional situations and materials for nursing, patient, community, and allied health-related education. Specific responsibilities for design and development of print, display, lecture support, slide/sound, video, and other audio-visual media materials. Requires a master's degree in instructional design and technology or related field, direct instructional design experience, a broad technical knowledge of instructional strategies and evaluation, working knowledge of audio-visual media design, and management skills for efficient planning of activities. Interpersonal communications skills and writing skills essential, previous experience in hospital, business, or media-related environment desirable.

Instructional Designer (Business)

Research and Development facility has an opening for an instructional designer. Responsibilities include needs analysis, design and development of technical courses, revision of available programs, and coordination of curriculum committee activities. Applicants should have experience in the application of instructional media.

Instructional Designer (Industry)

Specific responsibilities include assisting in the specification of training needs and tasks, instructional content and strategies, and the development, writing, and revision of course materials. A degree in the field of instructional technology, with courses in learning theory, systematic course development, and media utilization, is desired. Excellent organizational, interpersonal, time managment, and oral and written communication skills are also critical.

Educational Specialist (Business)

Responsibilities: To conduct front end analysis and develop instructional guides and media specifications for computer software training materials. Qualifications: Graduate degree in instructional technology or other evidence of competencies in instructional development, media design, and evaluation; experience in developing instructional material, preferably for a banking environment; a basic understanding of computers and computer based instruction; people skills.

Settings

Any milieu that has an instructional function can become a setting for instructional design. This includes ID efforts in international settings, business and industry, health and non-profit associations, and schools and informal education. All need systematic development of instruction that utilizes instructional media and technology.

Differences among these settings can lead to differences in ID processes and products. Joe Durzo (1983) cautions designers moving from the academic world to the consulting business world to remember the following: (1) you may have to do much of the analysis before you win a contract, and (2) you may have to propose a less costly project, even if it is a less desirable one, in order to be competitive.

Table 1.8   Dimensions of ID Products

Large	Curriculum Efforts	Correspondence Course	Telecourse	Computer-based Self-Instructional Course
Project Scope	Programs Units Workshops	Curriculum Unit	Mediated Workshop	Computer Simulation
	Modules Lessons Presentations	Workbook Exercises	Slide-Tape Presentation	Computer Game
Small				
	Low			*High*

IT Sophistication

Similarly, those moving from the academic world of higher education to the K–12 school system need to be aware that differing norms mean differing constraints. Higher education routinely constrains through admissions standards. Public schools routinely constrain through budget and community values.

The options in instructional design vary with settings, jobs, and products. These options are shown in Figure 1.1. In the figure each cell stands for an ID position and the limitations on that position.

Table 1.9   Avionics Troubleshooting Project Profile

Avionics Troubleshooting Project
Director: Alan Lesgold
Assistant Director: Susanne P. Lajoie
1986

Source: Learning Research and Development Center, University of Pittsburgh.

Purpose: One purpose has been to identify the basic job skills that constitute troubleshooting proficiency in the manual avionics career field. The second purpose has been to develop an intelligent tutoring system that will train less skilled airmen to become proficient troubleshooters.

Description: Our tutor has explicit representations of skilled and less skilled performance which are used to monitor a student's competence and provide feedback based on an individual's performance level at a particular decision point in the problem.

Developmental Process: This project is a two-stage process. We have completed stage one and found the cognitive components of troubleshooting that distinguish skilled from less skilled airmen. We are now in stage two of the process, which involves building and testing our tutor in the real world.

Results: The cognitive task analysis research led to important methodological developments. We developed an interviewing technique that we referred to as decision tree analysis. This technique consisted of using experts to map out a problem space that indicated both the skilled and less skilled branches of decision-making for troubleshooting problems. We then tested our decision trees on novices and filled out the tree to reflect additional branches of problem solving. Thus, we had a way for a layperson to interview airmen and understand where they are in the problem space so that they could probe airmen at appropriate decision points. Subsequently this technique was refined and termed effective problem space mapping. The strategies and skills that are involved for each of the major decisions in this tree were added. We are now using this effective problem space methodology as the basis of our tutor diagnosis of individual differences in problem solving. We map out the problem space for each problem and provide instruction and remediation at decision points (node level) based on these differences.

Table 1.10   Project Profile for College Course

Applied Phonics Courses
Directors: Barbara A. Petry
Mayhouse Edwards
1984

Source: Syracuse University Communicative Disorder Program

Purpose: The course was individualized in order to meet the needs of a diverse population of students (graduate, undergraduate, international, linguistics majors, communicative disorders majors). The course requires a high level of skill development, and traditional instruction was not resulting in this level for all students.

Description: Elaboration theory was selected as a theoretical base so the course begins with an overview of sound and speech, then proceeds to specific classes of sounds and skill development. Laboratory sessions were designed to closely correspond with class sessions. Parameters affecting the difficulty of transcription tasks were identified and manipulated through easy-to-difficult sequences. Students were allowed to work at their own speed until mastery was achieved.

Development process: A team from the University Center for Instructional Development used an instructional development (ID) model. The components developed included a student manual, a workbook and accompanying audio tapes, laboratory exercises, and tests answers for all except the final test in the workbook.

Results: Students' scores remained the same although content and skill requirements were increased. Students reported more positive attitudes towards the revised course. Although the project's scope expanded beyond the original intent, the investment was returned in improvement of instruction (Petry & Edwards, 1984).

ID COMPETENCIES

Instructional design is an intellectual process requiring higher-level thinking skills (Nelson, Macliaro, & Sherman, 1988). To perform this activity you will need entering skills and aptitudes plus training and education. Clint Wallington (1981) lists the generic skills

Figure 1.1   Products, Settings, and Jobs

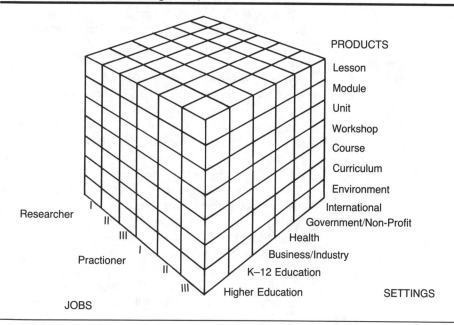

necessary to perform instructional design as interpersonal skills, communication skills, problem-solving skills, and skills in extracting and assimilating chunks of information and working them into a logical framework, applying principles of behavioral sciences, and systematically searching for related information. To develop your ID competencies, try to improve your basic aptitude areas, such as writing and editing skills, while continuing to work on professional competency areas, such as knowledge of instructional strategies.

Personal Aptitudes

In addition to study of the field there are aptitudes relevant to instructional design. An instructional designer needs to be able to think both in the abstract and the concrete. A great deal of design work involves checking for logical consistency of ideas. At the same time a designer is looking at the general and abstract, however, he or she must also attend to details. Thoroughness is required for quality products.

A designer must enjoy working with visual presentation modes and writing because a good deal of design work entails writing or editing. If you don't like to write or work with visuals, don't become an instructional designer.

Designers need to be task-oriented and yet still be able to work productively with people because much design work is done in teams. Designers must be open to ideas and be able to accept constructive criticism. Their tolerance for ambiguity should be high.

Gagné (1973) describes the personal characteristics of instructional technologists as falling into three categories: attitudes or values, specialized knowledge, and intellectual skills or methodologies. According to Gagné (1985), a designer needs to value empirical evidence as a basis for action, and needs to be able to analyze learning outcomes and conditions, use measurement techniques, and construct tests. In addition, a designer needs statistical and communication skills (Gagné, 1987).

When Mountain Bell Corporation wanted to develop their own designers from employees without training in ID, they considered writing, oral, and analytical skills. They found these skills were basic to the functions an instructional designer had to perform (Maxwell & Seyfer, 1984).

You will also need the interpersonal and process skills synonymous with consultant skills. Whether you are contracted temporarily to solve a specific problem or are assigned to give instructional advice as part of your regular duties, as an instructional designer you will often be in a consulting role. You will be asked to help a client temporarily with judicious sharing of your knowledge. You will need to be able to determine what the instructional problem is, whom it affects, and how it can be dealt with. You will need to be able to convince people to work with you voluntarily. You do not want to make the organization dependent on you; rather, you want to share your skills. The combination of enthusiasm and restraint which characterizes the effective consultant also characterizes the effective instructional designer.

Certification

You need to know the competencies required of instructional designers so that you can gain these competencies. The National Society for Performance and Instruction and the Division of Instructional Development of the Association for Educational Communications and Technology have jointly appointed a task force to investigate the feasibility and desirability of certifying instructional designers.

The task force established a foundation to help promote this effort. The debate as to the desirability of certification continues within each organization. Against those who argue that certification can be a standard-setting device for the field are those who argue that fixed standards will stunt the growth of the industry. Measurement issues are also debatable. Until it is clear whom should be certified, who should certify, and why, how, and what behaviors really define competence, it is unlikely that certification will be required. It may be offered, however, as an option.

The task force is proposing a list of competencies for certification. This list is shown in Table 1.11. Some instructional design positions do not require all these competencies. For example, planning and monitoring (project management) skills may not be required.

On the other hand, there are large competency areas, such as design of computer-based instruction, that are suggested only indirectly by the list. Because the ID field is changing rapidly, this competency list needs continual revision.

It is important to be prepared to demonstrate your competence in ID. There are many ways to demonstrate competency when you go job hunting. You can use letters of recommendation, transcripts, portfolios of work, including project reports, or internship projects. Competencies can be developed through courses, field experiences, projects, workshops, professional meetings, and independent study. Another strategy to increase competence is to read the periodicals that represent the profession, such as *Educational Technology Research and Development* and *Performance and Instruction Journal*. In addition, you can attend the conventions and meetings of organizations such as the Association for Educational Communications and Technology, the National Society for Performance and Instruction, and the many educational computing organizations. An organization of professors in instructional design and technology meets every year. Students can apply to attend.

An Exercise Designed to Help You Assess Your Strengths in ID Skill Areas

Directions: This exercise is for your use only. It is not designed as a test. First check the column that reflects your perception of each skill. Next indicate a method to develop that skill in the To Improve column—for example, take a course, do an internship, complete an independent study project. Be specific about courses, books, and sites. Finally, have your instructor read the exercise and comment on your ideas.

Basic

The basic competency areas are defined as follows: Communication skills are abilities in the areas of language. Interpersonal skills are abilities in the area of interactions with other people. Self-concept means how one sees oneself. A strong self-concept is important for skill in communications. Self-awareness and acceptance can increase openness and clarity of expression. Analytical skills are thinking skills in the area of analysis which enable you to determine the parts of a problem.

Competencies	Little Skill	Some Skill	Strong Skill	To Improve
1. Communication Skills				
a. Writing				
b. Editing				
c. Speaking				
2. Interpersonal				
a. Listening				
b. Self-concept				
c. Coping with Emotions				
3. Analytical				
a. Break a problem into parts				
b. Design a solution strategy				
c. Evaluate solution				

Applied

1. Determine Appropriate Projects

2. Conduct Needs Assessment

Competencies	Little Skill	Some Skill	Strong Skill	To Improve
3. Assess Learner Characteristics				
4. Analyze Jobs, Tasks, Content				
5. Write Statement of Outcomes				
6. Analyze Setting				
7. Sequence Outcomes				
8. Specify Instructional Strategies				

Table 1.11   Instructional/Training Development Competencies

A competent instructional/training development specialist is able to

1. Determine Projects Appropriate for Instructional Development
    Analyze information regarding potential projects and decide if instructional development is appropriate.
    Discriminate situations requiring instructional solutions from those requiring other solutions (e.g., job design, organizational development, etc.).
    Judge the appropriateness of project selection decisions and provide a rationale for judgment.

2. Conduct Needs Assessment
    Develop a needs assessment plan including selection of procedures and instruments.
    Conduct a needs assessment and interpret results to suggest appropriate actions.
    Judge the appropriateness, completeness, and accuracy of given needs assessment plans and results.

3. Assess Learner/Trainee Characteristics
    Distinguish among entry skills assessment, prerequisite assessment, and aptitude assessment.
    Identify a range of relevant learner/trainee characteristics and determine methods for assessing them.
    Develop and implement a plan for assessing learner/trainee characteristics.
    Judge the appropriateness, comprehensiveness, and adequacy of a given assessment of learner/trainee characteristics.

4. Analyze the Structural Characteristics of Jobs, Tasks, and Content
    Select and use a procedure for analyzing the structural characteristics appropriate to a job, task, or content and state a rationale for the selection.

5. Write Statements of Learner Outcomes
    Distinguish objectives stated in performance/behavioral terms from instructional goals, organizational goals, learner activities, teacher activities, and objectives written in other styles.
    State an outcome in performance terms which reflects the intent of instruction.
    Judge the accuracy, comprehensiveness, and appropriateness of statements of learner outcomes in terms of the job, task, or content analysis, and/or judgment/opinion of the client (e.g., subject matter expert, faculty, etc.).

6. Analyze the Characteristics of a Setting (Learning Environment)
    Analyze setting characteristics and determine relevant resources and constraints.
    Judge the accuracy, comprehensiveness, and appropriateness of a setting analysis.

7. Sequence Learner Outcomes
    Select a procedure for sequencing learning outcomes appropriate to a given situation, sequence the outcomes, and state a rationale for the sequence.
    Judge the accuracy, completeness, and appropriateness of a given sequence of learner outcomes.

8. Specify Instructional Strategies
    Select a strategy which is appropriate to information about the learner characterstics, resources,

Competencies	Little Skill	Some Skill	Strong Skill	To Improve
9. Sequence Activities				
10. Determine Instructional Resources				
11. Produce Materials				
12. Evaluate Instruction				
13. Monitor Projects Implementation				
14. Promote Diffusion and Adoption				

Table 1.11 (continued)

and constraints, desired learner outcomes, and other pertinent information, and state a rationale for the selection.

Judge the appropriateness of a specified instructional strategy for a given situation.

9. Sequence Learner Activities

Specify a sequence of learner activities appropriate to the achievement of specified learner outcomes and state a rationale for the sequence.

Judge the appropriateness and completeness of a given sequence of learner activities.

10. Determine Instructional Resources (Media) Appropriate to Instructional Activities

Develop specifications for instructional resources required for explicit instructional strategies and learner outcomes.

Evaluate existing instructional resources to determine appropriateness for specified instructional strategies and learner outcomes.

Adapt existing instructional resources.

Prepare specifications for the production of materials where required (e.g., storyboards, lesson plans, script outlines, etc.).

11. Evaluate Instruction/Training

Plan and conduct a formative evaluation (e.g., trials with subjects, expert review, analysis of implementation considerations, etc.).

Develop a range of information-gathering techniques (e.g., questionnaires, interviews, tests, simulations, observations, etc.).

12. Create Course, Training Packages, and Workshop Management Systems

Determine the components of a course/training package/workshop management system and state a rationale for the selection.

Judge the appropriateness, comprehensiveness, and adequacy of a given management system.

13. Plan and Monitor Instructional Development Projects

Develop and monitor an instructional development project plan (including timeliness, budgets, staffing, etc.) appropriate to the nature of the project and the setting.

14. Communicate Effectively in Visual, Oral, and Written Form

15. Demonstrate Appropriate Interpersonal, Group Process, and Consulting Behaviors

Demonstrate interpersonal behaviors with individuals and groups and state a rationale for using the behaviors in given situations.

Demonstrate consulting behaviors with individuals and groups and state a rationale for the behaviors in given situations.

Judge the appropriateness of interpersonal, group process, and consulting behaviors in given situations.

16. Promote the Diffusion and Adoption of the Instructional Development Process

Select strategies appropriate for promoting the diffusion and adoption of the instructional development process in a given setting and state a rationale for the strategies.

After "Professional Certification: Will It Become a Reality?" by B. Bratton, 1984, *Performance & Instruction*, *23*, pp. 6–7.
Reprinted with permission from *Performance & Instruction*, copyright National Society for Performance and Instruction, 1984.

FROM THE READING

Define the following terms.

Instructional Design   ID Researcher

Generic ID Model   ID Practitioner

ISSUES FOR DISCUSSION

1. What should be the requirement for admission to the study of instructional design?

2. What should be the relationship between research and practice in ID? How can the contributions of each be enhanced?

3. Is certification of instructional designers desirable? Why or why not?

4. Which role would you choose in ID and why?

5. How does instructional design differ from other approaches to instruction?

REFERENCES

Bratton, B. (1984). Professional certification: Will it become a reality? *National Society for Performance & Instruction Journal, 23,* 4–7.

Briggs, L.J. (1980). Thirty years of instructional design: One man's experience. *Educational Technology, 20,* 45–50.

Burt, C.W., & Geis, G.L. (1986, April). Guidelines for developmental testing: Proposed and practiced. Paper presented at the 70th annual meeting of the American Educational Research Association, San Francisco, CA. ED 270500.

Campbell, C.P. (1980, December). An instructional systems development process. Paper presented at the annual convention of the American Vocational Association, New Orleans, LA. ED 194 805.

Durzo, J.J. (1983). Getting down to business: Instructional development for a profit. *Journal of Instructional Development, 5* (2), 2–7.

Gagné, R.M. (1985). "What Should a Performance Improvements Professional Know and Do? *Performance & Instruction, 24,* (7), 6–7.

Gagné, R.M. (1987). Characteristics of instructional technologists. *Performance & Instruction, 26* (3) 26–28.

Geis, G.L., Burt, C.W., & Weston C. (1984, April). Instructional Development: Developmental testing. Paper presented at the annual 68th meeting of the American Educational Research Association, New Orleans, LA. ED 243 793.

Gibbons, A.S. (1981). The contribution of science to instructional development. *National Society for Performance & Instruction Journal, 20* .

Hannum, W.H., & Briggs, L.J. (1982). How does instructional systems design differ from traditional instruction? *Educational Technology, 22,* 9–14.

Hannum, W.H., & Hansen, C. (1989). *Instructional Systems Development in Large Organizations.* Englewood Cliffs, NJ: Educational Technology Publication.

Jurgemeyer, F.H. (1982). Programmed instruction: Lessons it can teach us. *Educational Technology, 22* (5), 20–23.

Kennedy, P., Esque, T., & Novak, J. (1983). A functional analysis of task analysis procedures for instructional design. *Journal of Instructional Development, 6* (4), 10–16.

Maxwell, K., & Seyfer, C. (1984). Selection by design. *Performance and Instructional Journal, 23,* 8–10.

Melmed, A.S. (1986). The technology of American education: Problem and opportunity. *Technological Horizons in Education, 14* (2), 77–81.

Nelson, W.A., Macliaro, S., & Sherman, T.M. (1988). The intellectual content of instructional design. *Journal of Instructional Development, 2* (1), 29–35.

Petry, B., & Edwards, M.L. (1984). Systematic development of an applied phonetics course. *Journal of Instructional Development, 7* (4), 6–10.

Ritchey, R. (1986). The theoretical and conceptual bases of instructional design. NY: Nicols Publishing.

Salisbury, D.F., Richards, B.F., & Klein, J.D. (1985). Designing practice: A review of prescriptions and recommendations from instructional design theories. *Journal of Instructional Development, 8* (4), 9–19.

Seels, B. (1989). The Instructional Design Movement in Educational Technology. *Educational Technology, 29* (5), 11–15.

U.S. firms and employers still balk at retraining. (1984, August). *Training and Development Journal,* 9–10.

Vandergrift, J.D. (1983, September). Instructional systems without the big bang. *Training and Development Journal, 37,* 20–23.

Wallington, C.J. (1981). Generic skills of an instructional developer. *Journal of Instructional Development, 4* (3), 28–33.

Weston, C., Burt, C.W., & Geis, G.L. (1984, April). Instructional development: Revision practice. Paper presented at the 68th annual meeting of the American Educational Research Association, New Orleans, LA. ED 243794.

Wileman, R.E., & Gambill, T.G. (1983). The neglected phase of instructional design. *Educational Technology, 23* (11), 25–32.

Chapter Two
Psychological Basis for Instructional Design

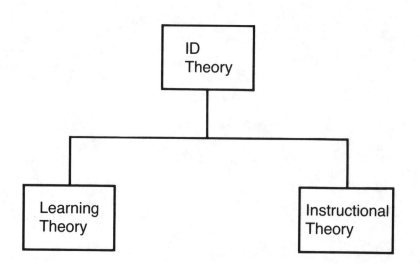

Objectives

- Given learning outcomes, classify them according to the three learning domains.
- Given learning outcomes from each of the three domains and associated learning taxonomies, classify the learning outcomes according to the taxonomies.
- Given learning taxonomies, state their similarities and differences.
- Given true/false statements, distinguish between behavioral and cognitive schools of psychology.

Overview

Evidence of learning is a relatively permanent change in behavior due to experience. The goal of the instructional designer is to plan the experiences that will change current behavior to some new, as yet unlearned behavior. We begin by identifying the skill to be learned. Human capabilities are divided into three domains: cognitive, psychomotor, and affective. The cognitive domain deals with mental tasks such as remembering facts and the intellectual skills involved in thinking; the psychomotor deals with physical actions such as manipulative skills and gross motor skills; and the affective domain deals with feelings and emotions such as attitudes, interests, and values.

Consider the job of the coach of a Little League baseball team. To prepare the team to play baseball, the coach must have the team develop capabilities in all three domains. Hitting the ball, running, and catching are the psychomotor skills the players will need to develop. Knowing the rules of the game and making judgments about when to attempt to steal a base are two of the cognitive skills of baseball. The coach will also have to motivate the players to put forth the effort necessary for winning.

Not all learning is the product of instruction. In fact, most learning occurs without the benefit of any deliberate instruction. We learn how to behave socially from our parents, then later from other sources such as television and our peers. Emotional learning, which includes our attitudes, values, and beliefs, comes from the same sources. Experience from everyday life is constantly shaping and molding our behavior in unpredictable ways. These changes are defined as learning.

Instructional design is a deliberate process that tries to control and direct learning toward predictable ends. It begins with a defined learning deficiency and concludes with a plan to overcome the deficiency. That plan specifies the instructional events and materials that will provide the conditions for learning. "Instruction" is planned by the instructional designer and performed by teachers, materials, and other mediators. While instruction is intended to provide the conditions for learning, it never provides learning. "Learning" is done by students; it is an internal phenomenon. Instruction, however, is an external phenomenon. Thus, what a designer can do is limited to the choice and arrangement of external conditions that will help the internal process of learning to occur. Out of theory and research, a substantial body of knowledge has evolved about how to control conditions effectively to enhance the likelihood that learning will occur.

Study Questions

1. What is learning?
2. What are the different types of learning?
3. How can taxonomies be used in the instructional design process?
4. What implications do theories of learning have for instructional design?

TYPES OF LEARNING

While we can distinguish three domains conceptually, in practice the relationship among them is not clear. How much difference is there between what we know and what we feel about a subject? What is the cognitive component of a psychomotor task? Actually, all learning involves the three domains to varying degrees. Attitudes consist of a cognitive component and an affective one. The cognitive component of an attitude refers to the perceptions and information one has about the attitude object. The affective component refers to one's feelings or liking or disliking of the attitude object. Similarly, many psychomotor outcomes have a large cognitive component. When performance is highly proficient, the domains become so integrated that they are no longer distinguishable. Thus, when we classify a learning outcome as being in one of the three domains, we do so on the basis of its primary focus and intent.

Educators have developed classification schemes for defining the types of learning within each domain. These schemes, called taxonomies, are organized from the simplest to the most complex type of learning. This hierarchical organization means that the lower level skills must be learned before one can acquire the higher level skills. Look at the simple version of a hierarchy in Figure 2.1. Before a student can perform at the top level, he or she must acquire all the lower types of learning in the sequence shown in the taxonomy.

While taxonomies share certain general characteristics, it is difficult to make comparisons between any two of them. No two learning theorists break learning down into the same number of categories or the same types of learning. It is futile to try to equate definitions across taxonomies.

Despite these difficulties, taxonomies (1) assist the designer to determine the type of learning which is to be the object of instruction, (2) are useful for sequencing learning when the learning outcomes are known, and (3) reduce the work associated with planning the conditions of learning by grouping learning outcomes into similar types of capabilities.

Cognitive Domain

A number of educators have developed taxonomies for the cognitive domain (Committee of College and University Examiners, 1956; Gagné, 1977; Gerlach & Ely, 1980). The simplest level is usually some type of associative learning, such as naming, and the highest levels are complex intellectual tasks, such as might be performed by a debater in preparing to argue a position or an instructional designer attempting to solve a learning problem. Bloom's taxonomy for the cognitive domain is one of the best known and is summarized in Table 2.1.

The cognitive taxonomy was published in 1956, and its purpose was to develop a classification system to describe behavior and therefore enable educators to communicate about test items, educational goals, and testing procedures. The behaviors are divided into six categories with corresponding subcategories. The categories are arranged hierarchically from simple to complex, the simplest being recall of specific bits of information, and the most complex being judgments about the value of some object, idea, or process.

Figure 2.1   Model of a Simple Learning Hierarchy

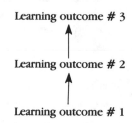

Table 2.1 The Cognitive Domain Taxonomy

Type of Learning	Definitions and Examples of Behavior
6. *Evaluation*	Making judgments about the value of ideas, works, solutions, methods, materials, etc. Judgments may be either quantitative or qualitative.
	Examples: to argue, to decide, to compare, to consider, to contrast.
5. *Synthesis*	Putting together elements and parts to form a new whole.
	Examples: to write, to produce, to plan, to design, to derive, to combine.
4. *Analysis*	Breaking down material or ideas into their constituent parts and detecting the relationship of the parts and the way they are arranged.
	Examples: to distinguish, to detect, to employ, to restructure, to classify.
3. *Application*	Knowing an abstraction well enough to apply it without being prompted or without having been shown how to use it.
	Examples: to generalize, to develop, to employ, to transfer.
2. *Comprehension*	Understanding the literal message contained in a communication.
	Examples: to transform, to paraphrase, to interpret, to reorder, to infer, to conclude.
1. *Knowledge*	Remembering an idea, material, or phenominon in a form very close to that in which it was originally encountered.
	Examples: to recall, to recognize, to acquire, to identify.

After *Taxonomy of Educational Objectives: Handbook I Cognitive Domain* (pp. 201–207) by Commitee of College and University Examiners, B.S. Bloom (Ed.), 1956, New York: David McKay Co.

Martin and Briggs (1986) summarize the studies to validate the psychological assumptions and hierarchical relationship of the taxonomy. Results of studies are mixed and inconclusive. However, there is fairly strong support for the hierarchical structure of the lower levels of the taxonomy, but less for the upper three levels. Criticisms of the taxonomy reported by Martin and Briggs are that (1) the categories are not mutually exclusive; (2) there are problems of consistently classifying behavior due to the vagueness of the descriptors; (3) although useful for formulating learning outcomes, structuring learning sequences and assessment procedures, it is of little value for curriculum development; and (4) the taxonomy is weighted toward knowledge rather than the higher mental processes (p.71).

Affective Domain

The best known of the affective taxonomies was developed by Krathwohl et al. (1964). It is summarized in Table 2.2. Affective capabilities are difficult to translate into behavior that reveals the learned capability. Since attitudes, interests, and values are not easily defined in behavioral terms, it is difficult to know when an attitude or interest is acquired. On top of this, it takes a long time, perhaps years, to achieve this type of learning. Martin and Briggs (1986) distinguish between long term and short term objectives for attitude learning. They note that

> an objective such as willingness to receive information on a fairly non-controversial, limited topic, such as soccer as a hobby or as an elective physical educational activity, may be quickly established. On the other hand, taking a studied position on a complex, highly controversial topic, such as abortion, may require a long period of information learning, debate, soul-searching, and position-taking. (p.365)

Krathwohl notes that instructional objectives are rarely set at the highest level of the taxonomy.

Table 2.2   The Affective Domain Taxonomy

Type of Learning	Definitions and Examples of Behavior
5. *Characterization by Value or Value Set*	Acts consistently in accordance with the values he or she has internalized.
	Examples: to revise, to require, to be rated high in the value, to avoid, to resist, to manage, to resolve.
↑	
4. *Organization*	Relates the value to those already held and brings it into a harmonious and internally consistent philosophy.
	Examples: to discuss, to theorize, to formulate, to balance, to examine.
↑	
3. *Valuing*	Willing to be perceived by others as valuing certain ideas, materials, or phenomena.
	Examples: to increase measured proficiency in, to relinquish, to subsidize, to support, to debate.
↑	
2. *Responding*	Committed in some small measure to the ideas, materials, or phenomena involved by actively responding to them.
	Examples: to comply with, to follow, to commend, to volunteer, to spend leisure time in, to acclaim.
↑	
1. *Receiving*	Being aware of or sensitive to the existence of certain ideas, material, or phenomena and being willing to tolerate them.
	Examples: to differentiate, to accept, to listen (for), to respond to.

After *Taxonomy of Educational Objectives: Handbook II: Affective Domain* (pp. 176–185) by D.R. Krathwohl, B.S. Bloom, and B.B. Masia, 1964, New York: David McKay Co.

The taxonomy is ordered according to the principle of "internalization." Internalization refers to the process whereby a person's affect toward an object passes from a general awareness level to a point where the affect is "internalized" and consistently guides or controls the person's behavior.

Validation studies reported by Martin and Briggs (1986) indicate that the categories seem to be correctly ordered. But, as with the cognitive taxonomy, the support is stronger for the lower categories of receiving, responding, and valuing, with tenuous support for the higher categories. Criticisms of the taxonomy cited by Martin and Briggs are that it is too general and abstract, overly dependent on cognition, and limited in scope because it fails to include the affective constructs of self-development (self-concept, self-esteem) and motivation.

Psychomotor Domain

The psychomotor domain is organized on the basis of the degree of coordination required. The lowest level is simple reflexes and the highest levels are tasks requiring complex neuromuscular coordination. The best known taxonomy is Anita Harrow's (1972). She classifies six types of capabilities and corresponding subcategories in the psychomotor domain. The classification scheme includes involuntary responses as well as learned capabilities.

The categories and examples of corresponding behaviors are presented in Table 2.3. Reflex movements in Category 1 are not learned capabilities; they are functional at birth. Harrow includes them because they are prerequisites for the development of higher order movement patterns learned during the first year of life. Obviously, instruction is not developed for reflexes. While the movements included in Category 2, basic fundamental movements, are learned capabilities, they unfold as the child matures, rather than being taught. Instructional designers do not usually develop instruction at this level either, unless a child is having problems in this area. Categories 3 and 4, perceptual abilities and physical abilities, are developed through maturation and learning. Structured learning programs facilitate the acquisition of these abilities. Category 5, skilled movements, builds upon the

Table 2.3 Taxonomy for the Psychomotor Domain

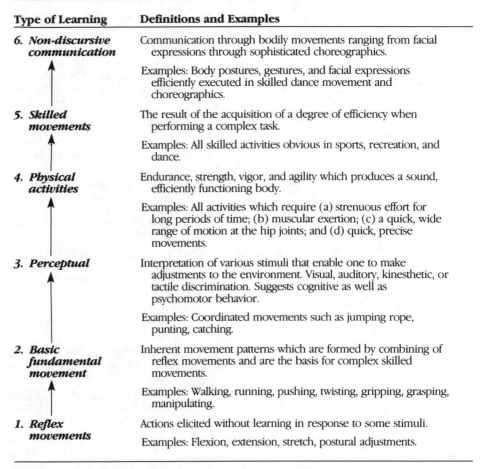

Type of Learning	Definitions and Examples
6. *Non-discursive communication*	Communication through bodily movements ranging from facial expressions through sophisticated choreographics.
	Examples: Body postures, gestures, and facial expressions efficiently executed in skilled dance movement and choreographics.
5. *Skilled movements*	The result of the acquisition of a degree of efficiency when performing a complex task.
	Examples: All skilled activities obvious in sports, recreation, and dance.
4. *Physical activities*	Endurance, strength, vigor, and agility which produces a sound, efficiently functioning body.
	Examples: All activities which require (a) strenuous effort for long periods of time; (b) muscular exertion; (c) a quick, wide range of motion at the hip joints; and (d) quick, precise movements.
3. *Perceptual*	Interpretation of various stimuli that enable one to make adjustments to the environment. Visual, auditory, kinesthetic, or tactile discrimination. Suggests cognitive as well as psychomotor behavior.
	Examples: Coordinated movements such as jumping rope, punting, catching.
2. *Basic fundamental movement*	Inherent movement patterns which are formed by combining of reflex movements and are the basis for complex skilled movements.
	Examples: Walking, running, pushing, twisting, gripping, grasping, manipulating.
1. *Reflex movements*	Actions elicited without learning in response to some stimuli.
	Examples: Flexion, extension, stretch, postural adjustments.

After *A Taxonomy of the Psychomotor Domain* (pp. 100–150) by A.J. Harrow, 1972, New York: David McKay Co.

student's perceptual abilities and stage of physical development. Skilled movements, in turn, are the prerequisites for the aesthetic movements patterns in Category 6, non-discursive communication. A proficiency continuum exists in both categories 5 and 6; that is, there are degrees of excellence that a learner may attain.

Gagné's Learning Taxonomy

The taxonomies just discussed are distinguished by their content. Bloom distinguishes between subcategories such as "knowledge of terminology" and "knowledge of classification categories," although the requirements for acquiring such knowledge are not distinguishable. Likewise, "acceptance of a value," "preference for a value," and "commitment" in the affective domain are difficult to distinguish on the basis of their requirements for learning.

Robert Gagné has approached the classification of learning from a different angle. Gagné's scheme includes five kinds of learned capabilities: intellectual skills, cognitive strategies, verbal information, attitudes, and motor skills. It can be characterized by its comprehensiveness and by its prescriptive nature. Learning outcomes are organized into categories that can be taught by similar instructional strategies. For each category the internal and external conditions for learning are prescribed. Internal conditions are those that must be present within the learner in order for the type of learning to occur. These are usually prerequisites, competencies that were previously developed or remembered. External conditions must be established by the instructional designer. The categories of Gagné's taxonomy and associated conditions for learning are defined in Table 2.4.

Table 2.4　Definitions of Gagné's Five Learned Capabilities

Type of Learning	Definitions and Examples of Behavior
Intellectual Skills	
Problem solving	Combining lower level rules to solve problems in a situation never encountered by the person solving the problem. May involve generating new rules which receive trial and error use until the one that solves the problem is found.
Rule using	Applying a rule to a given situation or condition by responding to a class of inputs with a class of actions. Relating two or more simpler concepts in the particular manner of a rule. A rule states the relationship among concepts.
	Examples: It is helpful to think of rules or principles as "if-then" statements. "If a task is a procedure, then use flowcharting to analyze the task." "If you can convert a statement into an 'if-then' statement, then it is a rule or principle."
Concrete concept	Responding in a single way to all members of a particular class of observable events. Seeing the essential similarity among a class of objects, people, or events, which calls for a single response.
	Example: Classifying music as jazz, country western, rock, etc.; saying "round" upon seeing a manhole cover, a penny, and the moon.
Discrimination	Making different responses to the different members of a particular class. Seeing the essential differences between inputs and responding differently to each.
	Example: Distinguishing yellow finches from house finches on the basis of markings; having to tell the differences between gauges on an instrument panel.
Cognitive Strategy	An internal process by which the learner controls his or her own ways of thinking and learning.
	Example: Engaging in self-testing to decide how much study is needed; knowing what sorts of questions to ask to best define a domain of knowledge; ability to form a mental model of the problem.
Verbal Information	
Labels and facts	Naming or making a verbal response to a specific input. The response may be naming or citing a fact or set of facts. The response may be vocal or written.
	Example: Naming objects, people, or events. Recalling a person's birthday or hobbies. Stating the capitals of the United States.
Bodies of knowledge	Recalling a large body of interconnected facts.
	Example: Paraphrasing the meaning of textual materials. Stating rules or regulations.
Attitude	An internal state which affects an individual's choice of action toward some object, person, or event.
	Example: Choosing to visit an art museum; writing letters in pursuit of a cause. (See Krathwohl's Affective Taxonomy).
Motor Skills	Bodily movements involving muscular activity.
	Example: Starting a car; shooting a target; swinging a golf club. (See Harrow's Psychomotor Taxonomy).

After *Principles of Instructional Design* (2d ed.) by Robert M. Gagné and Leslie J. Briggs, Copyright 1974, 1979 by Holt, Rinehart and Winston, Inc.

The Gagné taxonomy is probably the best known and most frequently used taxonomy in the field (Reigeluth, 1983). Its acceptance is most likely based on the fact that it alone, of the many taxonomies, helps the designer make the transition from the abstract definitions of learning to the concrete action which will bring learning about. Gagné's taxonomy concentrates largely on the intellectual skills central to school learning. Four levels of hierarchically-ordered intellectual skills are defined, with each requiring different instructional conditions. Martin and Briggs (1986) note several studies that validate the hierarchical order of the intellectual skills. In contrast, learning outcomes are not differentiated for motor skills, attitudes, and cognitive strategies because they are not distinguished on the basis of the internal or external conditions for learning. To promote learning of skills in the psychomotor domain, similar internal conditions (the acquisition of lower level prerequisite motor skills) and the same external conditions apply whether the motor skill to be learned is simple or complex.

Exercise to Classify Behavior According to Domain

Directions: Classify each statement by writing the correct letter as follows:

A—Affective Domain
C—Cognitive Domain
P—Psychomotor Domain

_____ 1. Chooses the best of two solutions to a geometry problem.

_____ 2. Displays good manners toward elders.

_____ 3. Lists the names and contributions of five key curriculum developers.

_____ 4. Knits a baby blanket.

_____ 5. Votes for a political candidate.

_____ 6. Plans daily menus in accordance with nutritional principles.

_____ 7. Reports to work on time, 100 percent of the time.

_____ 8. Defeats three inexperienced players at Ping-Pong.

_____ 9. Recites the Gettysburg Address from memory.

_____ 10. Voluntarily attends lectures on higher mathematics.

_____ 11. Relaxes using yoga breathing techniques.

_____ 12. Listens attentively when the instructor speaks.

_____ 13. Analyzes a painting for its design elements.

_____ 14. Evaluates conclusions drawn from a body of data.

Exercise to Classify Learning Outcomes According to Gagné's Taxonomy

Directions: Classify each of the learning outcomes according to Robert Gagné's taxonomy. Identify the type or level of learning required.

Learning Outcome	Type or Level of Learning
1. Wraps an ankle, given an elastic bandage and a plastic model of an adult's foot.	

Learning Outcome (continued)

Learning Outcome	Type or Level of Learning
2. Lists the U.S. Air Force enlisted and officer ranks from memory.	
3. Lists five causes of the Civil War as cited in *The Civil War and Reconstruction* by D. S. Randall.	
4. Given a list of chemical elements, recalls and writes the valences of at least thirty.	
5. Solves electrical circuit problems, using Ohm's Law.	
6. Interprets written instructions to determine sequence of two or more actions.	
7. Encodes data for radio and teletype transmission.	
8. Using a year's data from atmospheric data-gathering systems, computes the annual mean wind velocity.	
9. Finds West 33rd Street on a map of Manhattan.	
10. Labels the components of a carburetor.	
11. Participates in a public discussion on the transportation of hazardous materials.	
12. Changes an automobile tire in ten minutes.	
13. Attends the theater regularly.	
14. Volunteers to answer a crisis hot-line telephone.	
15. Contributes to a political party.	
16. Types sixty words a minute.	
17. Visually tracks a moving object.	
18. Pronounces German words correctly.	
19. Uses visual imagery to remember names.	
20. Troubleshoots defective equipment to detect cause of breakdown.	
21. Follows investment guidelines to obtain highest possible income.	
22. Diagnoses disease from clinical symptoms.	

Exercise to Classify Learning Outcomes According to One of Three Taxonomies

Directions: Classify each of the learning outcomes as cognitive, affective, or psychomotor, and then classify it according to the appropriate taxonomy. Identify the type or level of learning required.

Learning Outcome	Type or Level of Learning
1. Wraps an ankle, given an elastic bandage and a plastic model of an adult's foot.	
2. Lists the U. S. Air Force enlisted and officer ranks from memory.	
3. List five causes of the Civil War as cited in *The Civil War and Reconstruction* by D. S. Randall.	
4. Given a list of chemical elements, recalls and writes the valences of at least thirty.	
5. Solves electrical circuit problems, using Ohm's Law.	
6. Interprets written instructions to determine sequence of two or more actions.	
7. Encodes data for radio and teletype transmission.	
8. Using a year's data from atmospheric data-gathering systems, computes the annual mean wind velocity.	
9. Finds West 33rd Street on a map of Manhattan.	
10. Labels the components of a carburetor.	
11. Participates in a public discussion on the transportation of hazardous materials.	
12. Changes an automobile tire in ten minutes.	
13. Attends the theater regularly.	
14. Volunteers to answer a crisis hot-line telephone.	
15. Contributes to a political party.	
16. Types sixty words a minute.	
17. Visually tracks a moving object.	
18. Pronounces German words correctly.	

Learning Outcome (continued)

Learning Outcome	Type or Level of Learning
19. Uses visual imagery to remember names.	
20. Troubleshoots defective equipment to detect cause of breakdown.	
21. Follows investment guidelines to obtain highest possible income.	
22. Diagnoses disease from clinical symptoms.	

Exercise to Compare Taxonomies

Directions: Write a short essay comparing Gagné's taxonomy with those of Bloom, Krathwohl, and Harrow. Your essay must compare the following dimensions:

Comprehensiveness of each taxonomy

Implications for sequencing learning

Implications for specifying the conditions of learning

Ease and difficulty of using each

THEORIES OF LEARNING

Instructional designers look to the behavioral sciences for the answer to the question "What conditions lead to what outcome?" Out of theory about how learning occurs and associated research has come considerable knowledge regarding how to control conditions to increase the likelihood that learning will occur. Theory is a global term used to specify particular ways of looking at things, explaining observations, and solving problems. Two major theories of learning are behaviorism and cognitive psychology.

Behaviorism

Behaviorism is an orientation in psychology that emphasizes the study of observable behavior. It grew out of an attempt by early psychologists to make the study of behavior more objective. The premise of the behaviorist schools is that instead of trying to understand vague internal processes, psychologists should concentrate on actions that are plainly visible, thereby making the study of behavior more scientific. Stimuli (conditions that lead to behavior) and responses (actual behavior) are the observable aspects of behavior. Behaviorists are concerned with discovering the relationship between stimuli and responses in order to predict and control behavior. That does not mean they are not concerned with thinking. Rather, they are interested in discovering the external controls which affect internal processes. They are less concerned with mental processes, since they can only be inferred.

First Application of Behaviorism to Instructional Design. B.F. Skinner, one of the more prominent American behaviorists of the past half century, was chiefly interested in the learning process. He applied laboratory findings to complex forms of human learning by a technique called "programmed learning." In this technique the information to be learned is broken down into very small steps. At each step a single new term or idea is introduced and material previously covered is reviewed. Students respond to each step in a manner appropriate to the instruction, for example by answering a question or filling in a blank. The student is immediately told whether the answer is right or wrong. As the student progresses through the programmed materials, his or her behavior is gradually shaped until the learning objective is achieved. Textbooks, audiovisual devices, and the computer have been used to present programmed materials.

Behaviorism influenced the course of instructional design for many years and continues to do so. It has provided precise prescriptions about what conditions lead to what outcomes. Its basic approach has been controversial, however, because it eschews references to mental events and does not adequately explain some complex human performance. For example, it cannot adequately explain how children learn grammar (Chomsky, 1969).

Cognitive Psychology

Psychologists have always been interested in mental processes. The first psychologists were chiefly interested in studying human consciousness and used a form of self-analysis called "introspection" to analyze the processes of their minds. This approach was rightly criticized as unscientific and merely another name for philosophizing about learning. In fact, behaviorism was a reaction against these methods, and for many years it was the major force in psychology.

More recently, there has been a shift from behaviorism to an interest in the organization of memory and thinking. Among the factors that have shaped the cognitive movement are computer programming and the work on artificial intelligence. For cognitive scientists, the basic model of the mind is an information processing system. Their orientation is a relative lack of concern with stimuli and responses and an interest in more holistic, internal processes (e.g., problem solving, comprehension, etc.).

Information processing and computer simulation are techniques used for theorizing about cognitive processes. Information-processing analysis is a technique for describing the presumed flow of information during cognitive processes. The flow diagrams show decision points and the sequences of the cognitive processes under study. In computer simulation a theory of cognitive operations is translated into a computer language and run as a program. If the performance of the computer matches human performance on the same task, then the theory that underlies the computer program is presumed a plausible one for human performance.

While the recent emphasis on cognition has focused attention on areas previously neglected, implications of the research for the instructional designer are tentative. There are two reasons. First, current research on cognitive processes is based on a number of assumptions that are not easily verified, for example, that human thinking is analogous to computer programming. Likewise, the diagrams used to hypothesize about cognitive structures cannot be verified by direct means. In fact, it is generally true in cognitive psychology that the same performance can be accounted for by different theories about mental processes (Gagné 1985).

Implications for Instructional Design

Richey (1986) discusses the implications of behavioral and cognitive theory for instructional design. She notes that instructional design has been affected by both theories of learning, with the cognitive school having prominence at this time. As a result of the cognitive theorists's interest in mental processes, there is now interest in building instruction to facilitate thinking processes. However, Richey points out that instruction is still focused on behavioral outcomes. Her discussion of behavioral theories concludes with the following:

> Ultimately, the most fundamental application of behaviorist thought in instructional design is the reliance on observable behaviors as the basis for instruction. Performance, or behavioral, objectives describe goals using action verbs. All knowledge is cast in terms of the observable evidence of such knowledge. Test items relate to such statements, and the entire delivery process is directed toward facilitating new learner behaviors. This orientation can also be extended to instruction related to values or attitudes. This is an almost universal approach among designers, and it stems directly from the behaviorist learning theories. (p.65)

Exercise to Identify Facts About Schools of Psychology

Directions: Read the following statements and check the ones that are true.

_____ 1. Programmed learning principles grew out of the behaviorist school of psychology and influenced instructional design for many years.

_____ 2. Flowcharting is a technique for describing mental processes.

_____ 3. The computer is capable of replicating virtually all mental processes.

_____ 4. Cognitive psychologists are primarily interested in the organization of memory and thinking.

_____ 5. Gestalt psychology is mainly concerned with stimulus/response relationships.

_____ 6. Behaviorism is concerned only with the psychomotor domain.

_____ 7. It is basic to instructional design that all learning must be cast in observable evidence of that learning.

_____ 8. Behaviorism does not adequately explain all types of learning.

FROM THE READING

Define the following terms.

Learning   Taxonomy

Cognitive domain   Behaviorism

Affective domain   Cognitive Psychology

Psychomotor domain   Theory

ISSUES FOR DISCUSSION

1. How important is it that an instructional designer support a particular theory of learning?

2. Are social scientists subject to social and political influences in the viewpoints they support?

3. What are the implications of current trends in cognitive psychology for instructional design?

REFERENCES

Chomsky, N. (1969). *The acquisition of syntax in children 5 to 10*. Cambridge, MA: M.I.T. Press.

Committee of College and University Examiners. (1956). *Taxonomy of educational objectives: Handbook I: Cognitive domain*, B.S. Bloom (Ed.). New York: David McKay Co., Appendix p.201.

Gagné, R.M. (1985). *The Cognitive Psychology of School Learning*. New York: Little, Brown, & Co.

Gagné, R.M. (1977). *The conditions of learning* (3rd ed.). New York: Holt, Rinehart & Winston.

Gagné, R.M. & Briggs, L.J. (1979). *Principles of instructional design* (2nd ed.). New York: Holt, Rinehart & Winston.

Gerlach, V.S., & Ely, D.P. (1980). *Teaching and media: A systematic approach*. Englewood Cliffs, NJ: Prentice-Hall.

Harrow, A.J. (1972). *A taxonomy of the psychomotor domain*. New York: David McKay Co., pp. 100–150.

Krathwohl, D.R., Bloom, B.S., & Masia, B.B. (1964). *Taxonomy of educational objectives: Handbook II: Affective domain*. New York: David McKay Co., Appendix A, p. 176.

Martin, B.L., & Briggs, L.J. (1986). *The affective and cognitive domains: Integration for instruction and research*. Englewood Cliffs, NJ: Educational Technology Publications.

Reigeluth, C.M. (1983). *Instructional design theories and models: An overview of their current status*. Hillsdale, NJ: Laurence Erlbaum Associates.

Richey, R. (1985). *The theoretical and conceptual basis of instructional design*. New York: Nicols Publishing Co.

Chapter Three
The Instructional Design Process

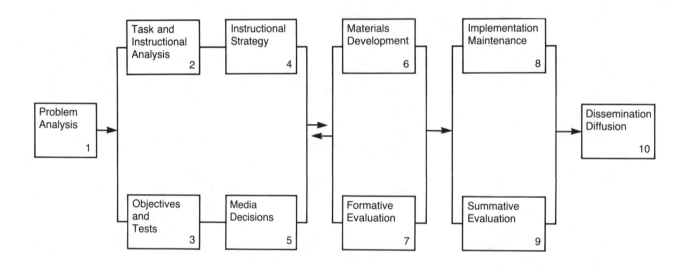

Objectives	■	Given true/false questions on common elements of ID models, answer correctly.
	■	Given descriptive phrases, match each phrase with one of these categories: common elements of ID models or errors in application of ID models.
	■	Given authors and descriptions for ID models, match a schematic or phrase with each author.
	■	Given the steps, match the steps in the generic ID model to the steps in the Seels and Glasgow model.
	■	Given an essay question, explain the steps and flow of the Seels and Glasgow model.
	■	Given a chart, compare and contrast these characteristics of ID models: date, shape, steps.

Overview

Instructional design models serve as analogs for the process used to complete an instructional design task. The tasks or steps of a model can be applied in different settings. Some of the models have made unique contributions to the ID process.

Models are visual or verbal representations of a process comparable with the generic ID process. Different models emphasize different aspects of the process. Media selection models, for example, are one type of ID model; other models are applicable when materials are to be produced. Comparable ID models for product research and development are the IDI model, the Air Force model, the Briggs model, the Gagné and Briggs model, the Kemp model, the Dick and Carey model, and the Seels and Glasgow model used in this text.

The IDI (Instructional Development Institute) Model has three phases: define, develop, and evaluate. The Air Force Model is iterative in nature: the steps are repeated and revisions made as new information is revealed at a later step. Leslie Briggs's model is accompanied by thorough detail, especially about the design step. He also adds the step of diffusion planning to be done concurrently with other steps. The Gagné and Briggs model uses Gagné's theories about types and conditions of learning as a basis for analysis and design decisions.

Kemp's model is the most flexible. The order of steps can be modified to suit the situation. Kemp's model emphasizes choice of teaching/learning pattern as an important determinant in media selection. Dick and Carey's model emphasizes the instructional analysis step and includes clear directions on how to perform this step.

Like the other models, the Seels and Glasgow model is a variation of its predecessors. It is iterative because the products of the steps can be revised as the process proceeds. Thus the design is continually being refined and polished by returning to a step and making adjustments. For example, you can complete a task analysis before writing objectives; however, you may expand the task analysis and rewrite the objectives as new insights are revealed.

When an instructional design process is used to solve problems, decisions must be made about which model to use and what adjustments, if any, need to be made in the model chosen. A design team may choose to develop their own model instead.

Study Questions

1. What is an ID model?
2. What purposes can these models serve?
3. What are the similarities and differences among major ID models?
4. What is the Seels and Glasgow model?

FUNCTIONS OF MODELS

Models can take many forms: verbal, visual, or three-dimensional. Whatever form they take, their purpose is to present a view of reality. Although models can be part of a theory, they are not in themselves theories. They are used to give form and substance to concepts or procedures. Although models represent a reality, they can never be a complete representation because you must abstract in order to translate reality into theoretical terms. Models can show variables and their interrelationship or they can represent steps in a problem-solving process.

Instructional design models give visual form to the procedures used in the ID process. Often this is done with an accompanying description in verbal form. An ID model is modified as it is implemented in different settings and situations.

Imagine you've finished your studies and accepted a position as instructional designer. You are assigned your first project, which is a relatively ambiguous task, such as improving the instruction in a course or changing the behaviors of employees who do performance appraisal, or creating an environment for learning how to learn. How do you keep control of your anxiety? You break the task into parts. The first part is to decide on procedures you will follow in solving this problem.

The instructional design model is a representation of the process you or your team agrees to follow when doing instructional design. ID models serve several purposes:

1. They visualize a systematic process, thus allowing those involved to reach consensus on that process.
2. They provide a tool for managing the process and project.
3. They allow you to test theories by integrating them within a practical model that can be applied.
4. They set tasks for the designer that can be used as criteria for good design.

Instructional design models are based on assumptions about tasks and order of tasks. Always question these assumptions. Like all models, the ID model is not reality; rather, it is a way to simplify and make reality visible. There are more aspects to each step than known in the model. Each step breaks down to many substeps.

Usually ID models are adaptations of the generic model. This is because a model must be modified to fit specific situations or localities. What is new in the model is not the process, but rather the interpretation of the process.

ID models differ in many ways. Some are accompanied by annotations or descriptions of how to implement a step. Others include only brief descriptions of a step. Most require doing each step in a prescribed order; a few allow more flexibility. Some are linear and others are iterative. The order of steps and what steps are included differ from model to model.

COMPONENTS OF MODELS

Models are constructed by showing the relationship between the steps and how the steps occur chronologically. A step is a task or phase that must be completed in order to develop an instructional design solution.

The generic model represented in Chapter 1 consists of five steps: analysis, design, development, implementation, and evaluation. These steps are simply listed or shown in a line of five rectangular blocks connected by arrows. This model defines the process as five steps in fixed order done one at a time. Other models may vary the steps, show more steps, or suggest more flexibility.

Diana R. Carl (1976) compared instructional development models used in instructional television. She found great differences in their components. The general categories common to many of the models were found to be needs assessment and goal generation, learner or audience analysis, content identification, objective identification, strategizing (media, format), and formative and summative evaluation.

Andrews and Goodson (1980) compared thirty ID models on the basis of fourteen dimensions taken from a list developed by George Gropper. To that list they added four dimensions: problem identification, alternative solutions to instruction, identification of constraints, and cost of instructional programs. Their review of models led Andrews and Goodson to these conclusions:

> The general tasks constituting a model of instructional design, though differing in sequence, are generic in that they may be applied across differing purposes, emphases, origins, uses, and settings. This attests to the robust qualities of the systematic approach to instructional design. (p. 13)

At the same time, Andrews and Goodson caution that many of the models represent a series of mechanical or linear steps rather than the complex analytical and cybernetic process required in order to apply the systems approach effectively.

Richey (1986) examined Andrews and Goodson's "Comparative Analysis of Models of Instructional Design." Their list of fourteen common elements was reduced to the six core elements shown in Table 3.1, "A Definition of the Six Core Elements."

Table 3.1   "A Definition of the Six Core Elements"

Core Elements	Andrews/Goodson Tasks
Determine learner needs	Assessment of needs, problems identification, occupational analysis, competence or training requirements
	Characterization of learner population
Determine goals and objectives	Formulation of broad goals and detailed subgoals stated in observable terms
	Analysis of goals and subgoals for types of skills/learning required
	Sequencing of goals and subgoals to facilitate learning
Construct assessment procedures	Development of pretest and post-test matching goals and subgoals
Design/select delivery approaches	Formulation of instructional strategy to match subject-matter and learner requirements
	Selection of media to implement strategies
	Development of courseware based on strategies
	Consideration of alternative solutions to instruction
Try out instructional system	Empirical tryout of courseware with learner population, diagnosis of learning and courseware failures, and revision of courseware based on diagnosis
Install and maintain system	Formulation of system and environmental descriptions and identification of constraints
	Development of materials and procedures for installing maintaining, and periodically repairing the instructional program
	Costing instructional program

The question of whether ID models are or should be linear is an interesting one. The word linear means arranged in a line, taking the form of a line. In programmed instruction linear style means each learner follows the same path or line. Using this meaning, some of the models to be discussed, such as Briggs and IDI, are linear; others, such as Kemp and the Air Force model, are not.

The issue is whether an ID model when applied should require a fixed sequence of steps or whether there should be some flexibility in the steps or order of steps in an ID model. The flexibility in the Kemp and Air Force models is for different purposes. Kemp's model uses flexibility to adapt to situations; the Air Force model uses it to adapt to information resulting from a previous step. The Air Force model still requires a prescribed sequence of steps. The consensus of ID models is that there is a fixed order of steps to be followed but that the process is iterative.

Several ID models provide for flexibility in the order of steps either by being iterative or by leaving openness. Some of the ID models that provide for simultaneous and interacting steps as well as linear ones are the Air Force, Dick and Carey, Kemp, and Seels and Glasgow models.

VISUAL DIFFERENCES

One of the reasons for using visual models is that you can see at a glance the nature of the process. Differences between processes are shown through shapes and connections between shapes. There are two aspects of the ID process that can be interpreted through shapes. One is the subprocesses used to reach the goal, such as operations (rectangles) or decision-making (diamonds). The other is the overall configuration of all the shapes together. What basic shape does the whole process take? If you know this, you've learned something about the process from the model.

Look at Figure 3.1, Different Configurations of Models. It presents five shapes that are common to ID models. Shape A is an oval. It could also be drawn as a circle. This shape suggests no beginning and no end. The operations are connected so that wherever you start you complete all the steps. (This is not to be confused with an oval as used to begin and end a flowchart.)

Shape B is basically a short line of steps. It is a simple path to follow. Shape C is more complex. The basic shape is a large rectangle made from a path that allows for many steps in a line that starts at the top left corner and loops like a maze to the bottom right corner. More steps can be represented in a single path using this shape.

Shape D is a variation on B. You follow one path, but at points along that path you deal with two steps alternately or simultaneously. This path can be long or short and the number of concurrent steps can vary.

Shape E is a cross. The circle in the center is an intersection through which information passes. In this model, the steps are done in a specified order, but a step can be returned to at any point. The crucial element is the cross point, where information from each step is checked against information from another step and a decision is made to return to a step or proceed.

The basic shapes—oval or round, line, rectangle, cross, and line with squares projecting above and below—are some of the configurations ID models can take. The oval indicates a flexible starting point; the line, a predetermined path; the rectangle, a long series of steps in a predetermined path; and the cross, steps that are returned to as information from other steps is checked. There are other configurations, but these examples show how the configuration of a model can reveal differences among ID processes.

COMMON ERRORS

According to Richard Boutwell (1979) there are eight common errors in applications of models. Although none of these common errors is inherent in the ID process or model,

Figure 3.1   Different Configuration of Models

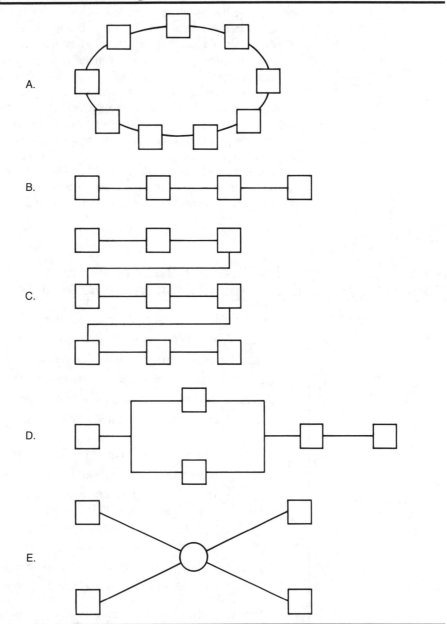

a designer should be aware of them as potential sources of invalidity that must be avoided. Here is Boutwell's list of errors:

1. Social variables are not taken into account.

2. Most systems are situational to the training.

3. Other solution strategies are often ignored.

4. Courses and materials are evaluated as single entities rather than interacting components of a larger whole.

5. Task analysis lacks realism.

6. The design and development phase of an [ID] model are often overgeneralized.

7. [ID] models are often blindly adopted rather than creatively adapted.

8. There is too much reliance upon [ID] development manuals (Boutwell, 1979, p. 33).

One problem with the use of an ID model is the use of an essentially structural model as if it were the complete procedure or paradigm. Because models are static and simplified, they lack the detail and dynamic interaction that must be provided in the ID process. Designers should be aware of this and adjust accordingly. For example, some models lack a problem analysis phase and start with the assumption an instructional problem exists. Yet for non-academic settings, the problem analysis phase is important.

Therefore, when you adapt a model for the process you'll use to design instruction, don't do it blindly. Understand the assumptions of the model such as fixed path or starting point and why you choose it. Be aware of the limitations of a model such as few steps. Avoid these problems with implementing the model: not faithfully executed; implemented superficially; rushed completion of steps due to unrealistic timeliness, such as omission of steps when a decision is made just to do revisions (Hannum, 1983). In each of these cases, if you report that the model was used for your problem-solving process, you are not reporting accurately because the process was not followed completely.

An Exercise Designed to Give Feedback on Your Knowledge of Functions and Limitations of ID Models

1. Answer these questions with true and false.

   _____ a. Models set tasks which can serve as criteria for good instructional design.

   _____ b. Instructional design models can serve as theories.

   _____ c. Instructional design models reproduce the reality of the design process.

   _____ d. Models can translate theory into many forms.

   _____ e. One purpose of an instructional design model is to make the process visible.

   _____ f. A step common to most models is determining learner needs.

   _____ g. Few models include a step for writing objectives.

   _____ h. There is little agreement among models about the necessity of planning for dissemination and diffusion of the innovation.

   _____ i. Models with the configuration of a circle convey a process different from models with the configuration of a straight line.

   _____ j. When an ID process is adopted, other solution strategies are often ignored.

   _____ k. ID models emphasize social and environmental variables.

2. Match each phrase with the category it refers to.

   C–Components of models
   E–Error in application of ID models

   _____ a. Steps are shown as operations, procedures, or processes.

   _____ b. The designer assumes the model represents the process as it exists in reality.

   _____ c. Design and development phases are stated too generally.

   _____ d. Team members omit or rush steps.

   _____ e. Materials are designed and delivery approaches selected.

   _____ f. An ID model is accepted without questioning assumptions.

   _____ g. Field testing is a requirement.

ID MODELS

Models for instructional design fall under several rubrics, depending on the scope of the project. At the simplest level are models for media selection that explain how to select media and use them systematically. Media selection models are a form of instructional design model. At the next level are models that represent procedures to be followed in designing programs and materials. At the top level is the sophisticated ID model, which is used for massive design projects like telecourses, open university courses, or interactive video courses. Models at the top level are a combination of ID models and project management models. This chapter will review models for designing programs and materials.

IDI Model (1973)

In 1965 a consortium was formed by instructional technology departments at the University of Southern California, Syracuse University, Michigan State University, and the U.S. International University in Corvallis, Oregon. In 1973–74 the consortium changed its name to the University Consortium for Instructional Development & Technology (UCIDT), and Indiana University became a member (Wittich & Schuller, 1973).

The U.S. Office of Education gave the consortium a grant to create Instructional Development Institutes (IDIs) for public school personnel. In the early 1970s the IDIs were used to train teams of administrators, teachers, and curriculum and media specialists in principles of instructional systems design. After a thorough review of the literature on systems approaches and design, the institute materials were developed by institutional members of the consortium. (UCIDT, 1968). About 400 Instructional Development Institutes were conducted in twenty states. The subsequent evaluation was not thorough enough to determine impact. However, since then the components of the IDI workshops have been modified and used nationally and internationally with much success (Schuller, 1986).

The IDI project has nine steps in three stages called decision points in instructional development. Explanatory detail accompanies each step (Stamas 1973, p. 23). Figure 3.2 shows the IDI model.

The IDI model is noteworthy for its "organize management" step, which is missing from other models. This model also has the strength of being very detailed.

Air Force Model (1975)

The Air Force has been a pioneer in the application of instructional systems design concepts. It was the military that emphasized a systematic procedure for assuring application of instructional technology to course planning and development. The Air Force was among the first organizations to use a systematic approach to ID. Today the Air Force annually trains thousands from its ranks as instructional designers. Manuals for training instructors in ID concepts were published from 1975.

Because training using the ID approach is so important, Air Force policy states that ID should be used to produce all training materials. The five-step model used by the Air Force is shown in Figure 3.3.

The process requires the following:

1. Determining job performance requirements

2. Determining training requirements (what is necessary to bring them to a skill level)

3. Writing behavioral objectives and test items

4. Designing instructional procedures and materials

5. Conducting and evaluating the instruction

There is interaction between steps of the model, so sometimes portions of several steps can be revised simultaneously. The output of one step is intended to provide the information needed to accomplish a later step.

The Air Force Model is accompanied by adequate detail. Generally it is used by a team, although sometimes one person uses the model to perform the ID process. This model

Figure 3.2   IDI Model

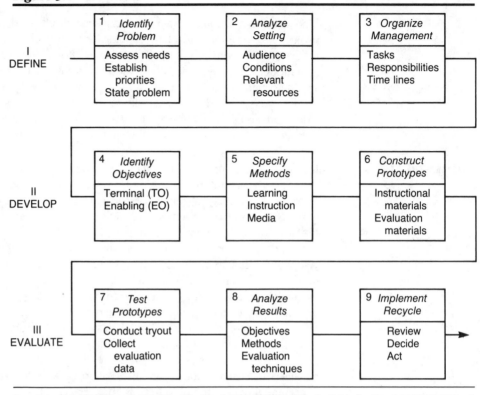

From *Instructional Technology: Its Nature and Use*, 5th ed. Walter Wittich and Charles F. Schuller. Copyright 1973 by Walter A. Wittich and Charles F. Schuller. Reprinted by permission of Harper & Row Publishers, Inc.

Figure 3.3   Air Force Model

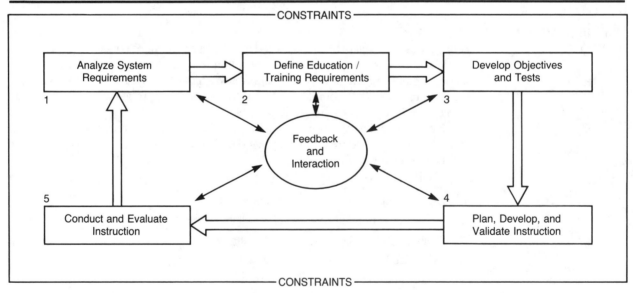

From *Instructional System Development* (1975), U.S. Air Force, UF Manual, 50–52.

emphasizes a thorough systems analysis before moving to the design phase. A lengthy process of collecting information on the learners, instructors, environment, subsystems, purposes, and policies is conducted, and task analysis is done thoroughly. The problem is examined until it is proved to be an instructional problem. After the first phase, decisions in other phases are based on the conclusions reached during the analysis stage. Classroom management techniques and individual differences are stressed at the "plan instruction" stage. The "conduct and evaluate" instruction stage includes support functions such as instructor training and facilities maintenance. Evaluation is conducted in both the field and the learning environment. This military model emphasizes analysis of content requirements and stresses instructional and systems management.

Briggs Model (1977)

Leslie Briggs was an important scholar in the instructional design field. He is known for the thoroughness with which he pursued the study of each step, especially media selection. Figure 3.4 presents his 1977 model.

Note that the Briggs 1977 model differs in its emphasis on planning for diffusion of the innovation, or in other words, preparing for the adoption and maintenance of the instructional program.

His model works very well for program or course design. The suitability to school settings is revealed in the steps where attention is given to adapting instruction to students and providing remedial programs. If you invest the time to follow Briggs's prescriptions, the model is effective. Overall, the model presents an approach to program development that has been tested and works well.

Gagné and Briggs Model (1979)

In 1979 Gagné and Briggs published the revision of their 1974 text, *Principles of Instructional Design*. The model used in their text is summarized in Table 3.2.

This model incorporates Briggs's theory on the use of levels of objectives to organize a course. Levels of objectives mean developing objectives from goals to specific objectives for each component of a course. When Briggs's ideas were combined with Gagné's theories on types of learning and differing conditions for instruction, the Gagné and Briggs model (1979) was developed. The core steps of this model are, in order, the following:

1. Do system level analysis.
2. Specify the outcomes of instruction.

Figure 3.4 Briggs 1977 Model

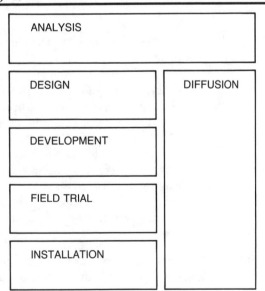

From *Instructional Design Principles to Applications* (p. 284) by L. Briggs, 1977, Englewood Cliffs, NJ: Educational Technology Publications. Copyright 1977 by Educational Technology Publications. Reprinted by permission.

Table 3.2 Gagné–Briggs Model (1979)

Stages in Designing Instructional Systems

System Level
1. Analysis of Needs, Goals, and Priorities
2. Analysis of Resources. Constraints, and Alternate Delivery Systems
3. Determination of Scope and Sequence of Curriculum and Courses: Delivery System Design

Course Level
4. Determining Course Structure and Sequence
5. Analysis of Course Objectives

Lesson Level
6. Definition of Performance Objectives
7. Preparing Lesson Plans (or Modules)
8. Developing, Selecting Materials, Media
9. Assessing Student Performance (Performance Measures)

System Level
10. Teacher Preparation
11. Formative Evaluation
12. Field Testing, Revision
13. Summative Evaluation
14. Installation and Diffusion

From *Principles of Instructional Design*, 2nd ed., by Robert M. Gagné and Leslie J. Briggs, Copyright 1974, 1979 by Holt, Rinehart and Winston Inc. Reprinted by permission of the publisher.

3. Analyze the learning task.

4. Define performance objectives.

5. Design instructional sequences.

6. Specify events of instruction.

7. Select media.

8. Assess performance.

9. Evaluate instruction.

Dick and Carey Model (1985)

This model was presented in a text for instructional designers published in 1978 and was revised in 1985.

The text is used extensively in colleges to train instructional designers. The Dick and Carey model is shown in Figure 3.5.

This model describes the instructional design process from stating goals and writing objectives to developing materials, assessing instruction, and grading. The Dick and Carey model is for practitioners. The theory is linked with skills to implement that theory. The model is an excellent guide for the instructional design process. Their book describes an approach to instructional analysis that should be required knowledge for every instructional designer. Still, the instructional analysis approach used by Dick and Carey does not adequately handle the analysis of affective objectives, though their attempt to relate affective objectives to cognitive components is useful.

Kemp Model (1985)

Kemp's model differs the most from the other models. As it has evolved over the years, it has moved further from linearity. The model was introduced in a text in 1971. Figure 3.6 shows the 1985 model.

Figure 3.5 Dick and Carey Model

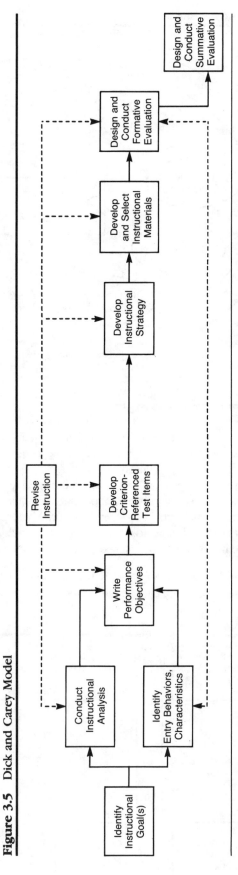

From *The Systematic Design of Instruction* (pp.2–3) by Walter Dick & Lou Carey, 1985, Glenview, Il.: Scott, Foresman & Company. Copyright 1985 by Scott, Foresman & Company. Reprinted by permission.

Figure 3.6   Kemp Model

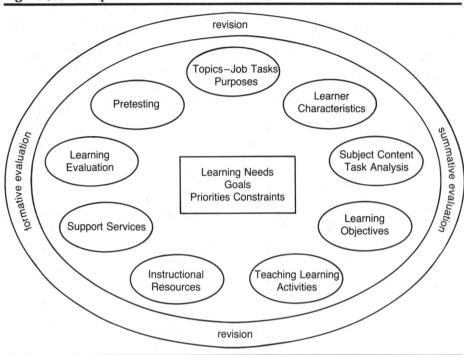

From *The Instructional Design Process* by Jerrold Kemp, 1985, NY: Harper & Row. Copyright 1985 by Harper & Row Publishers, Inc. Reprinted by permission of the publisher.

The 1985 model presents ten design elements that can be approached by different paths as long as the starting point is the step in the center, needs and goals. One problem with the model is a lack of specificity on some of the steps (e.g., goal setting), at least at the level required by a professional designer. Another problem is insufficient attention to instructional analysis. A strength of the model is its step of identifying teaching/learning activities (large group, small group, independent study) before resource selection.

This model is helpful to novice designers. Kemp's model allows more latitude in writing objectives. He suggests using expressive as well as instructional objectives.

Seels and Glasgow Model (1990)

As you have probably surmised by now, these models are variations on the generic ID model and on each other. They are adaptations or redefinitions of previous models. This

Figure 3.7   Seels and Glasgow ID Model

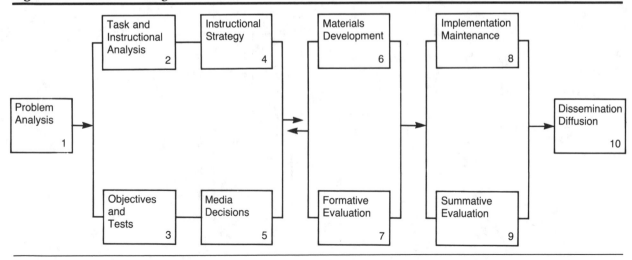

text introduces a new adaptation or variation intended for beginning students in instructional design. This is the Seels and Glasgow model presented in Figure 3.7.

An Exercise Designed as a Test of Your Knowledge and Understanding of ID Models

1. Match the schematic in Figure 3.8 with the name of the model it represents.
    1. Air Force Model
    2. Kemp Model
    3. Briggs Model
    4. IDI Model
    5. Dick and Carey Model

2. Match the phrase with the model it describes.

    _____ a. Start with determining job performance and training requirements.

    _____ b. Design elements can be approached by different paths.

    _____ c. Do instructional analysis and identifying entry behaviors concurrently.

    _____ d. Diffusion planning should be conducted concurrently with other stages.

    _____ e. A strategy for management should be developed during the first stage.

    1. Briggs Model
    2. Air Force Model
    3. Kemp Model
    4. IDI Model
    5. Dick and Carey Model

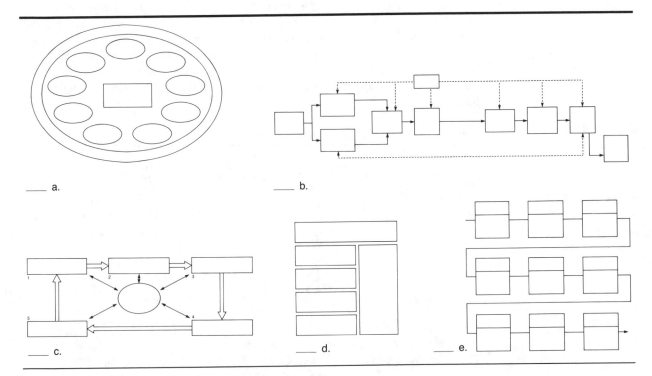

_____ a.

_____ b.

_____ c.

_____ d.

_____ e.

The ID process presented in the Seels and Glasgow model (p. 50) is based on the assumption that a project management plan is formulated and revised as necessary. The project management plan establishes roles, tasks, timelines, budget, checkpoints, and supervisory procedures. The steps are undertaken within the parameters of the project management plan.

These are the steps in the Seels and Glasgow model:

1. Analyze the problem, determine whether there is an instructional problem, collect information through needs assessment techniques, and write a problem statement.

2. Through task analysis collect more information on performance standards and skills and on attitudinal requirements. Then do an instructional analysis to determine the prerequisites.

3. Write behavioral objectives and criterion-referenced tests to match those objectives.

4. Determine the instructional strategy or components of instruction, such as presentation or practice conditions.

5. Select methods and media that will allow you to meet these conditions.

6. Plan for production. Develop the program or materials. Monitor materials development to assure project integrity.

7. Plan a formative evaluation strategy. Prepare to collect data on achieving objectives. Revise as feasible and re-evaluate.

8. Plan for implementation and maintenance of the instruction.

9. Conduct summative evaluation.

10. Arrange for dissemination and diffusion of the innovation.

Some of these steps are characterized by back and forth activity with the preceding step. Thus, step 2 (instructional analysis) and step 3 (objectives) are considered together. Step 2 is the starting point and the step 3 the finishing point, but until both tasks are finished there will be much coordination between these steps. The difficulty of formulating a criterion item may suggest problems with the instructional analysis, for example. At times, the tasks may be done concurrently, as with step 4 (instructional strategy) and step 5 (media decisions). Media factors may affect instructional strategy decisions and vice versa. This model allows for doing other steps concurrently, such as steps 2 and 4. Media decisions may lead to changes in objectives, or instructional strategies may lead to changes in the instructional analysis. Step 6 (materials development) and step 7 (formative evaluation) form the same pattern, as do steps 8 and 9 (implementation and maintenance and summative evaluation). Table 3.3 compares the Seels and Glasgow model with the generic ID model.

Table 3.3   A Comparison with the Generic ID Model

Steps in Generic ID Model	Steps in Seels and Glasgow Model	Questions Answered
1. Analysis	1. Problem Analysis	What is the problem? Who is the learner?
2. Design	2. Task/Instructional Analysis	What is the specific content?
	3. Objectives and Test	How are the objectives classified?
	4. Instructional Strategy	How should the content be organized?
	5. Media Decisions	What media (hardware/ software) should be used?
3. Development	6. Materials Development	
4. Implementation	7. Formative Evaluation	Does the material work?
	8. Implementation and Maintenance	
5. Evaluation	9. Summative Evaluation	Are the objectives achieved?
	10. Dissemination and Diffusion	

An Exercise Designed to Give Feedback on Knowledge and Understanding of the Seels and Glasgow Model

1. Match the steps in the Seels and Glasgow model with the corresponding step from the generic ID model.

   _____ 1. Problem Analysis   a. Analysis

   _____ 2. Task/Instructional Analysis   b. Design

   _____ 3. Objectives and Tests   c. Development

   _____ 4. Instructional Strategy   d. Implementation

   _____ 5. Media Decisions   e. Evaluation

   _____ 6. Materials Development

   _____ 7. Formative Evaluation

   _____ 8. Implementation and Maintenance

   _____ 9. Summative Evaluation

   _____ 10. Dissemination and Diffusion

2. In an essay explain the steps and flow in the Seels–Glasgow model.

An Exercise Designed to Help You Distinguish Among Models

Complete the following chart for each of the models presented in the text.

Developer	Date	Shape of Model	Steps
1.			
2.			
3.			
4.			
5.			
6.			
7.			

FROM THE READING

Define the Following Terms

ID Process   Iterative

ID Steps

ISSUES FOR DISCUSSION

1. Which model seems to be most practical for the setting you are preparing to work in? Why?

2. What must happen for a product to be called an instructional design?

3. What criteria would you establish for selecting a process for instructional design?

4. How can common errors in the use of instructional design models be avoided?

REFERENCES

Andrews, D.H., & Goodson, L.A. (1980). A comparative analysis of models for instructional design. *Journal of Instructional Development, 3,* (4), 2–15.

Boutwell, R.C. (1979). Instructional systems in the next decade. *Journal of Instructional Development, 2,* (3), 31–55.

Briggs, L. (1977). *Instructional design principles and practices.* Englewood Cliffs, NJ: Educational Technology Publications.

Carl, D.R. (1976). Instructional development in educational television. *Educational Technology, 16,* 10–24.

Dick, W., & Carey, L. (1985). *The systematic design of instruction.* Glenview, IL: Scott Foresman.

Gagné, R.M., & Briggs, L.J. (1979). *Principles of Instructional Design.* NY: Holt, Rinehart & Winston.

Gropper, G.L. (1977). On gaining acceptance for instructional design in a university setting. *Educational Technology, 17,* 7–12.

Hannum, W.H. (1983). Implementing instructional development models: Discrepancies between models and their applications. *Performance and Instruction Journal, 22,* 16–19.

Kemp, J. (1985). *The instructional design process.* NY: Harper & Row.

Reiser, R.A., & Gagné, R.M. (1983). *Selecting media for instruction.* Englewood Cliffs, NJ: Educational Technology Publications.

Richey, R. (1986). *Theoretical and conceptual bases of instructional design.* NY: Nicols Publishing.

Schuller, C. (1986). Some historical perspectives on the instructional technology field. *Journal of Instructional Development, 8* (3), 3–6.

Stamas, S. (1973). Instructional models. Division of Instructional Development Occasional Paper. Washington, DC: Association for Educational Communications and Technology.

U.S. Air Force, (July 31, 1975). *Instructional system development,* Washington, DC: UF Manual, 50–2.

University Consortium for Instructional Development and Technology. (UCIDT) (1968). Instructional Development Institutes. Syracuse, NY: Syracuse University, Instructional Design, Development and Evaluation.

Wittich, W. & Schuller, C. (1973). *Audiovisual materials and their use.* NY: Harper and Brothers.

Chapter Four
Problem Analysis

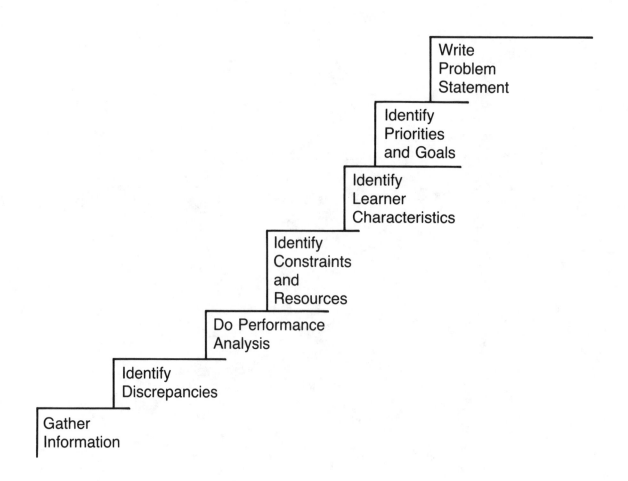

Write
Problem
Statement

Identify
Priorities
and Goals

Identify
Learner
Characteristics

Identify
Constraints
and
Resources

Do Performance
Analysis

Identify
Discrepancies

Gather
Information

Objectives	· Given problem areas and a checklist of the decisions to be made in planning a needs assessment, use the checklist to develop a plan for assessing needs in one of the areas.
	· Given an outline for an interview, complete the outline with questions that could be asked for each part of the outline.
	· Given problems, identify them as instructional, non-instructional, or a combination of both.
	· Given a situation, list the kinds and sources of information about constraints, resources, and learners.
	· Given a situation, describe learner characteristics and complete a learner profile.
	· Given needs, apply the card sort method for determining priorities.
	· Given a form, use the RUPS method to write a problem statement.
	· Given a form, use the IDI method to write a problem statement.

Overview

The problem analysis step is completed by using a needs assessment process. There are seven components or substeps to the needs assessment process: (1) gathering information, (2) identifying discrepancies, (3) analyzing performance, (4) identifying constraints and resources, (5) identifying learner characteristics, (6) identifying priorities and goals, and (7) writing a problem statement. The purpose of the needs assessment process is to identify goals and describe the context in which a problem will be solved. The instructional design process is appropriate only when performance analysis determines that a problem is an instructional problem.

According to Kaufman and English (1979, p. 83), there are several types of needs: resources, processes, products, outputs, and outcomes. The instructional designer improves the instructional process in order to change learner outcomes. For a problem to be instructional it has to involve deficiencies in knowledge, skills, or attitudes.

You need to analyze the setting by gathering information on constraints and resources. This information helps the designer define the parameters of the problem. The same information will be helpful in later stages of the ID process. A problem statement should summarize the nature of the problem, constraints, resources, and decisions on goals.

Study Questions

1. How do you distinguish between instructional and non-instructional problems?
2. How do you develop a plan for needs assessment?
3. How do you collect information about constraints, resources, and learners?
4. How do you write a problem statement?

PURPOSE OF PROBLEM ANALYSIS

You are entering the analysis stage, the first step in the generic ID model. During this stage, you will complete problem, task, and instructional analyses in order to arrive at instructional goals, content, and prerequisites.

Ken Silber describes the instructional design process succinctly:

If we carefully analyze what happens to and within the developer during the ID process, something like the following pattern emerges:

1. The developer is presented with some problem related to learning and/or performance.

2. The developer must gather information about the problem, analyze it, synthesize it into some coherent statement, and evaluate the statement in terms of reality.

3. The developer is presented with a body of content, usually in verbal or written form, that he or she must learn or develop a cognitive structure for.

4. The developer must analyze that body of content and restructure (or synthesize) it into a form that takes into account both the integrity of the content and the learning and instructional principles to be applied to it.

5. The developer must evaluate the accuracy and adequacy of this restructuring and restructure again if the original attempt is not successful.

6. The developer must translate the verbal written form of the content into other communication formats, such as visual and oral media. (Silber, 1981, p. 34)

The process Silber describes is an interactive (feedback loops) one in which (1) and (2) are problem analyses, and (3) and (4) are task and instructional analyses.

The purpose of problem analysis is to define the parameters of the problem to be solved by instruction. The term "needs assessment" is often used to describe the problem analysis phase.

NEEDS ASSESSMENT

What does "assess needs" mean in the context of instructional design? It means a plan for gathering information about discrepancies and for using that information to make decisions about priorities. The priorities that must be determined are the goals for the problem-solving effort. The data collected by needs assessment procedures should provide a basis for stating goals.

As an instructional designer you may be given the results of a needs assessment in the form of goal statements or you may be asked to develop goal statements from an existing needs assessment. You could be asked to gather the information and identify priorities. In each of these situations, it is your responsibility to consider the integrity of the goal statements and the needs assessment process.

There are several components to the needs assessment or problem analysis phase. One way to visualize the process is as a ladder leading to a problem statement that defines the goals. Figure 4.1 presents the components in a specific sequence. They are not always done in this order, however.

The first step on the ladder is gathering information. There are many ways to do this. The designer must know what questions to ask.

The second step is determining discrepancies. A discrepancy is a gap between desired behavior and actual or predicted behavior. An instructional design problem analysis is always done from the point of view that needs are gaps or discrepancies in instructional outcomes.

The third step in needs assessment is performance analysis. It requires asking these questions: (1) Is this an instructional problem, one that can be solved by instruction?, and (2) What is causing the problem? The performance analysis step results in identifying the nature of the problem and its causes.

After analyzing performance you should be able to decide whether an instructional design solution is feasible and sufficient. In many cases instruction may be part of but not the whole solution, so it is important to justify any commitment of resources to instruction. During problem identification you ask what caused the problem and whether it can be

Figure 4.1   Components of Needs Assessment

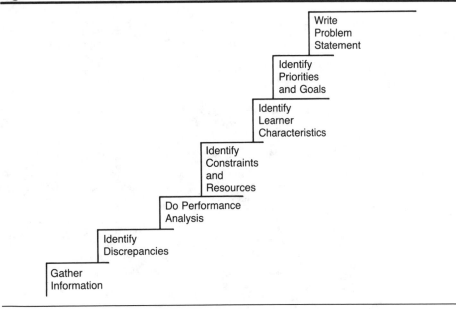

eliminated by instruction. You may even find that solutions other than instructional design is warranted.

The fourth and fifth steps on the ladder require identifying parameters of the problem: constraints, resources, and learner characteristics. This information establishes the context in which the problem is to be solved. Information about the context of the problem helps the designer make decisions about feasible directions.

The sixth step is identifying goals and priorities. It is not enough to identify the needs as gaps or discrepancies. The designer must determine which of these needs should have priority. Information gathered on constraints, resources, the learner, and the nature of the problem is helpful at this point. In addition, methods for determining priorities can be used.

Finally, the designer reaches the top of the ladder where a problem statement can be formulated. A problem statement serves many purposes. It communicates the agreed-upon priorities and goals. If the team approach is used, the writing of the statement can become a process that facilitates the development of a common conceptual framework. If you are working independently, a problem statement is a way to clarify your thinking and facilitate communication with those you approach for assistance.

Table 4.1 gives the input, action, and output of each step in the needs assessment process.

Each step helps define the problem more completely and sharply. The rest of this chapter will cover ways to accomplish these steps.

STEP 1: GATHER INFORMATION

The designer needs to collect information that will reveal who can do what, who knows what, who needs to learn, and what constraints, resources, and learner characteristics affect the situation. In order to develop a plan for needs assessment a series of decisions must be made. While there is no one model or conceptual framework for needs assessment, a model developed by Witkin for a project funded by the National Institute of Education is widely used in educational settings (Witkin, 1978a; 1978b). Witkin (1984) defines needs

Table 4.1 Outputs to Steps in Needs Assessment

Input	Action	Output
Data collection methods	Gathering information	Information on discrepancies, nature of problem, constraints, resources, learner characteristics, priorities
Information on gaps between ideal and status quo	Identify discrepancies	Statements of needs
Information on nature of problem	Analyze performance	Whether it is an instructional problem
Information on constraints and resources	Identify constraints and resources	Context of problem
Information on learner characteristics	Identify learner characteristics	Learner profile
Information on discrepancies, context, and learner characteristics	Determine priorities	Goal statements
Goal statements	Write problem statement	Problem statement

assessment as using information to make decisions, set priorities, and allocate resources. Her model includes nine questions:

1. Who wants a needs assessment?
2. Why is a needs assessment wanted?
3. What should be the scope of the needs assessment?
4. On whose needs will you focus and at what level?
5. What kinds and amounts of data should be collected for your purposes?
6. What sources and methods might you use for data collection?
7. What are your constraints on data collection?
8. What can you invest in people, money, and time?
9. What needs assessment products meet your purposes, constraints, and resources? (pp. 33–36)

It may be easier for you to remember that to devise any data collection plan you must answer at least three questions: (1) What do I need to know? (2) How will I collect information? (3) Whom or what will I use as a source of information? You can make a table to summarize your plan by completing columns for the questions you'll ask, the information you'll need, and the sources or methods you'll use. You can also build a matrix to show your plans for data collection (Stufflebeam, McCormick, Brinkeroff, & Nelson, 1985). Across the top, list the questions you have developed. Down the side, list the data collection procedures you will use. Wherever a collection procedure will answer a question put an x.

Another approach to planning data collection is to use the checklist given in Table 4.2. This checklist requires answering six questions.

Data Collection Methods

Later in this text you will be given practice in choosing data collection methods. You can use these methods for needs assessment. Each of the methods has advantages and disadvantages. For example, questionnaires reach a large number of people in a short time, but

Table 4.2   Checklist for Decisions in Data Collection

1. What will be the scope of the needs assessment?

    _____ A. Phases

    _____ B. Resources

    _____ C. Schedule

2. What categories of information are needed?

    _____ A. Facts/Knowledge

    _____ B. Skills/Competencies

    _____ C. Feelings/Opinions

    _____ D. Causes/Relationships

3. What data collections methods will be used?

    A.   Interviews

    _____ 1. Consultations

    _____ 2. Group debriefing

    _____ 3. Individual

    _____ 4. Forum/Panel

    _____ 5. Questionnaire

    B.   Documents

    _____ 1. Records

    _____ 2. Literature

    _____ 3. Newspapers

    _____ 4. Tests

    C.   Observation

    _____ 1. Products

    _____ 2. Samples

    _____ 3. Settings

    _____ 4. Sociodata, e.g., sociogram

    D.   Priority

    _____ 1. Card sort

    _____ 2. Delphi technique

    _____ 3. Storyboarding

    _____ 4. Nominal groups

    _____ 5. Other

4. What sources will be used?

    _____ A. People? Specify. _____

    _____ B. Services? Specify. _____

    _____ C. Reporting techniques? Specify. _____

    _____ D. Other? Specify. _____

they take time to develop and may obtain only superficial information. Records are a ready source, but require skilled review and often reflect the past rather than the current situation. Although interviews can be very revealing, the data collected may be biased. Observation provides useful *in situ* data but requires highly skilled observers. Tests can determine if deficiencies are causes but do not measure on-the-job use. Further, group discussion permits immediate synthesis, but the data is difficult to quantify (Newstrom & Lilyquist, 1979, pp. 52–56). The commonly used methods for needs assessment are compared in Table 4.3.

Table 4.3   Methods for Assessing Training Needs

Data Collection Techniques	Primary Strength	Primary Weakness
Business data review	Provides objective data	May take a long time
Interviews	Obtain in-depth information	Usually labor intensive
Focus groups	Provides qualitative focus	Direction of discussion may be swayed by informal leader
Questionnaires	Narrows direction of further investigation	Doesn't give in-depth information
Critical incident	Gathers observable investigation	Usually labor intensive
Observation	Provides a reality check	Usually labor intensive
Performance data reviews (e.g., performance appraisals)	Establishes criteria	May be confounded by other variables
Informal discussions	Provides input for other techniques	May be biased due to unsystematic approach
Job requirements review (e.g., job descriptions)	Provides objective data (if accurate)	Usually takes a long time

From "Maximize the Return on Your Training Investment Through Needs Assessment" by D. Georgenson and E. Del Gaizo, August 1984, *Training and Development Journal,* p. 46. Copyright 1984 by *Training and Development Journal,* American Society for Training and Development. Reprinted with permission. All rights reserved.

Some methods are better suited for one phase of needs assessment than others. When you want to gather just enough preliminary information to enable you to decide whether to pursue the problem, a review of records or a phone interview is quick and adequate. At the next phase or level where you need to collect information, tests and questionnaires are useful. If you want to be sure the information gathered from other methods is reliable, in-field observation is a good method. Forums, interviews, nominal groups, storyboarding, and card sort are useful for ranking priorities. Forums and group discussions are also effective ways to begin collecting information.

There are other less commonly used techniques. Sociodata collection methods include sociograms, where preferences for friends or work relationships are gathered, the data is graphed, and interactions are analyzed. Another sociodata collection method is interaction analysis, where observers code verbal behaviors and interactions.

Content analysis involves examining texts, articles, reports, or other print or nonprint material in order to determine themes.

An Exercise to Practice Developing Plans for Gathering Information

Use the checklist in Table 4.2 to develop a plan for gathering information in one of the problem areas listed below. Report your plan in essay form, using graphics if you wish. Then repeat the exercise with another problem area.

1. There is a need to serve more nursing students with a limited professional faculty. One place to start is to develop a center for independent learning on certain aspects of the beginning nursing curriculum. There is first a need to identify what aspects should be

programmed and to develop a procedure for producing software based on these aspects. The new learning resources center's director has experience in both nursing and media. The budget and clerical staff are limited, and the faculty is resisting involvement. It is felt that the best way to start is with a plan of attack in a specific area.

2. The social studies department wants to change to a more relevant curriculum. It plans to have units on economics throughout the world instead of organizing the curriculum by regional areas. The fear is that the content will be too diffuse to be retained. Teachers have been asked to submit proposals for this new curriculum, relating to activities, sequencing, content themes, and materials. The school is a suburban middle school.

3. A traditional elementary school reading program for grades K–6 has been re-evaluated. The results show that a majority of students are not reading at their grade levels. Library-use records document students's lack of interest in reading, which is probably due to poor reading skills. The reading supervisor has been charged with coordinating efforts to remedy the situation. After many group brainstorming sessions, the feeling is that too many unrelated ideas are being presented. It is suggested that some systematic goals be developed before further major policy changes are considered.

4. Students in high school biology fail to work on their own to discover concepts and facts about the subject. The school is located in a suburban area where the community income is above the national average. The school board and administration wish to try some innovative programs in the area of higher level thinking skills for biology. The BSCS series is being considered, but teachers are not enthusiastic.

5. The health educators for the county health department have recently been charged with upgrading the inservice training program for patrolman recruits in casualty care. The recruits represent the police for a city of 100,000. The previous program for recruits in casualty care consisted of lecture, textbooks, and films. It is important that the course be successful because patrolmen are usually the first on the scene of accidents, and their immediate first aid procedures may result in saving or losing a life. The department has considered determining the effectiveness of different learning situations (cognitive vs. predominantly psychomotor) in improving the retention and application of casualty care skills.

6. A large corporation is considering having all its management employees improve communication skills through training in areas such as transactional analysis, communication style, and listening skills. No determination has been made concerning the extent of the problem, or whether the problem exists at all.

Instruments

In order to gather information, you have to prepare for writing questions and developing instruments. What kinds of questions do you want to ask? How do you want to phrase them? How will you analyze the answers? Before you develop an instrument, such as a survey questionnaire or interview protocol, you need to think about these questions.

Allison Rossett's (1982, p. 30) typology for generating needs assessment questions is helpful. Her typology includes five areas of questioning: nature of the problem, priorities within the problem, subject matter/skills, attitude toward the problem, and cause of problem. You don't have to use all the questions and categories at once; you may omit some questions or categories completely.

Type 1 includes questions on problem finding. These questions deal with the discrepancy and the nature of the discrepancy. Rossett gives these examples:

"Compared to other job seekers, I think that I . . ."
"What experiences have you had that have led you to enroll in this engine safety class?"

Type 2 questions cover problem selecting. It is important to give clear directions in this section. The respondents need to know on what basis you want them to rank items and whether you want them to describe their needs or a group's needs. Questions are longer in this section because you want them to select from several items or assign priority. For example:

> "Mark the skills below with the number that reflects how important it is to you to know how to do it."

Type 3 questions are on knowledge/skill proving. These items are like sample pre-test items. They will tell you what the learners know, if anything, about the skills. For example:

> "Please examine this resume. Render a judgment on its strengths and weaknesses."

Type 4 items deal with finding feelings. How does the learner feel about the problem? What are his or her emotions and attitudes? For example:

> "Which best describes your feelings about taking a class on alcohol abuse and automobile safety? Check one."

Type 5 questions center on cause finding. What do the learners think is causing the problem? For example:

> "Which of the following are contributing to your problem selling frangarams this year? Check all that apply to you."

The use of questionnaires to collect data is discussed later in this text. Poorly designed questionnaires yield little information. When you prepare your instruments follow these basic rules (Spitzer, 1979; Maher, Jr., & Kur, 1983). First, avoid ambiguous and technical language, negatively worded questions, hints at responses, and unnecessary or obvious questions. Second, don't put the important items at the end. Third, begin with easy items and personal data. Fourth, emphasize crucial words, leave adequate space for comments, group and vary items, and include clear instructions and incentives. Fifth, print your questions neatly and try them out first. Finally, plan how you'll analyze the data.

An Exercise to Give Practice in Developing Questions in Topical Categories for Needs Assessment

Complete this outline for a needs assessment instrument by formulating three questions in each category. Choose a problem area, such as one of those listed in the previous exercise, and relate all questions to that area.

Part I. Nature of the Problem

    1.

    2.

    3.

Part II. Priorities within the Problem

    1.

    2.

    3.

Part III. Skills/Knowledge

    1.

    2.

    3.

Part IV. Attitudes

    1.

    2.

    3.

Part V. Causes

    1.

    2.

    3.

Note: Remember that in a needs assessment the questions should provide a basis for writing goals and for deciding what parts of the problem are instructional.

STEP 2: IDENTIFY DISCREPANCIES

It is at this point that the Organizational Elements Model by Kaufman and English (1979) is used. The Organizational Elements Model (OEM) is shown in Figure 4.2.

The OEM has five elements that relate means to ends and the individual to organizations and society. Two of the elements (inputs and processes) are means, or what organizations use and do. Three of the elements (products, outputs, and outcomes) are ends. Of the five, one element (outcomes) is external to the organization because it represents impact on society; the other four are internal to the organization.

Each of the elements in the model is defined. Inputs (things we use) and processes (things we do) are supportive of effects on individuals, organizations, and society, not effects in themselves. Examples of inputs are instructor or learner characteristics, and examples of processes are testing or managing.

Products and outputs are difficult to distinguish. They are results produced by an intervention through inputs or processes. Needs for products or outputs are internal to any organization. The difference between products and outputs is that outputs have more scope. Output refers to an aggregate of products and thus is a product of the organization as a whole rather than of an individual. A completed physics course is a product, whereas graduation is an output. A product must be combined with other products to create a useful output.

Figure 4.2   Categories of Needs

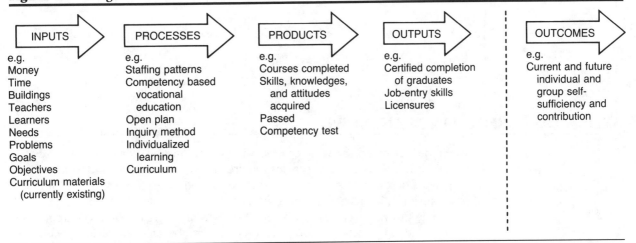

INPUTS

e.g.
Money
Time
Buildings
Teachers
Learners
Needs
Problems
Goals
Objectives
Curriculum materials
  (currently existing)

PROCESSES

e.g.
Staffing patterns
Competency based
  vocational
  education
Open plan
Inquiry method
Individualized
  learning
Curriculum

PRODUCTS

e.g.
Courses completed
Skills, knowledges,
  and attitudes
  acquired
Passed
Competency test

OUTPUTS

e.g.
Certified completion
  of graduates
Job-entry skills
Licensures

OUTCOMES

e.g.
Current and future
  individual and
  group self-
  sufficiency and
  contribution

Outcomes are individual or organizational changes that contribute to society's survival. There should be logical consistency among all the elements. Each element should lead to the next element. By determining the status quo for each element and comparing it with the desired results, it is possible to identify gaps or discrepancies.

Suppose you are employed as a curriculum supervisor in a school district in Pennsylvania. In that state each district is required to administer a statewide test of achievement called the TELLS, or Testing for Essential Learning and Literacy Skills, in third, fifth, and eighth grades. You therefore have an existing database that must be considered when goals for curriculum improvement are established. In your subject area, math, thirty percent of the students in the district were identified as needing remedial help. Fifteen percent of those students are already enrolled in special programs to help them with math.

An obvious discrepancy exists, but to define it specifically, you need to determine how congruent the content of the test and cut-off levels are with your district's stated aims and policies on math instruction. You may need to reexamine the school's math goals in light of the TELLS objectives. You may also need to obtain more specific information on the gaps identified by doing another needs assessment. Teachers' perspectives on the implications of the test can be useful.

Kaufman is describing a global societal level when he defines outcomes as the end result of the combined effects of inputs, processes, products, and outputs. Most instructional designers are concerned with less global needs. Designers cannot deal at the level of long-term benefits to individuals or society; time constraints confine them to short-term goals. This does not mean that the designer ignores long-term outcomes. Each need interacts with the other categories of needs (Kaufman, 1983; Kaufman & English, 1979). Typically, the instructional designer writes a problem statement that includes the input (resources, such as development team), the action (processes to be used, such as systems models), and the product (results, such as competencies and attitudes).

An Exercise in Applying the Organizational Elements Model

Drawing on your own experience, fill in each of the elements in Kaufman and English model.

Inputs	Processes	Products	Outputs	Outcomes

STEP 3: DO PERFORMANCE ANALYSIS

When you have determined discrepancies through information gathering, you are ready to identify which of these discrepancies require an instructional plan and which require other types of solutions, such as new management policy, better organizational structure, or improved equipment, tools, or materials.

To do this you need to determine causes. Why are there deficiencies? Are the deficiencies due to instruction? Information on causes can be gathered during needs assessment. At this point problems are stated as goals to be accomplished and causes have yet to be clarified. You may find that to reach a goal, it is necessary to attend to both instruction and management policy. The instructional designer may opt to deal only with the instructional aspect.

As an instructional designer you effect changes in people. You must learn to distinguish among problems that call for effecting changes in knowledge, skills, and attitudes, and problems that call for alternative solutions, such as management or communication problems. For example, students forget to register by a certain date. This problem might be solved by posting a sign or by advertising the date. It could be a communication problem, not an instructional problem.

Your first task as a consultant may be to advise your client on whether the problem can be solved by instruction. The approach taken in this field is that instructional problems can be differentiated from non-instructional problems by whether the problem is due to a deficiency in knowledge/skills/attitudes or to poor organizational conditions. Both conditions can influence attitudes towards performance of tasks. The instructional design field deals only with deficiencies in knowledge, skills, or attitudes that can be remedied by formal training or practice (Kaufman, 1986).

Nadler (1982, p. 17) distinguishes between problems stated in terms of obtaining or organizing resources and problems stated in terms of instruction. The distinction is useful because it reminds us that there are solutions other than training and that not all human resource problems are instructional problems. Instead of training, you may need to change the person in the job, the work team, the workplace, or the contingencies and rewards. Similarly, not all instructional problems require complex instructional design solutions. A job aid or on-the-job training may be sufficient.

Thomas Gilbert (1982), a psychologist/performance engineer, uses another approach, PROBE. PROBE, shown in Table 4.4, uses a list of questions designed to elicit more than yes/no answers. Gilbert recommends PROBE when you are doing needs assessment on training for jobs. The more difficult the job, the more useful PROBE questions are. Gilbert has designed PROBE so that there are questions about two areas that affect behavior: environment and repertoire. Gilbert's PROBE approach yields information needed to determine whether a problem can be solved by instruction. If the answers indicate the problem lies in the behavioral repertoire, the solution is likely to be instruction; if the answers indicate the problem is the environment, instruction is not likely to be the solution.

There are several flowcharts available for the designer to use for performance analysis. Roger Kaufman (1986) offers an algorithm for identifying human performance problems. His flowchart requires identifying whether it is possible to solve the problems by changing the environment, people, or people's performance. Mager and Pipe's flowchart (1970) for determining performance problems is probably the most popular guide to performance analysis.

Mager and Pipe separate performance discrepancies into those due to skill deficiencies and those due to obstacles to and rewards for performance. Their method for analyzing whether performance problems are due to lack of instruction or lack of rewards includes these steps:

1. Evaluate whether the discrepancy is important enough to warrant consideration.

2. Determine whether there is a lack of critical knowledge or skills. If yes, look for an instructional solution; if no, look for a problem with motivation or obstacles.

3. Determine whether the workers ever had the required skills or knowledge.

4. If they had the skills and knowledge, determine whether there has been opportunity for practice.

5. If the skill is used frequently, determine whether the feedback on performance is adequate.

6. If training, practice, and feedback are found adequate, consider simpler ways of solving problems, such as job aids (charts, diagrams, etc.), job redesign, or on-the-job training.

Table 4.4   Gilbert's PROBE Approach

E—QUESTIONS ABOUT THE BEHAVIORAL ENVIRONMENT

A.   DIRECTIONAL DATA

1. Are there sufficient, readily accessible data (or signals) to direct an experienced person to perform well?

2. Are they accurate?

3. Are they free of confusion—"stimulus competition"—that slows performance and invites errors?

4. Are they free of "data glut"—stripped down to simple forms and not buried in a lot of extraneous data?

5. Are they up-to-date and timely?

6. Are good models of behavior available?

7. Are clear and measurable performance standards communicated so that people know how well they are supposed to perform?

8. Do they accept the standards as reasonable?

B.   CONFIRMATION

1. Is feedback provided that is "work-related"—describing results consistent with the standards and not just behavior?

2. Is it immediate and frequent enough to help people remember what they did?

3. Is it selective and specific—limited to few matters of importance and free of "data glut" and vague generalities?

4. Is it educational—positive and constructive so that people learn something from it?

C.   TOOLS AND EQUIPMENT

1. Are the necessary implements usually on hand for doing the job?

2. Are they reliable and efficient?

3. Are they safe?

D.   PROCEDURES

1. Are the precedures efficient and designed to avoid unnecessary steps and wasted emotion?

2. Are they based on sound methods rather than historical happenstance?

3. Are they appropriate to the job and the skill level?

4. Are they free of boring and tiresome repetition?

E.   RESOURCES

1. Are adequate materials, supplies, assistance, etc. usually available to do the job well?

2. Are they efficiently tailored to the job?

3. Do ambient conditions provide comfort and prevent unnecessary interference?

F.   INCENTIVES

1. Is pay for the job competitive?

2. Are there significant bonuses or raises based on good performance?

3. Does good performance have any relationship to career advancement?

4. Are there meaningful non-pay incentives (recognition, and so on—for good performance (based on results and not behavior)?

5. Are they scheduled well, or so frequently as to lose meaning and so infrequently as to be useless?

6. Is there an absence of punishment for performing well?

7. Is there an absence of hidden incentives to perform poorly?

8. Is the balance of positive and negative incentives in favor of good performance?

P—QUESTIONS ABOUT BEHAVIORAL REPERTOIRES

G.   KNOWLEDGE AND TRAINING

1. Do people understand the consequences of both good and poor performance?

2. Do they grasp the essentials of performance—do they get the "big picture"?

3. Do they have the technical concepts to perform well?

4. Do they have sufficient basic skills—reading and so on?

5. Do they have sufficient specialized skills?

6. Do they always have the skills after initial training?

7. Are good job aids available?

H.   CAPACITY

1. Do the incumbents have the basic capacity to learn the necessary perceptual discriminations with accuracy and speed?

2. Are they free of emotional limitations that would interfere with performance?

3. Do they have sufficient strength and dexterity to learn to do the job?

I.   MOTIVES

1. Do incumbents seem to have the desire to perform when they enter the job?

2. Do their motives endure—e.g., is the turnover high?

7. Determine whether workers are able to change. If not, transfer or terminate them.

8. Look at the reward structure. What kinds of behaviors are rewarded or punished?

9. Determine whether performance matters. Are the tasks worth accomplishing? How can you make the tasks worth accomplishing?

10. Determine whether there are obstacles to performance, such as policies, environment, expectations, demands on time.

Mager and Pipe distinguish between competence (can do) and performance (does do). If workers can't do a task, then formal training is advised. If they can't do it but used to do it, practice and feedback are advised. If they can do it but don't do it, management of rewards and consequences (behavior management) is recommended. Mager and Pipe discuss performance problems that fall into the skill deficiency category. By skill deficiency they mean psychomotor or cognitive behaviors. They do not provide for instruction to develop attitudes. To determine whether a problem is instructional, an important question is whether workers could perform the task if their lives depended on it.

Instructional problems can be identified using the Mager and Pipe approach if knowledge and skills are considered competencies or instructional problems. Mager and Pipe do not deal with the distinction between attitudes affected by instruction and attitudes affected by organizational conditions.

An Exercise Designed to Help You Distinguish Between Instructional and Non-instructional Problems

A problem could be described by more than one category. What categories describe each of the problems below? Explain your classification of each problem.

Categories

I. Non-instructional

    A. Contingencies and rewards

    B. Work conditions

    C. Work procedures

    D. Other

II. Instructional

    A. Skills

    B. Knowledge

    C. Attitudes

    D. Other

Problems

1. An instructional designer is asked to develop additional training in telephone skills for volunteers at a United Fund Agency. The volunteers have already had two hours of training in how to represent the organization on the phone and in person. But they continue to give their opinions about controversial matters rather than merely stating the organization's position.

2. A training consultant is asked to develop training to make maintenance workers more productive. She analyzes the knowledge and skills needed and finds the workers already possess these competencies. She also finds that except for the end-of-the-year evaluation, there is no feedback on performance after the first three months.

3. An instructional designer is asked to improve the remedial reading curriculum for ninth-grade students. He finds that students are continually tested and evaluated on reading, that the current objectives are appropriate and clear, and that the materials for teach-

ing are excellent. But the teacher is not using the materials as designed nor is she reporting results correctly because she has minimal competencies in design and evaluation.

4. A government agency asks an instructional design consultant to develop instruction for repair technicians. When the designer does the needs assessment he finds the existing training program is excellent, but repair technicians are not performing well in the field. The technicians report that they are hampered by unavailability of parts, an impossible work load, and incompetent colleagues.

5. A school district has decided to offer enrichment social studies because many of the students already have the current curriculum competencies and are bored in class. The district will purchase materials and design a program to use these materials so that additional teacher time requirements will be minimal.

6. An educational specialist in a hospital setting is asked to improve the required certification course for radiation safety. He finds the current course teaches concepts well but gives no practice in safety skills. Consequently, workers return to their labs and continue to perform manual tasks carelessly. The course teaches concepts only, not attitudes or skills.

An Exercise Designed to Provide Practice in Performance Analysis

Label each item true or false.

_____ 1. Analyzing performance problems is necessary because a manager may fail to realize how best to solve performance problems.

_____ 2. A performance problem is a discrepancy between existing and expected performance.

_____ 3. An analysis of performance problems is not appropriate for every ID effort.

_____ 4. An analysis of performance problems is especially necessary when nuclear plant operators are being trained on a new maintenance system.

_____ 5. Formal training is indicated when those who were once able to do a job are now unable to do it well.

_____ 6. Practice and feedback are useful for preventing the formation of bad work habits.

_____ 7. When workers or students receive punishment for performing well, poor performance often results.

_____ 8. Inadequate tools are obstacles to good performance.

_____ 9. Performance analysis can be done solely on the basis of available documents.

_____ 10. To determine whether an ID solution is appropriate, you need to ask "Could they do what is expected of them if they had to?"

_____ 11. Formal training is usually the best solution when the proper sequence of steps in a procedure is not being followed.

_____ 12. If the learner is able to do what is required but still won't do it, a non-instructional solution could be warranted.

_____ 13. Formal instruction tends to be one of the more expensive ways to solve an instructional problem.

_____ 14. If a worker lacks the physical or mental capabilities to handle the job, either change the job to match the worker's capabilities or change the worker to match the job's requirements.

_____ 15. Obstacles obstruct performance.

From *Module 9. Problem Analysis* by A. Chenzoff, 1983, Contract No. F41689-83-C0048, Randolph AFB, TX: USAF Occupational Measurement Center (ATC).

An Exercise Designed to Give Further Practice in
Distinguishing Types of Instructional and Non-instructional Problems

For each problem, decide whether an instructional or non-instructional solution, or both, would be required.

1. Three graduates of a technical school motorcycle repair program are employed by Honda Corporation to be field representatives for sales and service. They stay in these roles for two years. During this time they do no maintenance; they consult on parts and procedures. Their duties are unrelated to their study in technical school. When they are re-assigned to the main service center as repair personnel, they find they have forgotten how to execute motorcycle maintenance procedures. Is this an instructional problem? If yes, what kind of instructional solution would you suggest? (Chenzoff, 1983)

2. An oxygen bottle in a college chemical laboratory blows up when lab maintenance personnel try to fill it to 1850 psi, using an adapter without a blowout plug. The oxygen system has no relief valve. Maximum pressure is 450 psi. The directions placard had been painted over. The maintenance person had not been checked out on that piece of apparatus. The lab supervisor recommends all lab maintenance personnel receive a course on servicing the oxygen equipment. Discuss the wisdom of this recommendation. What would you recommend? (Chenzoff, 1983)

3. Students in music are anxious to improve their skills in choral singing. The ninety-member chorus meets twice a week for forty minutes. Most of the time is spent on furious preparation for frequent musical events. The more talented members are frustrated and complain about the lack of opportunity to try innovative numbers or improve skills. Is this an instructional problem? What would you recommend?

4. You are operating the swimming program in a community center similar to a YWCA. The center is supported by county tax funds, and anyone can attend for a nominal fee. There are four age groups for which instruction is available: adults (over 18), teens (13–18), juniors (6–13), and beginners (6 and under). Average attendance at each instruction section is 100 per swim period. The swim periods are a half-hour long. There are one or two instructors, two lifeguards, and three in-the-water aides present at each period. The center would like to do a better job of teaching rules of water safety. They are planning to illustrate through media as well as class instruction. A lecture room is available nearby. Should they proceed as planned?

5. The student council at a junior high school is responsible for all after-school functions. The council has not been able to control the students or groups performing at council functions. As faculty advisor you would like to assure proper functioning of the council's activities. You would like to avoid problems which seem to be created as a result of student council action. For example, recently some students at a dance provoked the band members into a fight. Council members couldn't cope effectively with the disturbance; either the students involved in the fight didn't respect them, or the members themselves were reluctant to exert their authority. The council has discussed the problem many times. What is the nature of the problem? Is instruction recommended?

6. A private training school in an urban setting offers a thirty to thirty-six-week secretarial training program for high school graduates. About sixty percent of the students are middle-class; forty percent come from lower socioeconomic groups. Although graduates have quite a bit of manual and office practice skill, they are not careful about details. Therefore, graduates tend not to advance in their jobs. What, if any, instruction is recommended?

7. Several average classes of fifth-graders from a school district in a high socioeconomic area are found to be inadequately prepared for fifth-grade work. It is important that their problem-solving motivation and skills improve in order to meet the pre-entry criteria for a new middle school. Most of the students are unable to comprehend almost any fifth-grade textual material. They seem to lack enthusiasm for projects and problems. Many of

the students have been frightened by their relatively sudden academic failure and are with-drawing in confusion. Is instruction the solution? What do you recommend?

STEP 4: IDENTIFY CONSTRAINTS AND RESOURCES

It is useful to know about the constraints and resources that will have an effect on the project. A constraint is a limitation on the project. A resource is something available for you to use on the project. People, funds, and equipment are examples of constraints and re-sources. Constraints and resources can include time, facilities, space, materials, group size and composition, philosophy, personnel, money, and organization. The same variable can function as either a constraint or a resource depending on whether it limits or expands the designer's flexibility.

An Exercise on Gathering Information Relevant to Constraints and Resources

Describe a situation in which you have identified the problem as instructional. You are now gathering information on the constraints and resources that will be helpful later in the ID process.

In a team or individually, make a list of the kinds of information you could gather (e.g., topic, budget, personnel) and the sources of information you could use. Do this in re-sponse to each of these questions (UCIDT, 1986).

1. Kinds of information about the community or society. Sources of such information in-clude interviews with VIP's, reports, statistics, projections, and media events. Give exam-ples of types of information (e.g., perceptions) one can gather about a community, and suggest appropriate sources of information.

2. Kinds of information about the corporation or district. Sources of information include annual reports, proposals, statistics, and policy statements. Give examples of types of in-formation (e.g., products) one can gather about a district or corporation, and suggest ap-propriate sources of such information.

3. Kinds of information about the division or department. Sources of such information in-clude reports, charts, statistics, and interviews. Give an example of types of information (e.g., budget) one can gather about the organizational unit and suggest appropriate sources of such information.

4. Kinds of information about personnel. Sources of such information include employee records, questionnaires, evaluation reports, and statistics. Give an example of types of in-formation (e.g., educational level) one can gather about personnel and suggest appropri-ate sources of information.

5. Kinds of information about the learners or audience. Sources of such information in-clude peers, employers, parents, teachers, tests, sociograms, interviews, and observations. Give examples of types of information (e.g., attitude) one can gather about an audience, and suggest appropriate sources of such information.

6. Kinds of information about time. Sources of such information include schedules, cal-endars, deadlines, and opinions. Give examples of types of information (e.g., flexibility) one can gather, and suggest appropriate sources of such information.

7. Kinds of information about facilities. Sources of such information include inventories, floor plans, room schedules, and supervisors. Give an example of types of information (e.g., availability) one can gather about resources, and suggest appropriate sources of information.

STEP 5: IDENTIFY LEARNER CHARACTERISTICS

It is useful to collect information on the learner as part of the needs assessment process. You can use this information to outline the characteristics of the intended learner in a profile that can include age, sex, educational level, achievement level, socioeconomic background, learning style, experience, attitudes, role perceptions, and perceived needs. Such information may be useful when you decide on objectives and when you choose an instructional strategy or evaluation technique. For example, some research suggests high-ability students achieve less when provided with more instructional support such as cues, structure, and provision for frequent responding. You can take this information about the learner into account when selecting instructional strategies (McGowan & Clark, 1985). If you know the learners have low verbal skills, you will be more careful about the verbal form of your test items. You will not use all the information, but it is difficult at this point to know which information may be useful. The best strategy is to collect any information you think may be useful. If you are sure you will not need certain kinds of information, such as sex or educational level, don't waste time collecting it.

An Exercise to Give Practice in Developing a Learner Profile

Here are the results of a needs assessment done by interviews and an examination of records. Use this information to complete the learner profile.

Students in eighth-grade enrichment science classes range in age from twelve to fourteen with the mean and mode being thirteen. There are three sections with a total of eighty-seven students (twenty-eight, thirty-two, and twenty-seven students per class). Forty-five are girls and forty-two are boys. Each section uses one self-contained classroom with fixed chairs and tables. There are lab tables around the walls of the classroom.

Eighty percent of the students are in other enrichment classes. The Dakota Achievement Test scores on areas related to scientific concepts and skills range from the 92 percentile to 99 percentile for their grade level. On the Metropolitan Aptitude/Achievement Test, last year's eighth-grade enrichment science students all scored well-above average. Last year's students were representative of this year's students. The Metropolitan Test checks measurement, reading, logic, and graphing concepts relevant to science.

Students must maintain a B average overall to stay in this class and have an A average in science to be recommended for the class. Most of the students come from upper-middle-class families where at least one of the parents is a professional or business executive. Many of the parents are scientists or in science-related occupations. Most of the students are well-traveled.

The students have had infrequent trips to a local science center and one year's experience with an independent study approach to science (Learning Activity Packages). Generally, in science they have been taught for the last three years by the traditional lecture/discussion method. In other classes, such as social studies, they frequently do independent projects. They have a range of learning style preferences and ways of approaching problem solving. About two-thirds of the students prefer hands-on activities and a variety of instructional strategies. The other third prefer to take notes from lecture/presentation and to be checked by tests. Four of the students have placed in the school science fair and one in the regional science fair.

As is usual, some of the students are very verbal and quick to respond; others are quiet and consider carefully before responding. All of the students have high verbal ability, as seen in their reading, writing, and speaking. They almost all have a positive attitude toward school. However, they find enrichment science as taught by lecture/discussion and lab experiments one of their least interesting classes. When asked, they report they need science for future careers but that it's not one of their favorite subjects. They are vague when asked what they need to know in science. When pressed, many say they like to dissect and are disappointed there won't be dissecting this year.

Learner Profile		
	Representative Learner	**Range for Learners**
Age		
Sex		
Educational level		
Achievement level		
Socioeconomic background		
Learning style		
Verbal ability		
Relevant experience		
Attitudes toward subject		
Role perceptions		
Perceived needs		
Other		

STEP 6: IDENTIFY GOALS

Because the intent of needs assessment is to determine goals, a needs assessment is not complete until priorities have been identified. The purpose of a needs assessment is to clarify the scope of problem-solving efforts. The process must lead to a statement of priorities. The product of needs assessment should be goals, descriptions of intent stated in broad, not measurable, terms. Kaufman (1983, p. 14) defines needs assessment as "the process for identifying, documenting and justifying the gaps between what is and what should be for results—products, outputs, and/or outcomes—and placing the gaps (needs) in priority order for closure."

Needs assessment is the process of defining the results (end) of the curriculum sequence (means). In instructional design the needs to be identified are the effects on individuals and organizations. The processes used to achieve the ends are needs of the designer, not of the learner. Assessed needs must always be stated as learner needs or outcomes.

There are several techniques for determining priorities from the data collected. Priority-ranking techniques include the Delphi Technique, card sort, Q-sort, nominal group, and storyboarding. These methods are described in many sources: Kaufman & English, 1979; Murray-Hicks, 1981; Scott & Deadrick, 1982; Stufflebeam, McCormick, Brinkeroff, & Nelson, 1985; Witkin, 1984. Two of these methods for ranking priorities will be discussed briefly: storyboards and card sort.

Storyboarding as a technique for creative thinking was developed by the Walt Disney Corporation. As used in needs assessment to establish priorities, it starts with many colors of index cards, soft display areas for tacking, tacks, and a group of people given a topic, theme, or question. Like the Delphi Technique, storyboarding requires a series of rounds. Participants are asked to write down as many ideas as they can in response to a question. Using different-colored cards, participants can generate categories, combine ideas, move, delete, or add ideas. Discussion is interspersed with the use of cards to visualize and manipulate ideas until categories and priorities in each category are generated and agreed on.

In card sort declarative sentences or themes are written on cards; then the cards are sorted and ranked. This is a forced choice method that usually requires sorting into five or fewer piles that represent degree of importance. This technique is often used when large numbers of goals must be put in priority.

An Exercise in Applying a Method for Determining Priorities

This is a team exercise in using a card sort technique for establishing priorities. You are part of a team charged with developing a Master of Arts in Teaching (MAT) program for a university. In order to create a curriculum, the team has decided to begin by establishing goals for the program.

Each team member has been asked to imagine what successful graduates of the program will do, think, or feel. The next step is for each team member to write statements (one to a card) that describe how MAT graduates will be expected to perform. The statements should be complete sentences in active voice. Some of the other team members have written statements such as these:

MAT graduates will accurately perceive their strengths and weaknesses.

An MAT graduate will want to help others.

Each MAT graduate will understand the role nonverbal communication plays in successful teaching.

MAT graduates will understand how to identify and use learner characteristics.

Your first task, then, is to spend five to ten minutes writing goal statements for an MAT program on separate cards. After each team member has finished writing goals, the cards are sorted. Each team member sorts his or her cards into groups that indicate priorities. In this case, sort your cards into the categories of (1) essential and critical, (2) very useful, and (3) slightly useful. After you have sorted your cards, rank order them within each group with no ties. If a statement seems vague, rewrite it.

Once statements have been written, sorted, and ranked individually, lay all the cards out on a table or display them on a board. The team members can inspect all the cards and ask questions beginning with the lowest category, slightly useful. The discussion continues until the cards in each category can be merged into a team rather than individual list. The decision-making process should be one of compromise, consensus, and creativity. Cards can be moved as decisions are made.

When the goal statements in each category are agreed on, the team must decide whether to include all the categories or all the cards in a category in the final goals. The team could decide that the program must focus on achieving essential goals only. Or the team could say that all "essential" goals and the first three "very useful" goals will become priorities.

As a team, use index cards and the card sorting technique to generate priority goals for a Master of Arts in Teaching program.

After "The Card-Sort: A Tool for Determining Clients' Goals" by D. F. Leitzman and G.-R. Sisakhti, 1981, *National Society for Performance and Instruction Journal*, pp. 13–15. Copyright 1981 by *National Society for Performance and Instruction Journal*.

STEP 7: WRITE PROBLEM STATEMENT

At the end of the problem analysis process, you should write a problem statement to guide you through the instructional design process. The problem statement will summarize what you have determined about the problem. Problem statements should not be long. Usually one to three pages of discussion will suffice, but fewer or more can be acceptable. The problem statement itself is usually no more than a sentence to a paragraph or two. The rest of the information is background material on the problem.

RUPS Problem Statement

One easy format to use is RUPS, or Research Utilizing Problem Solving (Jung, Pino & Emory, 1970). The purpose of the RUPS problem statement is to establish the background and context for the problem, state what type of problem it is, and give a general goal for

Table 4.5   Guideline for Writing a RUPS Statement.

1. Who is affected?

   You? Another person? A teaching team? Another group? An entire organization? The community or society?

2. Who or what is the cause?

   Is it a person or group? An entire organization or community? Is it lack of attention to details? Poor organization? Poor materials?

3. What kind of problem is it?

   Disagreement or confusion about goals? Lack of skills? Lack of resources? Lack of accurate communication? Lack of adequate means? Lack of support? Conflict about decision-making? (Obviously, not all these problems are instructional problems. In fact, only lack of skills should be solved by instruction. Perhaps instruction is related to accurate communication or adequate means, but why it is related has to be made clear.)

4. What is the goal for improvement?

   What will be different when the goal has been achieved? Who will be doing what to achieve what? What is the target? (Be as specific as possible. The goal is not just improved skills, but specific skills at a specific level.)

improvement. The problem is stated as a goal. Table 4.5 contains the guidelines for writing a RUPS problem statement. Use these guidelines to complete the exercise on writing a RUPS problem statement. The RUPS technique works best when you answer the questions in complete sentences.

You can use a RUPS problem statement to establish that your other team members or a client agree on the problem. Thus the process of writing a RUPS problem statement becomes a way to develop a common conceptual framework. That is, you can use the statement to communicate with others about your goals, or you can use the statement to gather input on the importance of the problem. The RUPS statement becomes a summary of the needs assessment and the nature of the problem.

Table 4.6 gives an illustration of a RUPS problem statement.

Table 4.6   Example of RUPS Problem Statement.

Students and graduates in instructional design practica and positions sometimes prepare flowcharts and hierarchies incorrectly. Although they can pass tests on flowcharting symbols and prepare simple hierarchies and flowcharts, they make mistakes when they try to represent more complicated content. The instructor is causing this problem by not giving sufficient attention to the use of visual conventions in instructional design. A contributing cause is the frequency with which authors of articles and books in the field incorrectly label or draw hierarchies and flowcharts.

Thus there is a gap between what students know about hierarchies and flowcharts, such as recognition of symbols, and their ability to distinguish between correct and incorrect use of visual symbols and to develop flowcharts and hierarchies for complex content. This is an instructional problem because a deficiency in knowledge, skills, or attitudes must be eliminated. The goal will affect students' use of flowcharts and hierarchies on the job by ensuring their competency in using visual conventions correctly when they produce flowcharts and hierarchies. Students will be taught to differentiate between correct and incorrect use of flowchart and hierarchy conventions and to use symbols and conventions correctly when representing complex content. They will be taught to value correct use of visual conventions as a communication tool and as a way to establish professional credibility.

Table 4.7 IDI Problem Definition Stage

A. Definition Stage

    1. Identify the problem (gather data)

        a. Assess needs

            1. Status quo

            2. What is desired

        b. Establish priorities

        c. State the problem (problem statement)

            1. Who is involved

            2. Solution processes

            3. Scope

    2. Analyze the setting (gather data)

        a. Audience characteristics

        b. Conditions for change

        c. Relevant resources

            1. Human

            2. Physical facilities, equipment

    3. Organize management (gather data)

        a. Tasks

        b. Responsibilities

            1. Lines of authority

            2. Lines of communication, input

        c. Time lines

IDI Problem Statement

The Instructional Development Institute method of problem identification leads to a problem statement that proposes solution processes (UCIDT, 1968). The results of your needs assessment can be summarized in an expanded problem statement using the IDI format shown in Table 4.7. Notice that while the IDI problem definition process includes analyzing constraints, resources, and learner characteristics, this information is not summarized in the problem statement.

The IDI problem statement narrows the goal stated in the RUPS problem statement and forces the designer to be clear about the solution process. The IDI problem statement includes information on needs, priorities, scope, and solution. It draws this information from the needs assessment.

List the discrepancies identified from the needs assessment. Then explain which discrepancies are to be given priority and why. Finally, state the problem as how to achieve a goal. Tell who will accomplish the solution and how. Tell whether he or she will work on one phase of the problem (proposed solution) or on the whole problem.

Table 4.8 is an example of the IDI problem statement that addresses the same problem presented in the RUPS problem statement in Table 4.6.

An Exercise to Give Practice in Writing A RUPS Problem Statement

Choose a problem that meets the criteria for an instructional problem. Answer these questions about the problem. Then summarize your answers in a problem statement that includes the problem stated as a proposed solution.

RUPS Analysis:

    1. Who is affected?

Table 4.8   Example of IDI Problem Statement

Instructional design students know visual conventions for flowcharting and hierarchies. However, when presented with examples from books or articles, they cannot distinguish between correct or incorrect use of visual conventions.

They can draw flowcharts and hierarchies for simple content, but make mistakes when asked to represent more complex content. When they accept practica assignments or positions in the field, they need to know visual symbols and conventions more thoroughly. They need to be able to distinguish between correct and incorrect use of visual/conventions and to construct flowcharts and hierarchies for complex content. It is also important that the students value using visual symbols and conventions correctly.

The most frequently used technique is flowcharting. This is also the most confusing technique because the conventions vary from field to field. The first priority will be to develop competencies related to flowcharting conventions. The instructor for the instructional design courses will develop improved instructional strategies for teaching and testing flowcharting competencies from the knowledge to the evaluation levels and from the responding to the valuing levels. An instructional design process will be used to improve the lecture and exercises on flowcharting.

2.   Who or what is causing it?

3.   What kind of a problem is it?

4.   What is the goal for improvement?

An Exercise to Give Practice in Writing IDI Problem Statements

Choose a problem that meets criteria for an instructional problem. Answer these questions about the problem. Then summarize your answers in a problem statement that proposes a solution.

Problem Identification: IDI Method

1.   Needs (status quo, what is desired, discrepancies)

2.   Priorities

3.   Problem Statement (who is involved, solution processes, scope)

Summary

In this chapter we have presented a seven-step approach to problem analysis: (1) Information Gathering, (2) Identifying Discrepancies, (3) Performance Analysis, (4) Identifying Constraints and Resources, (5) Identifying Learner Characteristics, (6) Identifying Goals, and (7) Writing a Problem Statement. Together these steps constitute the needs assessment process used for problem analysis. When you complete your problem analysis, you are ready to undertake task and instructional analysis where the goals statements will be refined into content and prerequisites.

FROM THE READING

Define the following terms:

Needs Assessment	Constraints
Goals	Resources
Instructional Problem	Problem Statement

ISSUES FOR DISCUSSION

1. What is a needs assessment strategy?
2. What would be the advantages and disadvantages of:
   a. using several needs assessment methods in a short period of time?
   b. using a single method?
   c. using several methods over a longer period of time?
3. What is the purpose of writing problem statements?

REFERENCES

Chenzoff, A. (1983). Module 9. Problem analysis. Contract No. F41689-83-C0048. Randolph AFB, TX: USAF Occupational Measurement Center (ATC).

Georgenson, D., & Del Gazio, E. (1984, August). Maximize the return on your training investment through needs assessment. *Training and Development Journal*, 42–47.

Gilbert, T. (1982, October). A question of performance—Part II: Applying the PROBE model. *Training and Development Journal, 17*, 85–89.

Jung, C., Pino, R., & Emory, R. (1970). *Research utilizing problem solving (RUPS)* (Leaders manual). Portland, OR: Northwest Regional Educational Laboratory.

Kaufman, R. (1983). A holistic planning model. *Performance and Instruction Journal, 22*, 3–12.

Kaufman, R. (1986). An algorithm for identifying and allocating performance problems. *Performance and Instruction Journal*, 21–23.

Kaufman, R., & English, F. W. (1979). *Needs assessment: Concept and application*. Englewood Cliffs, NJ: Educational Technology Publications.

Leitzman, D. F., & Sisakhti, G.-R. (1981). The card-sort: A tool for determining clients' goals. *National Society for Performance and Instruction Journal, 20*, 13–15.

Mager, R., & Pipe, P. (1970). *Analyzing performance problems*. Belmont, CA: Fearson.

Maher, J. H., Jr., & Kur, E. (1983, June). Constructing questionnaires. *Training and Development Journal, 37*, 17–19.

McGowan, J., & Clark, R. E. (1985). Instructional software features that support learning for students with widely different ability levels. *Performance and Instruction Journal, 14*, 17.

Murray-Hicks, M. (1981). Analysis techniques for management skills. *National Society for Performance and Instruction Journal, 20*, 15–20.

Nadler, L. (1982). *Designing training programs: The critical events model*. Reading, MA: Addison-Wesley.

Newstrom, J. W., & Lilyquist, J. M. (1979, October). Selecting needs analysis methods. *Training and Development Journal*, 52–56.

Rossett, A. (1982). A typology for generating needs assessment. *Journal of Instructional Development, 6* (1), 29–33.

Scott, D., & Deadrick, D. (1982, June). The nominal group technique: Applications for training needs assessment. *Training and Development Journal*, 26–33.

Silber, K. (1981). Applying Piaget's stages of intellectual development and Guilford's structure of intellect model to training instructional developers. *Journal of Instructional Development, 4* (3), 33–40.

Spitzer, D. (1979, May). Remember these do's and don't's of questionnaire design. *Training HRD*, 34–37.

Stufflebeam, D. L., McCormick, C. H., Brinkeroff, R. O., & Nelson, C. O. (1985). *Conducting educational needs assessment*. Boston: Kluvner-Nijhoff.

University Consortium on Instructional Development and Technology (UCIDT). (1968). Syracuse, NY: Syracuse University, Instructional Design, Development & Evaluation (IDDE).

Witkin, B. R. (1984). *Assessing needs in educational and social programs*. San Francisco: Jossey Bass.

Witkin, B. R. (Ed.). (1978a). Before you do a needs assessment: Important first questions. Hayward, CA: Office of Alameda County Superintendent of Schools.

Witkin, B. R. (Ed.). (1978b). Needs assessment product locator: Available needs assessment products and how to select them for local use. Hayward, CA: Office of the Alameda County Superintendent of Schools.

Chapter Five
Basic Skills

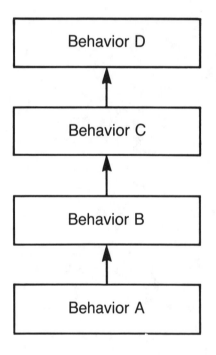

Objectives	■ Given statements of learning outcomes, identify those that are observable and measurable.

Objectives

- Given statements of learning outcomes, identify those that are observable and measurable.

- Given unacceptable statements of learning outcomes, rewrite them to make them acceptable.

- Given job titles and associated requirements, write statements that describe observable and measurable behavior.

- Given flowcharting conventions used incorrectly, correct the errors to display the information properly.

- Given a list of tasks, develop a flowchart.

- Given a hierarchy, answer questions about the relationship of the tasks.

- Given an incomplete hierarchy and a list of tasks, complete the hierarchy.

- Given a list of tasks, use the list to construct both a flowchart and a hierarchy.

- Given task descriptions, write three-part statements that describe the conditions of performance, the action taken, and the outputs.

- Given a task analysis situation, select the most appropriate method for collecting task data.

- Given a subject matter expert (SME) for a procedure, interview the SME to elicit the information needed to flowchart the procedure.

Overview

When children enter first grade, instruction is directed at teaching them to read, write, and do simple arithmetic. Mastery of these skills is important; they are the basis for all future school learning and they are necessary for effective day-to-day living. Because they are prerequisites for virtually all future learning, they are called basic skills.

A prerequisite is a task that enables or aids the learning of another task. And just as reading, writing, and arithmetic are basic to everyday living, certain competencies are prerequisites for the instructional design process. Gagné and Briggs (1979) define two types of prerequisites: essential and supportive. An essential prerequisite is a subordinate task essential to the learning of a higher order task. For example, before a child can learn division, he or she must first learn to add and subtract. Addition and subtraction are essential to learning division because they are actually part of the total skill of dividing.

Supportive prerequisites, as the name implies, support learning by making it easier. A child who enjoys math is likely to learn math skills, but the child's attitude is not essential for learning. That is, it is supportive of learning math skills, but not essential.

This chapter deals with certain essential prerequisites: the ability to use verbal and visual connections to describe learning outcomes and the ability to collect information in unfamiliar fields. These skills are essential prerequisites because they are integral to many instructional design tasks.

Verbal conventions are used to describe learning outcomes. The underlying premise of instructional design is that the behavior to be learned must be made explicit in order to design instruction to achieve objectives and to know when objectives have been achieved.

Visual conventions are analytical tools for identifying the subtasks, information flow, inputs, and decisions required to perform a function or job. As analytic tools, they reveal the relationships among elements and restructure them in accordance with an optimal learning design. Once these relationships are known, these same tools are used to communicate what students will learn, how they will learn it, and how they will demonstrate achievement of the objectives.

The ability to objectify behavior is fundamental to instructional design. As noted, there are certain verbal and visual conventions for describing learning outcomes in observable and measurable terms. When instructional designers are expert in the field to be taught, they draw on their own knowledge to define precisely the behavior to be taught. Usually, however, instructional designers are faced with the task of developing instruction in an unfamiliar field. Under these circumstances, designers must gather information from expert sources and translate it into a behavioral form. To do this, the designer must select from a repertoire of data collection methods those appropriate to the situation. The ability to work with unfamiliar subject matter is an essential prerequisite for virtually all designers.

Study Questions

1. What tools can we use to make others understand our instructional goals?
2. How can covert behavior be made explicit?
3. How are flowcharts constructed?
4. How are hierarchies constructed?
5. What does the instructional designer do when faced with an unfamiliar content area?

VERBAL SKILLS

We all have been students. Think back to those courses where you misunderstood what the instructor wanted. The instructor lectured on one thing and tested on another. Or remember the course you signed up for based on the course description. Partway through it, you realized that it was headed in a direction different from where you had intended to go. The course description had not clearly described the course's goal or purpose.

These and similar problems you encountered as a student are the very ones that as instructional designers you should strive to avoid. In order to design instruction that can be objectively measured, you need to precisely define the behavior to be taught.

Observable and Measurable Behaviors

A key concept in instructional design is that learning outcomes are described in terms of observable student activity; that is, what does the student do after instruction that indicates he or she has learned what was taught?

Why is this concept important? Simply because an instructor can't read the student's mind to see how well he or she understands; only through the student's observable activity can skill or knowledge be measured. Defining the precise behavior to be taught begins with the analysis step in the ID process. With a clear description of the topic or performance to be learned, you will be able to establish clearcut instructional goals that provide a basis for developing performance measures (tests), permit selection of the most suitable instructional techniques, and permit evaluation of the completed course's instructional effectiveness.

Statements that lead to these outcomes describe observable and measurable behavior. When you describe an observable action, focus on using precise verbs. Consider, for example, the two groups of statements in Table 5.1. Column A's verbs describe observable actions, and the statements communicate what a student will have to do on a test to determine whether learning has occurred. The verbs in Column B, however, are imprecise; it is not clear how learning will be evaluated. Does "Be familiar with fuses" mean the teacher will be satisfied with a definition of fuses? Will "critical thinking" be demonstrated by the answer to a multiple-choice question or by performing an experiment? Column B

Table 5.1   Observable and Unobservable Behaviors

Column A	Column B
Write the formula for Ohm's Law	Know Ohm's Law
Solve circuit problems	Think critically
Replace fuses	Be familiar with fuses

From *Module 9*: Preparing task/context hierarchies: *Student resource book* (p. 7) by D. Frezza, 1985, Randolph AFB, TX: USAF Occupational Measurement Center (ATC).

does not make clear what the teacher will observe in order to judge whether learning has taken place.

In addition to using precise verbs, you can further clarify behavior with active-voice, subject/verb/object sentence structure. In other words, say what the student is to do to what. The sentences in Column A leave no doubt as to how performance will be evaluated.

Good sentence structure doesn't always prevent confusion; sentences must contain unambiguous words. Consider these statements:

(a) **Handle classified defense documents.**
(b) **Analyze hazardous materials.**

"Handle" and "analyze" are certainly observable, but because the terms are open to interpretation, they are unacceptable. Does handle mean, for example, storing documents, following regulations for circulating documents, or labeling documents according to how they are classified? The term "analyze" also has a number of meanings. Likewise, "hazardous materials" is too general because there are different types of hazardous materials and different analytic techniques associated with each. The statement is ambiguous.

How can statements be improved? Making them specific will depend on the nature of the performance they describe. It may be possible simply to change the verbs. If "handle" means following a set of procedures for circulating the documents, then changing "handle" to "circulate" makes the statement acceptable. However, if a verb denotes a variety of actions, several statements must be written to describe each one. The statement on hazardous materials may have to be expanded into a series of statements in order to define the specific type of analysis required for each type of material.

In sum, to effectively communicate intentions that are not open to different interpretations, statements must describe observable, measurable, specific behavior.

Behaviors That Are Not Observable

Cognitive Operations. When information is related to a specific job or task, it isn't difficult to write statements of observable and measurable actions. In school settings, however, knowledge is not always directly related to an observable task. The goal of instruction is to instill knowledge and/or teach mental operations. When the behavior is covert, your job is to specify observable, measurable actions that the student can display as evidence that the knowledge or mental skills have been learned. Table 5.2 shows acceptable statements written for the cognitive domain.

Affective Behavior. In some settings, the instruction you develop will concern affective behavior. For example, you may wish to teach radiology technicians to maintain a professional relationship with their patients. It will be your job to define "professional relationship." You can define these behaviors in observable and measurable terms by getting good information during the task analysis about what technicians do when they demonstrate a professional relationship with patients. Most likely, the analysis will reveal several ways they exhibit this relationship and you will write several corresponding statements to make the behavior explicit so that it can be taught. Table 5.3 shows behavioral statements written for the affective domain.

Table 5.2. Statements of Observable and Measurable Behavior in the Cognitive Domain

Instructional Goal	Behavior Taken as Evidence of Learning
Recognize nutrients and their functions	Matches a list of nutrients to a list of their functions
Apply principles of planning	Constructs a plan for conducting a task analysis, given a description of the problem, a list of resources, and a due date
Classify levers according to their properties	Labels illustrations of levers as belonging to Class I, II, or III
Recognize symptoms of paranoid personality	Selects symptoms from a list of statements about behavior OR Identifies symptoms from video presentations of patients
Apply criteria for instructional design	Rates three instructional designs for adherence to criteria OR States which elements of an instructional design meet the criteria and where the design is deficient

Table 5.3. Statements of Observable and Measurable Behavior in the Affective Domain

Instructional Goal	Behavior Taken as Evidence of Learning
Interest in reading	Asks to read a book OR Selects statements consistent with an interest in reading OR Subscribes to a magazine OR Reports activities that involve reading (e.g., joins a book club, goes to the library)
Pleasure in gardening as recreation	Purchases a book on gardening OR Collects articles on gardening OR Responds favorably to statements about pleasure of gardening
Devotion to freedom of speech	Agrees with statements consistent with value OR Argues against limiting the expression of views with which the student strongly disagrees OR Reports protests against perceived infringements (e.g., writes letters to others to support freedom of speech, enlists aid of others in support of cause)
Alertness to nutrition principles	Voluntarily selects reading material on nutrition OR Rates high statements about sound nutrition

Exercise to Identify Correctly Stated Learning Outcomes

Directions: Check the statements of learning outcomes that can be readily observed and measured.

Example: A painting is an observable and measurable outcome for an art student. The painting is obviously visible. Art experts can evaluate the student's adherence to principles of design, use of color, and skill at manipulating the medium. But the student's innate artistic ability is not observable. It is an internal quality that manifests itself only when the student produces a product.

1. Possess interpersonal communication skills.
2. Complete maintenance data collection forms.
3. Develop manual dexterity.
4. Read a barometer and record the atmospheric pressure.
5. Read how to analyze a short story.
6. Translate a news report in a Russian newspaper.
7. Solve formulas containing statistical symbols.
8. Know when to notify a superior of a problem.
9. Perform safety procedures while repairing a malfunction in a stereo receiver.
10. Adhere to standards of good citizenship.

Exercise to Revise Poorly Written Learning Outcomes

Directions: Rewrite each of the statements from the previous exercise that did not meet the "observable and measurable" criteria. To be correct, your statements must be phrased in verb-object sequence and must describe an observable learning outcome. The statements may be written for any job or content area.

Exercise to Write Observable and Measurable Learning Outcomes

Directions: For each of the following jobs, write a statement that describes a readily observable and measurable learning outcome.

1. Job Title: Firefighter
   Ability to operate types of hand-held fire extinguishers.

2. Job Title: Statistician
   Ability to use visual conventions to display annual incomes.

3. Job Title: Communication Specialist
   Ability to use Morse code. Translates Morse code into English.

4. Job Title: Art Historian
   Ability to distinguish different painting styles.

5. Job Title: Pianist
   Ability to read music.

6. Job Title: Comptroller
   Ability to plan budget requirements. End product is a dollar amount.

7. Job Title: Geologist
   Dependability on the job.

8. Job Title: Climatologist
   Knowledge of specific facts about weather in northeastern U.S. cities.

9. Job Title: Soldier
   Knowledge of military convention for telling time.

10. Job Title: Electronics Technician
    Ability to apply Ohm's law.

11. Job Title: Woodworker
    Attitude consistent with good workmanship.

VISUAL TOOLS

Visual tools are graphic ways of making the components of a task explicit. Instructional designers commonly use flowcharts and hierarchies, and which visual tool to select will depend on the task and the intention of the analysis. Flowcharts are preferred for tasks where it is important to lay out the sequence of steps and decision points. Hierarchies are preferred if the purpose of the analysis is to determine learning prerequisites for a particular skill or knowledge.

There are at least four good reasons for using visual tools:

1. They help to focus on the specific practices that make experts out of novices. Graphic devices facilitate communication between the IDer and the subject matter expert (SME). They help to zero in on the subtasks critical to correct performance and provide a means of checking understanding.

2. They provide a systematic way to define subskills. Gaps and deficiencies are readily identified. Used correctly, visual tools often lead to a more rigorous analysis.

3. They lead to easier ways to perform tasks or expose dead-end steps. Procedures used by expert performers may be out of date or inefficient. SMEs continue using old ways out of habit. Visual displays help them see the task in a new light and consider alternative ways to achieve the same end.

4. The display may provide all the guidance necessary to perform a task. Many equipment-related tasks can be performed using only the information in a flowchart. Also, having reference sources at hand reduces dependence on memory. One instructional design project (Johnson, Schneider, & Glasgow, 1979) resulted in a set of flowcharts to describe complex rules for determining an insurance claimant's eligibility for benefits. Previous instruction on this task had consisted of having students learn the rules, but now, instead of trying to commit the complicated regulations to memory, students were simply taught to use the flowcharts. Instruction was thereby substantially reduced.

Flowcharts

Any procedure can be flowcharted. A flowchart is simply a description of the sequence of physical and mental actions and decisions involved in a procedure's performance. A number of different performances have been analyzed using flowcharts. Figures 5.1 through 5.4 illustrate flowcharts for various tasks.

Flowcharting Conventions.   Flowcharting has a language of its own. Following are the generally accepted conventions for flowcharting.

Start/End. ⬭ This symbol is used as the beginning symbol pointing to the first task and as a symbol indicating that no more tasks are to be performed. A flowchart has only one starting point; therefore there is only one START symbol. However, there can be more than one END point.

Input/Output. ▱ A parallelogram represents either an input task or an output task. An example of an input task is keying the account number of a savings account in a bank. An example of an output task is printing a report or displaying the results of a computation. An output at the end of a chain creates the input for the next step.

Process. ▭ A process is a simple procedure, an operation, or an instruction. Processes do not include tasks requiring a decision. A process is represented by a rectangle. Calculating simple interest, typing a report, or taking a test are examples of processes.

Decision. ◇ Decision symbols are used when two alternative sequences are possible depending upon the outcome of the decision. Usually decisions are posed as questions requiring a yes or no answer. However, any two-way alternative may be posed.

Connector. ⊙ A connector is represented by a circle and may serve one of two functions: (1) It is a junction point gathering flowchart segments leading to a common task. The

Figure 5.1   Flowchart for Determining Black Lung Claims

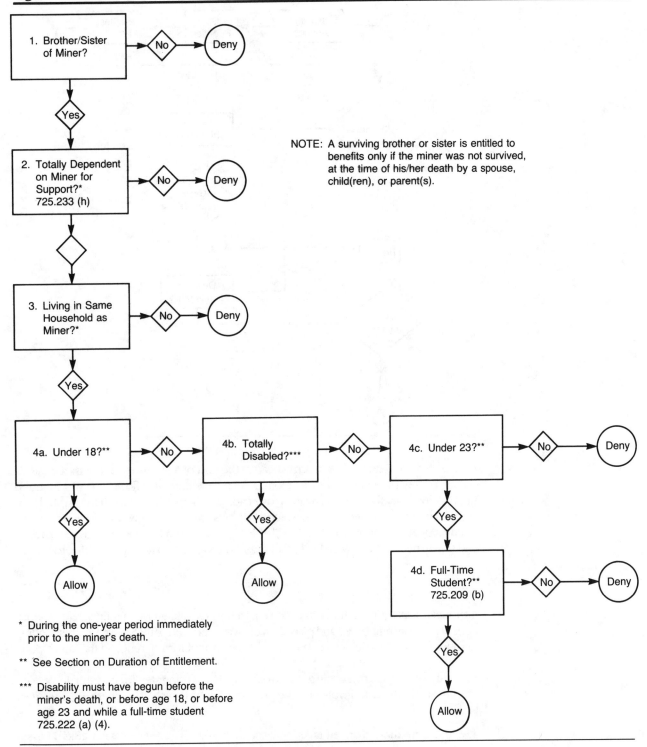

NOTE: A surviving brother or sister is entitled to benefits only if the miner was not survived, at the time of his/her death by a spouse, child(ren), or parent(s).

* During the one-year period immediately prior to the miner's death.

** See Section on Duration of Entitlement.

*** Disability must have begun before the miner's death, or before age 18, or before age 23 and while a full-time student 725.222 (a) (4).

From *Course for Black Lung Claims Examiners* by V. Johnson, G. Schneider, & Z. Glasgow, 1979.

junction point is given a label such as a capital letter. No two connectors can have the same label. (2) It connects flowchart segments from one page to another. This situation arises when space limitations make it necessary to continue a flowchart on a different page. In this case, the same label must be used.

Figure 5.2   Steps in the Planning Process

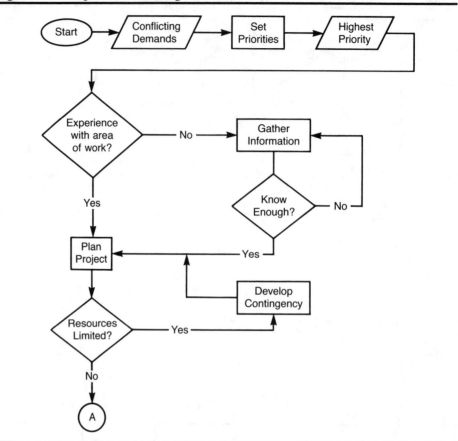

Lines with Arrowheads. ⟶ An arrowhead at the end of a line is used to indicate the direction of flow from one symbol to another. All the elements in a flowchart are connected in one way or another by lines with arrowheads. The sequence in which the symbols are ordered indicates the sequence in which steps must occur. This flowchart indicates the sequential order for steps A, B, and C. A→B→C   This flowchart indicates that steps A, B, and C may be taken in any order, but all must be completed before proceeding to step D.

Annotation. Descriptive notes may be required to explain a task in a flowchart. Annotations are usually numbered and placed on the lower portion of the sheet. A corresponding number is placed in the left-hand corner of the symbol for reference to the annotation.

Procedures for Constructing a Flowchart. The starting step for constructing a flowchart is a list of the tasks involved in the procedure to be flowcharted. There are three general steps.

1. If there are more than ten tasks, collapse them into five to seven major tasks. List and order the major tasks in optimal procedural order. Draw a simple flowchart to show the flow of the major tasks. Show any branching as a consequence of a decision point. If there are alternative ways to do the tasks, show them as branches.

2. Using the general flowchart as a starting point, draw an expanded flowchart that shows the flow of the subtasks for each major task. Continue expanding and elaborating the steps until you have arrived at an appropriate level of detail. All tasks should be at approximately the same level of description.

Figure 5.3   Flow Chart of the Instructional Objective "Given a list of mixed decimal fractions the pupil is able to order them from smallest to largest."

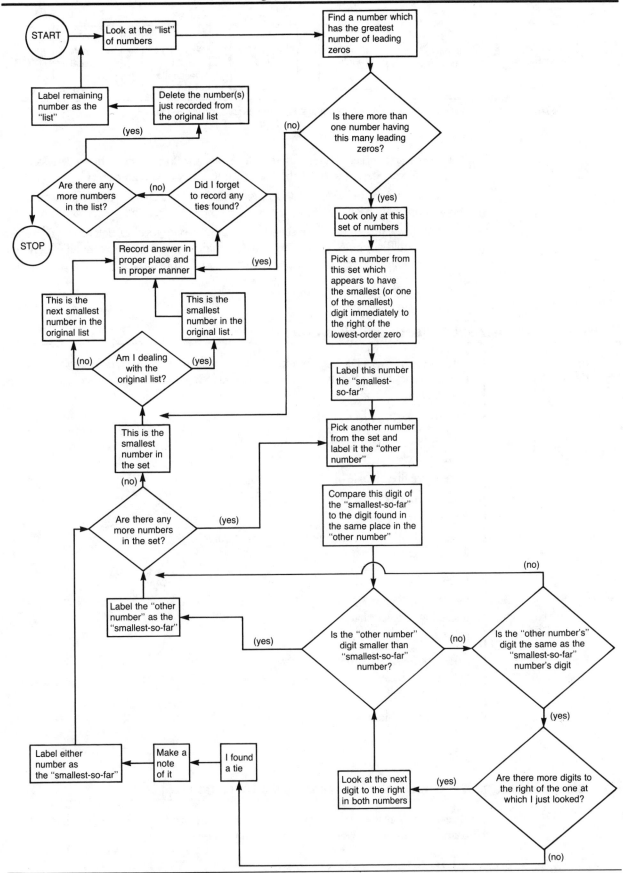

From *"Charting as a technique in instructional design"* by A. J. Nitko, 1976, in D.T. Gow (Ed.), *Design and development of curricular materials, Vol. 2,* Pittsburgh, PA: University of Pittsburgh.

Figure 5.4 Flowchart for performing a process analysis

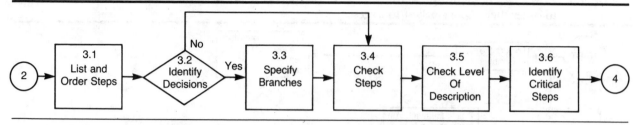

From *Task analysis procedure (ETAP): User's Manual* by C. H. Reigeluth, D. Merrill, R. K. Brandon, R. Begland, and R. Tarr, 1980.

3. Confer with a subject matter expert to determine the flowchart's accuracy. This step will be integral with Steps 1 and 2 if the construction is done with an expert.

    A. Ensure the presence of all decision points and that all steps are sequenced in the optimal order.

    B. Make sure all tasks are stated at the appropriate level of detail. The flowchart should not be so general as to be meaningless to anyone except an expert, nor should it be so detailed as to describe what is obvious even to the uninitiated.

Exercise to Construct Procedural Flowcharts

Directions: Here is a list of steps and decision points in the procedural task of changing a tire. Construct a flowchart using the symbols and the annotation methods described in this chapter.

Remove defective tire

Set brake

Lower vehicle

Place spare tire on axle

Place wheel block

Replace wheel cover

Obtain jack, lug wrench, and spare tire from trunk

Jack vehicle

Brake set?

Remove wheel cover

Install lug nuts alternately

Lift defective tire off axle

Type of jack?

Vehicle on grade?

Remove wheel block

Install serviceable tire

Exercise to Recognize Correctly Constructed Flowcharts

Directions: Consider the following flowchart. There are four errors in the use of flow-charting conventions. Correct the errors on the flowchart.

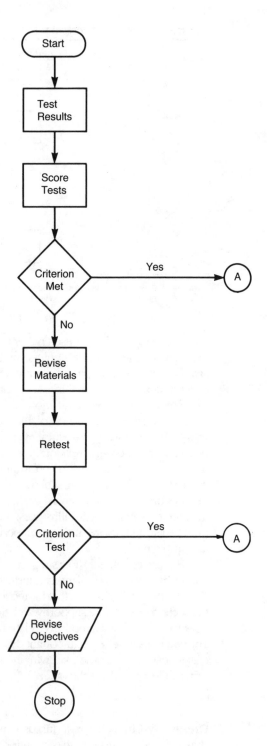

Hierarchies

A hierarchy is an organization of elements that, according to prerequisite relationships, describes the path of experiences a learner must take to achieve any single behavior that appears higher in the hierarchy (Nitko, 1976). Figure 5.5 illustrates a simple hierarchy. The order of learning proceeds upward. The sequential nature of the prerequisites is represented by the vertical axis of the hierarchy. A must be learned before B, which must be learned before C, and so on. The hierarchy does not preclude the possibility that a student may skip a particular learning step. In this figure, a student may begin the learning sequence at behavior B if he or she has already acquired behavior A. The top of the hierarchy represents the terminal behavior.

Figure 5.5   Simple Hierarchy of Learning Relationships

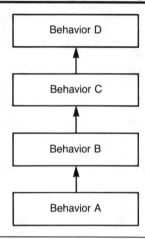

From *Module 9. Preparing task/content hierarchies: Student resource book* by D. Frezza, 1985.

The term hierarchy is used rather freely. For our purposes, a hierarchical relationship means you cannot do task B unless you know how to do task A. The question you will ask again and again in preparing hierarchies is this: What must the student already know in order to learn how to do this task or subtask? Figure 5.6 shows a visual display that looks like a hierarchy, but is not. It shows the temporal relationship of what is done. Although it has the vertical construction of a hierarchy, the display is in fact a flowchart.

Do not confuse a procedural relationship with a hierarchical relationship. Hierarchies do not show procedural relationships. In analyzing procedural relationships you ask "What does the experienced person performing this task do first? What is the next step? What step comes after that?" and so on. When analyzing procedural relationships you focus on the expert performer, but when analyzing hierarchical relationships you focus on the learner. As the hierarchy in Figure 5.7 illustrates, the concepts associated with an education problem must be learned before students can perform the more complex behaviors associated with the problem.

Hierarchies do not show supportive relationships. In supportive relationships, the various tasks may be so similar that transfer of learning takes place from one task to the other. Transfer of learning means that having learned one task, the student can more easily learn the second task when a supportive relationship exists between them. For example, "Drive a 1/4-ton truck" has a supportive relationship to "Drive a 2 1/2-ton truck" (and vice versa). The two tasks have some important differences, but for the most part learning one will facilitate learning the other; knowing how to drive one truck, however, is not essential in order to learn to drive the other.

Hierarchy Conventions. Just as you must follow conventions for constructing flowcharts, you also must follow conventions for constructing hierarchies that can be "understood."

Reading Hierarchies. Hierarchies are read from the bottom up. The block at the top is the end point. It contains the most comprehensive, complex action in the diagram. The blocks at the bottom—the starting points—contain the simplest, most basic action.

Levels. Subtasks of roughly equal complexity and without an essential prerequisite relationship are placed side by side. Blocks at the same level of the diagram are of equal rank and have no prerequisite relationship. There is no established method for showing supportive relationships in hierarchies.

Figure 5.6   Procedural Diagram for the Task: Remove Main Drive Shaft from
OH058 Helicopter

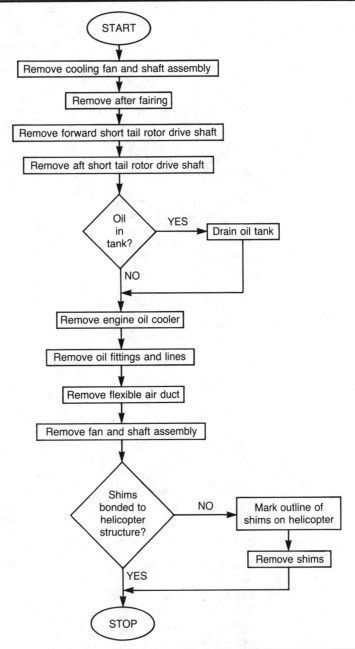

From *Module 9. Preparing Task/Content hierarchies: Student Resource Book* by D. Frezza, 1985.

Annotations. The boxes in a hierarchy may contain annotations. When they are too long, annotations are listed separately and referenced by numbers in the boxes.

Procedure for Creating Hierarchies.   The starting point for constructing a hierarchy is a comprehensive list of the tasks that make up a job or function. There are three major steps to constructing a hierarchy:

1. Cluster or group the tasks. For inclusion in a group, select tasks that bear a close relationship to each other. Each task must be included in at least one of the groups, but a task

Figure 5.7   Hierarchy for an Educational Problem

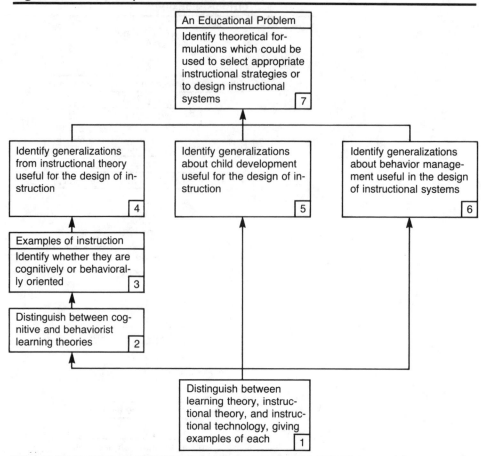

From "Unit 1. Goals of Education" by D. T. Gow (ed.), in *Design and development of curricular materials, Vol. 1,* 1976.

may also be common to several groups. Label the groups with terms that emerge from the job or function being analyzed. Initial clustering or grouping of tasks may be tentative. The composition of the groups may change as a result of decisions you make later on. Do not hesitate to regroup tasks when it seems appropriate.

2. Organize tasks within each group to show the hierarchical relationships for learning. Ask yourself "What would the learner have to learn in order to do this task?" Once the essential prerequisite relationships are shown, reevaluate the relationship between each pair of tasks with the question "Can this superordinate task be performed if the learner cannot perform this subordinate task?" The lower-level skill must be integrally related to the higher-level skill.

3. Confer with a subject matter expert to determine the hierarchy's accuracy. This step occurs concurrently with Steps 1 and 2.

Exercise to Apply Knowledge of Hierarchy Conventions

Directions: Refer to this hierarchy diagram in answering the following questions.

1. How does the subtask "Apply rules for direction for reading" relate to (contribute to the performance of) the subtask "Align points with scale"?

2. How does the subtask "Read compass values from scale" contribute to the performance of the subtask "Align points with scale"?

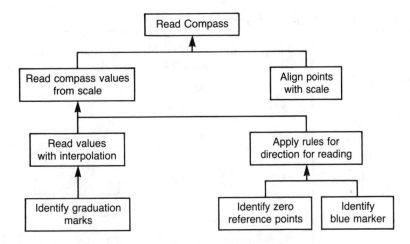

3. Which of the following subtasks is at the highest level?

    a. Identify graduation marks.

    b. Read values with interpolation.

    c. Align points with scale.

4. Which of these statements is correct?

    a. "Read compass values from scale" is essential for the performance "Read values with interpolation."

    b. "Read values with interpolation" is essential for the performance "Read compass values from scale."

5. Are "Read values with interpolation" and "Apply rules for direction for reading" jointly essential for performance of "Read compass values from scale"?

From *Module 9. Preparing task/content hierarchies: Student resource book* by D. Frezza, 1985.

Exercise to Construct Visual Displays

Directions: This is a group exercise. Divide into groups of three or four students. Each group will prepare a task hierarchy and a flowchart using the conventions described in this chapter. The reason for doing this exercise in a group is to emphasize the fact that in the real world, hierarchies and flowcharts are the product of input from several people.

Examine the sets of randomly listed tasks below for the job of troubleshooting FM radios. Your assignment is to use the tasks to construct both a flowchart and a hierarchy. All of the tasks must be included in the diagrams.

Recognize symptoms

Use Form XYZ to record results of troubleshooting

Identify component parts

Classify test results as normal or abnormal

Troubleshoot FM radios

Use test equipment

Obtain knowledge of normal test results

Source: Frezza (1985) p. 56.

Exercise to Construct a Hierarchy

Directions: Here is a blank hierarchy diagram and a list of tasks. Fill in the diagram by writing the appropriate task in each block.

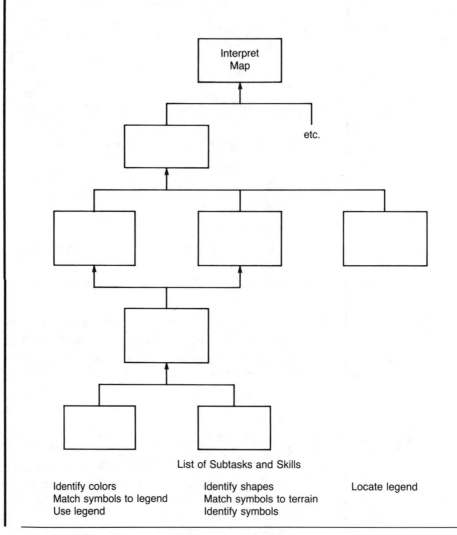

List of Subtasks and Skills

Identify colors	Identify shapes	Locate legend
Match symbols to legend	Match symbols to terrain	
Use legend	Identify symbols	

From *Module 9. Preparing task/content hierarchies: Student resource book* by D. Frezza, 1985.

COLLECTING INFORMATION IN UNFAMILIAR FIELDS

The object of the instructional designer working in an unfamiliar field is to document in behavioral terms what the competent performer does in response to the various conditions of performance. Documentation includes describing as objectively as possible all inputs to the performer, actions taken by the performer, and outputs produced by the action.

Types of Information

Inputs can be classified into four types: (1) cues that prompt performance, (2) resources used during performance, (3) organizational inputs affecting performance, and (4) environmental conditions affecting performance. Cues are any stimulus or event that starts the performance of a task (e.g., supervisor's or teacher's directions, completion of other tasks, other verbal, visual, or auditory signal.) Resources are performance aids or references used to guide performance. They consist of dictionaries, calculators, computers, meters, look-up charts, and tables. Resources also include the equipment or tools used to perform a task. Organizational inputs are the policies and practices, standard operating procedures, chains of command, and management directives put in place by an organization. Organizational inputs may facilitate or impose constraints on performance. Environmental conditions are physical and psychological factors. Physical factors include weather, lighting, time of day, temperature, noise levels, etc., when these conditions are relevant to performance of the task. Psychological conditions that may affect performance include fatigue, stress, anxiety, etc.

Actions are what the performer does. They are the overt actions that we can plainly see or hear and the covert actions that take place internally. Action statements describe how the job or function is done and in what sequence subtasks are performed.

Outputs are produced as a result of an action. Outputs may take many forms and include products as diverse as a written report, a painted surface, a speech, a typed letter, a completed project, or a correctly spelled word. Two characteristics of outputs are the following:

1. Indications or cues to the performer that mark the end of the tasks. (How do you know when you are done?) In some instances, task completion is self-evident. But for many tasks, what constitutes a satisfactory outcome must be learned. For example, a cook must learn when a sauce is at the right consistency, a woodworker must know when a wood finish is correct, and an instructional designer must be able to determine when one step is adequate before moving on to the next step in the design process.

2. Standards of acceptability. (How well must the task be performed?) The answer to this question will influence the standards of the instructional objectives. Sometimes standards of acceptance may be easy to set (e.g., a typist's words-per-minute rate), but sometimes they are difficult to define (e.g., esthetic criteria for a work of art). Often you will find that standards for a job or tasks do not exist and that poor performance may have resulted from the performers's not knowing what was expected of them. If this is the case, instruction may not be the best solution to the performance deficiency. The establishment of a clear standard may solve the performance problem. If, after you have investigated the problem, instruction remains the solution, you will have to arrive at a standard acceptable to the people involved.

Exercise to Define Inputs, Actions, and Outputs

Directions: Your assignment is to read job description narratives and record inputs, actions, and outputs. The first one is completed for you as an example.

1. An instructional designer interviews a soldier about the correct procedures for camouflaging and concealing a vehicle under field conditions. The designer is told that there are several steps in the procedure and that they are the same regardless of weather conditions or time.

2. An instructional designer observes the following on a job study for maintenance tasks. When a blue light flashes, the repair person replaces the XYZ component. When a red light flashes, the repair person turns off the equipment, calls the supervisor to report the problem, and requests a senior level repair person to handle the job.

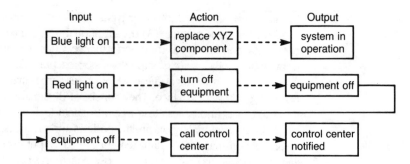

a.   Place the vehicle under natural vegetation.

b.   Cover all reflecting surfaces of the vehicle with natural or artificial materials.

c.   Ensure that the color and texture blend with the surrounding areas.

d.   Drape the net to conceal the vehicle.

e.   Brush and cover the vehicle's tracks.

Input	Action	Output

3. An emergency medical technician describes the following procedure for performing mouth-to-mouth resuscitation on a person who is apparently unconscious and not breathing: Check for breathing and consciousness. If the signs are negative, start resuscitation immediately and continue as long as there is a pulse, until the victim breathes on his or her own, until relieved by medically trained personnel, or until too exhausted to continue.

Input	Action	Output

Sources of Information

The ability to work with unfamiliar subject matter is one of the competencies that distinguish experienced designers from novices. Bratton (1981) asked ID practioners at six institutions of higher education, "How do experienced developers work in unfamiliar fields?" Most suggested that when embarking on a new project in an unknown area, they read texts and/or discussed the content area with an SME.

In collecting information about a field, there is no such thing as "one best source." Major sources are either some form of permanent documentation (either verbal or visual) or subject matter experts (SMEs). SMEs may be current or previous job holders, managers, or academicians.

Document Review

When you are faced with the challenge of designing instruction in an area about which you have little personal knowledge, it is a good idea to begin the task analysis by collecting all available written material about the job or function. This will give you a chance to become familiar with the terms and basic structure of the field before you encounter an SME.

Sources of written information include technical manuals, books, information sheets, professional journals, policy manuals, manufacturer's instructions, operating procedures, and job or performance aids. Existing instructional materials are another good source if the lesson plans and student materials are accurate. Finally, when the materials are too technical or too complex, go to the library and try to find the simplest possible presentation of the subject. When assigned to a project on mine safety, for example, one designer found that reading high school library books on mining practices was a good way to learn the basics about mining.

To come to grips with new topics, read actively. Outline, take notes, paraphrase key concepts, identify areas where you must seek further clarification, and write out specific questions to ask an SME. Constructing flowcharts, hierarchies, charts, and tables may help you discover the basics of the new discipline.

Interviews

The background you gain from written materials will help you work better with SMEs. Some of the information found in the documentation will be contradictory, some will be out of date, some will be redundant, and some will involve alternative ways of achieving the same objective. Accordingly, take nothing for granted. One of the goals of the SME interview is to clarify ambiguities. The designer who is afraid to ask the "dumb question" will probably generate deficient tasks data. But do your homework beforehand. Interviews are most productive when the designer is conversant with the basics and with the language of the new field.

The ID practitioners surveyed by Bratton suggested that a critical factor in learning about a new field from an expert is the interviewing strategy. The practioners reported interviewing the client with specific goals in mind; they used inductive, deductive, and inferential questioning strategies. As a means of clarifying their own understanding of the content, they offered analogies and presented tentative conclusions to the SME during the discussion.

If there are different points of view on a topic or different ways of performing a job, task analysis data should be collected from expert performers who represent the full range of approaches to acceptable performance. When a number of experts must be consulted and time is a constraint, or when differences regarding how tasks should be performed must be resolved, consider group interviews. Interviews are more difficult to control because the IDer must perform both task and maintenance functions for several people. The advantage of a group interview is that because the members of the group stimulate each other to recall information that otherwise might have been overlooked, it often elicits better information. Also, the pros and cons of each viewpoint are more likely to surface when they can be challenged by those holding differing opinions.

Face-to-face interviews probably elicit better information because it is easier to achieve rapport, there is usually more time to explore questions, and reference material can be consulted jointly. When travel time or money is a constraint, however, interviews can be conducted on the telephone—provided the occupation or function can be analyzed using verbal means only and the documentation is fairly good. Under these circumstances, telephone interviews allow contact with the SMEs for clarification and elaboration purposes.

Bratton notes that experienced interviewers he surveyed were not specifically trained during their professional development for conducting interviews in unfamiliar areas. He suggests that IDers adopt the interview strategies of ethnographers, scientists who study human cultures. His reasoning is that ethnographers and IDers have much in common since they both must rely on personal interviews as the primary means of gaining understanding. Bratton described three major types of questions for eliciting ethnographic information. The questions move from the general to the specific.

1. Descriptive questions are global; they are designed to encourage the respondent to talk. ("Describe to me what it is you do when you tune a guitar.")

2. Structural questions are more specific; they are used to gather detailed information about a particular topic. ("We've been talking about diagnosing a defective circuit. What are the symptoms of this type of problem?") Structural questions also can be used to confirm the interviewer's understanding of the content. ("Let's see if I understand that point. If the test is acceptable at this point, you assume that the trouble does not exist in this section of the circuit.")

3. The contrast question is still more specific. It is directed at discovering the meaning of discrete facts and concepts and the relationship among them. ("Some of the clinical signs of diabetes are also symptoms of other diseases. How do you clinically differentiate diabetes?")

Similarly, Gropper's (1971) strategy for interviewing starts with the "big picture" and systematically narrows the questioning to the appropriate level of specificity. The interview begins with an orienting question designed to get at the major areas of information; then more detailed questions are posed until the desired level of specificity is reached.

You can help focus the interview's general-to-specific movement by combining questioning with visuals. Use a chalkboard or flip chart during the interview, or diagram, flowchart, or outline the information. Relationships and sequences can be shown for each substep of the procedure or function under study. These are good techniques for verifying your understanding of the content. They are especially useful for group interviews because the visualizations help members to verify each other's perceptions and, when differences surface, to arrive at consensus. Also, if these illustrations are kept available for later reference, the interviewees will have the opportunity to review what was said and to revise, correct, or elaborate on information.

Critical Incident Technique

Interviews are useful for undocumented procedures that are complex or largely covert. When documentation is incomplete or absent, task information must be obtained from expert performers. The interview strategy discussed above is useful in most situations where performance can be described by expert performers.

There will be times, however, when what is considered expert performance will be difficult to describe or capture. For example, what is it that distinguishes the performance of an effective salesperson or a good manager from that of an average or poor one? What is the performance required to educate students for citizenship? The critical incident approach has been used effectively to define performance in such vague areas.

The critical-incident approach was developed by John Flanagan (1949) when faced with the problem of improving military flight training when too many trainees were cracking-up. He asked those pilot trainees who survived accidents what exactly they had done incorrectly.

Critical incidents are facts, not generalization or opinions. They're about performance that can be pinpointed as either very effective or very ineffective. They are not just routine steps habitually performed correctly. Rather they are behavioral descriptions of instances of extreme cases in performance. The respondent is asked to describe the action taken, the events leading up to the incident, and the specific outcome. After the analyst collects many such incidents, they are sorted into similar groups and labeled according to the type of performance they described.

Observation

The analyst watches an SME and writes down what the SME does. Observations may be made in-person or be videotaped for later observation. In either case, they analyst looks for connections between what is done and what is produced and is especially alert to sequencing. The analyst's job is to develop a behavioral description which consists of the inputs for the observed behavior, actions, and outputs. Observation methods of task analysis are especially useful in simple motor skill areas that include tasks such as machine repair, equipment assembly, and maintenance tasks.

Usually, however, after watching the job cycle until every move is known, the analyst must ask questions. "How did you know that was wrong just then?" "Why do you do A before B?" "How did you decide that the job was done?" Thus, few tasks can be described accurately through observation alone. Most tasks involving mental operations must be captured by questioning the expert performer.

Mailed Questionnaires

Ideally, the analyst should observe or interview performers face-to-face. But performers may be located far and wide. In organizations such as the military, there may be thousands of people performing similar jobs all over the world. Even under the best of circumstances, travel budgets may preclude in-person data collection, and even telephone interviews may sometimes be impractical. The problem then becomes one of devising a collection plan that will produce the best results within the resources available.

When jobholders are at many locations and performing under a variety of circumstances, consider using questionnaires—but understand their limitations. There are two major problems in obtaining accurate and valid responses through the use of questionnaires.

First, are the respondents willing to respond? Many people think questionnaires are a bother. Often, respondents are unwilling to devote the time and thought required to provide the kind of detailed task data necessary for analysis. Even when responding is mandatory, answers are likely to be perfunctory and, consequently, of limited value.

Second, will the respondents respond reliably? It is highly unlikely that most respondents will have the skills to define tasks in the behavioral terms needed for instructional design. If respondents are untrained and responses are unstructured, reducing the data to make sense of it will be an overwhelming task.

Although they are a good method for surveying large numbers of widely dispersed people, questionnaires should be used only when data collection is restricted to obtaining information about fairly straightforward, generally known tasks. The questionnaire's purpose should be to confirm which tasks are performed, where they are performed, and by whom, not to determine how the tasks are performed. Response requirements should be as simple and easy as possible—ideally, a check mark or a yes/no answer. Questionnaires are not useful for obtaining descriptions of how tasks are done because of problems of recording and interpreting results.

Exercise to Identify the Most Appropriate Task Analysis Data Collection Methods

Directions: Select the best method of data collection for each situation.

1. A department store receives complaints about its appliance department sales staff. No one is sure of the exact cause of the complaints. What data would you collect and emphasize? In each situation, you might also collect other types of data.

   a. Critical incident reports about the sales staff from customers

   b. Interviews with the sales staff

   c. Observations of the sales staff with customers

   d. Questionnaires surveying customer satisfaction with the sales staff

2. You are assigned to develop a basic course for aircraft maintenance jobs. The course is intended to teach tasks common to all aircraft maintenance regardless of the type of aircraft the job holder works on. After learning the tasks that are common to all jobs, students will be assigned to specialty training.

   a. Critical incident reports about employees in all jobs

   b. Study of maintenance manuals

    c. Observation of employees in all jobs

    d. Questionnaires surveying all employees, asking them to identify all tasks they do in their jobs

3. You are assigned to develop instruction for drug and alcohol abuse counselors.

    a. Critical incident reports about employees performing the job

    b. Interviews with counselors

    c. Textbooks and references on the subject

    d. a and b

    e. b and c

4. You are assigned to develop instruction for workers who assemble water sampling kits. Because of the high demand for the kit, the company is expanding its current ten-person assembly staff to one hundred people in the next month.

    a. Critical incidents about the ten employees

    b. Interviews with the ten employees

    c. Observation of the ten employees assembling the kits

    d. Study of manuals describing water sampling procedure

Exercise to Collect Information in an Unfamiliar Area

Directions: This is an exercise for two people. Each person will take a turn at playing an SME describing and demonstrating a procedural task and an instructional designer gathering information to define the task behaviorally.

    The SME should select a procedural task unfamiliar to the instructional designer. The task should be simple enough to describe in a single interview, for example, operating a VCR or playing a game of cards. Equipment or objects used during performance should be available for demonstration.

    The instructional designer should conduct the interview using whatever strategy and support materials are judged necessary. Afterward, the interviewer will prepare a task analysis report. The report will be evaluated by the SME using the following criteria:

1. All steps are correct.

2. The steps are arranged in logical and optimal order.

3. Flowchart conventions are used correctly.

FROM THE READING

Define the following terms.

flowchart

hierarchy

essential prerequisite

supportive prerequisite

behavioral statement

ISSUES FOR DISCUSSION

1. Select a task and cite its essential prerequisites as well as supportive prerequisites that may make learning the task easier or faster.

2. Can higher-order cognitive processes, such as problem solving or synthesis, be described using verbal or visual conventions?

REFERENCES

Bratton, B. (1981). Training the instructional development specialist to work in unfamiliar content areas. *Journal of Instructional Design, 4* (3).

Frezza, D. (1985). *Module 9. Preparing task/content hierarchies: Student resource book*. Randolph AFB, TX: Contract No. F41689-83-C-0048, USAF Occupational Measurement Center (ATC). Butler, PA: Applied Science Associates.

Frezza, D. (1985). Module 12. *Task analysis: Student resource book*. Randolph AFB, TX: Contract No. F41689-83-C-0048, USAF Occupational Measurement Center (ATC). Butler, PA: Applied Science Associates.

Gagné, R. M., & Briggs, L. J. (1979). *Principles of instructional design* (2nd ed.). New York: Holt, Rinehart & Winston.

Gow, D. T. (Ed.). (1976). Unit 1. Goals of Education. In *Design and development of curricular materials, Vol. 1*. Pittsburgh, PA: University of Pittsburgh.

Gropper, G. L. (1971). *A technology for developing instructional materials: Handbook A. Plan study of criterion behavior*. Pittsburgh, PA: American Institutes for Research.

Johnson, V., Schneider, G., & Glasgow, Z. (1979). *Course for Black Lung Claims Examiners*. Contract No. J-9-E-7-0188. Washington, DC: U.S. Department of Labor, Office of Workers' Compensation Programs, Employment Standards Administration. Butler, PA: Applied Science Associates.

Nitko, A. J. (1976). Charting as a technique in instructional design. In D. T. Gow (Ed.), *Design and development of curricular materials, Vol. 2*. Pittsburgh, PA: University of Pittsburgh.

Reigeluth, C. H., Merrill, D., Brandon, R. K., Begland, R., & Tarr, R. (1980). *Task analysis procedure (ETAP): User's Manual*. Fort Monroe, VA: U.S. Army Training Development Institute.

Part Two

Steps in the ID Process

Chapter Six
Task and Instructional Analysis

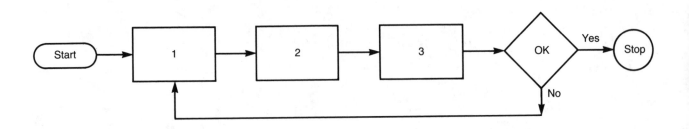

- Given learning requirements, select the format most appropriate for collecting task data.

- Given a list of tasks and criticality ratings, apply a set of rules to determine the instructional requirements.

- Given learning outcomes, select the information source for determining the entry level behaviors.

- Given a list of tasks and associated test results, select the tasks that can be considered entry level behaviors.

- Given a flowchart you constructed in an earlier exercise, describe the target audience and identify the entry level behaviors.

- Given a hierarchy you constructed in an earlier exercise, describe the target audience and identify the entry level behaviors.

- Given a task or function from your own experience, develop a plan to conduct a task analysis.

- Given a plan you developed in a previous exercise, perform the task analysis.

Overview

A systematic approach to instructional design uses analysis at several points. Writers on instructional design often fail, however, to distinguish among the different types of analysis; in fact, these distinctions are often blurred in system models as well. We will distinguish three types of analysis: needs analysis (discussed in Chapter 4), task analysis, and instructional analysis. The latter two are the topics of this chapter.

Different types of analysis are distinguished by the questions they are intended to answer more than by the techniques they use. Each type of analysis requires of the analyst a different mental set. When performing a needs analysis or a task analysis, you may interview jobholders. Although interviews are used to collect information in both instances, the purpose of the interviews is quite different. Needs analysis asks, What is the problem? Is instruction the best solution to the problem? Task analysis asks, What are the performance requirements for this job or function? Instructional analysis asks, What must be learned in order for someone to perform this task? What are the requirements for learning?

Needs analysis precedes task analysis, and task analysis precedes instructional analysis. But the instructional designer will find that he or she moves back and forth among the different types of analysis because analysis is an iterative process. It consists of collecting information for a specific purpose, analyzing the data, and making decisions based on that data. The data collection and analysis process moves from the general to the specific. It begins with the needs analysis phase, and once it is clear that some sort of instruction is the solution to the problem, it continues throughout the entire instructional design to answer increasingly specific questions about what to teach and the amount and type of instruction needed.

The three types of analysis do not have clearly defined beginning and end points. Task analysis begins when the needs analysis is completed. Data collected during the needs analysis, however, will be relevant to subsequent task analysis; therefore needs and task analyses overlap. Early on, the evidence from the needs analysis may indicate that instruction is needed to overcome a particular performance problem. But the data are usually still too general and diffuse for task analysis. Ordinarily the data tell you only what the next set of questions should be to answer questions about how tasks are performed. As the answers to initial task analysis questions are uncovered, new questions arise and additional information is collected. This process continues until, in the judgment of the designer, sufficient data exist as a basis for beginning the instructional analysis process.

Task and instructional analysis also overlap in that task analysis provides some of the answers to the questions posed during instructional analysis. Instructional analysis is intended to answer several questions: What learning outcomes must be achieved? What learning steps will lead to accomplishment of the learning outcome? Must learning steps be performed in a particular sequence?

The analysis process is akin to discovery learning. Information is gathered and examined. On the basis of the information, new hypotheses are formed and tested. Slowly, as an understanding of the instructional problem evolves and relationships among tasks and content become clear, answers emerge regarding what is to be learned to bridge the gap between the student entry level and the learning outcome to be accomplished.

Study Questions

1. How does data collected during needs analysis relate to task analysis?
2. What data is collected for a task analysis?
3. How can the results of task analysis alter the need for instruction?
4. How does an instructional analysis differ from a task analysis?
5. What are the outcomes of an instructional analysis?
6. What are the factors to consider when setting priorities for instruction?
7. How do you determine the entry requirements for a course?

TASK ANALYSIS

Task analysis is a process that moves from the general to the specific. First, the general topics or duties of a function or job are described, then subtasks are defined. Next, sub-subtasks are defined. The analysis continues until the designer arrives at a level of detail appropriate to define the task relative to the target audience. Difficult tasks will require more levels of analysis than easier tasks.

Many instructional design models offer guidelines and criteria for performing task analysis. One of the most comprehensive models is Gropper's *Technology for Developing Instructional Materials* (1971). The procedures are published in an eleven-volume *Handbook* developed to train educational R & D personnel in the development of instructional materials. The first volume is devoted to planning a task analysis. Gropper defines five steps in the planning process (p. 60).

1. Identify the type of criterion behavior to be taught and the type of target audience to which it will be taught. The problem statement developed in Chapter 4 provides the output for this step.

2. Identify the methods for obtaining information to describe and analyze the criterion behavior. The method or methods employed depend on whether an acceptable model of the criterion behavior is available. "Acceptable model" means a standard or agreed-upon way to perform the function or task. Generally speaking, people are more likely to agree upon one way of doing a task for behavior that involves some sort of person/object relationship, and is routine, relatively simple, and observable. Agreement is less likely for behavior that involves higher-level intellectual skills, creativity, alternative procedures, complexity, people-to-people relationships, and/or covertness.

3. Select information sources needed to describe and analyze criterion behavior. When a model is complete and agreed upon by experts, information about the criterion behavior may be collected by interviews with SMEs, observations of expert performers, extraction of information from documents, or some mix of these methods.

When a model is not available, obtain judgments from experts about performance, collect critical incidents, or prescribe behavior based on theory.

4. Plan the sequence in which information about the criterion behavior will be collected. Essentially data on procedural tasks are described in the same order in which they are performed. On tasks where no such dependency relationships exist, the preferred strategy is to move from the general to the specific.

5. Develop (or plan to use existing) information collecting instruments and procedures. The type of information to be analyzed and the methodology selected will determine the design of the instruments to collect data. The best forms are those designed to elicit the type of information needed and allow the data to be recorded in a manner to facilitate later analyses. Ideally, there should be minimal rerecording or transcribing of data to another form for analysis, and the data should be collected in an easily summarized form. Finally, a method for cross-referencing forms will be necessary to relate the different levels of detail.

Formats for Collecting Data

The format used for collecting data will depend on the type of data under study.

Procedural Tasks. Flowcharts are appropriate for procedural tasks consisting of complex and conditional behaviors. Motor skills and intellectual procedural tasks lend themselves to flowcharting. Analysts have employed this technique for jobs such as medical diagnosis, computer repair, and insurance claims processing. The procedure, described in Chapter 5, is fairly straightforward. The SME explains what he or she is doing or thinking while performing the task. A process/decision flowchart is developed and revised until it is correct. Figure 6.1 shows a section of a very large and complex flowchart for the procedures miners should follow when fighting small fires in underground mines.

Figure 6.2 summarizes the general steps for carrying out an analysis for procedural tasks which lend themselves to collecting data by observation. Note that the analysis procedure continues until the flowchart can serve as a set of instructions to do the task. According to Yelon (1971), a task analysis is complete when "a student can proceed through the task . . . though not as quickly or as accurately as a trained person" (Yelon, pp. 8–17). When practical, flowcharts that meet Yelon's standard should be developed. If the task can be performed simply by following the flowchart, the need for instruction will have been reduced or eliminated. If the student is not sufficiently proficient at the task, all that may be needed is practice using the flowchart as a performance aid to bring him to the required level. If the student's performance using the flowchart is satisfactory, no instruction will be needed. It is not always possible or desirable to use the results of the task analysis for instructional purposes. The designer should be alert, however, for such opportunities to reduce the time and effort of downstream development activities.

Intellectual Skills. Tabular or columnar formats are effective for problem solving, rule learning, concept learning, and discrimination learning because they allow the distinctions and commonalities to be made explicit. Table 6.1 shows how a columnar format is used to distinguish the attributes for the concepts "noun" and "verb." It makes explicit the basis of exclusion or inclusion in a class, and lists examples of each concept. Table 6.2 (p. 114) shows an example of the format applied to rule learning.

Verbal Information Learning. Outlines are often the simplest and best format of all for verbal information learning, as shown in Table 6.3 (p. 115).

Attitudes. The designer attempting to perform a task analysis of attitudes must specify the overt behavior that will be accepted as evidence that an attitude is learned. The student will

Figure 6.1   Flowchart for the Procedures Miners Should Follow

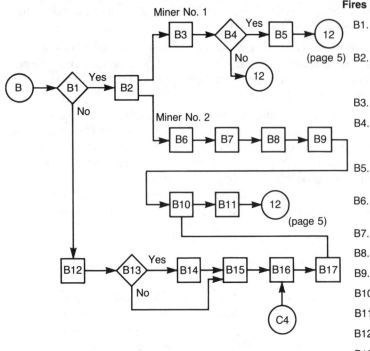

Fires Involving Electrical Equipment With Trailing Cables

B1.   If at least two miners are present at the fire site, go to Step B2. If not, go to Step B12.

B2.   Miner No. 1 (probably equipment operator) performs Steps B3 through B5. Miner No. 2 (probably equipment helper) performs Steps B6 through B11.

B3.   Shut off equipment power switch.

B4.   If the equipment has automatic fire suppression gear, go to Step B5. If not, go to Step 12 of General Procedure.

B5.   Activate automatic fire suppression gear. Go to Step 12 of General Procedure.

B6.   Shut off all section power at power distribution boxes.

B7.   Report fire to Section Foreman.

B8.   Alert other nearby miners to fire.

B9.   Call for mechanic.

B10.   Return to fire site with dry chemical extinguisher.

B11.   Go to Step 12 of General Procedure.

B12.   Shut off equipment power switch.

B13.   If the equipment has automatic fire suppression gear, go to Step B14. If not, go to Step B15.

B14.   Activate automatic fire suppression gear.

B15.   Shut off all section power at power distribution boxes.

B16.   Tell other miners to report fire to Section Foreman.

B17.   Call for mechanic. Go to Step B10.

From *Development of a training program for fighting small fires in the mining industry,* Contract No. J.0395060. by W. Laird, S. Bhatt, T. Bajpayee, Z. Glasgow, and D. Scott, 1981.

undertake some action, make a statement, or make a choice consistent with the attitude. The overt behavior will be a psychomotor skill, an intellectual skill, or verbal information. The task analysis technique appropriate for the overt behavior is used to describe the attitude.

Table 6.1   Columnar Format Used to Distinguish Attributes for the Concepts Noun and Verb

Personal Pronouns	Use Present Tense of Verb "To Be"	Correct Subject-Verb Pair
He *She* *It*	Say "Is"	Singular Pair
We *You* *They*	Say "Are"	Plural Pair and Singular "You" Exception
I	Say "Am"	First Person Singular Pair

Figure 6.2 Collecting Data by Observation

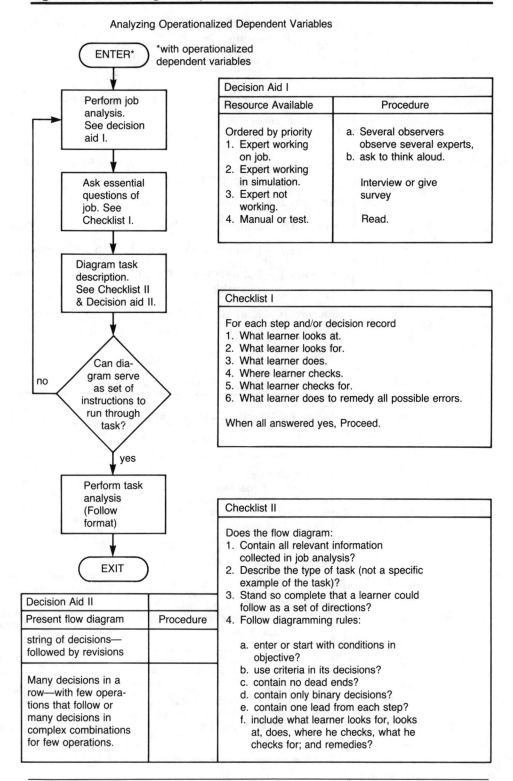

Analyzing Operationalized Dependent Variables

ENTER*   *with operationalized
          dependent variables

Perform job analysis. See decision aid I.

Ask essential questions of job. See Checklist I.

Diagram task description. See Checklist II & Decision aid II.

Can diagram serve as set of instructions to run through task?

no

yes

Perform task analysis (Follow format)

EXIT

Decision Aid I

Resource Available	Procedure
Ordered by priority 1. Expert working on job. 2. Expert working in simulation. 3. Expert not working. 4. Manual or test.	a. Several observers observe several experts, b. ask to think aloud. Interview or give survey Read.

Checklist I

For each step and/or decision record
1. What learner looks at.
2. What learner looks for.
3. What learner does.
4. Where learner checks.
5. What learner checks for.
6. What learner does to remedy all possible errors.

When all answered yes, Proceed.

Checklist II

Does the flow diagram:
1. Contain all relevant information collected in job analysis?
2. Describe the type of task (not a specific example of the task)?
3. Stand so complete that a learner could follow as a set of directions?
4. Follow diagramming rules:

   a. enter or start with conditions in objective?
   b. use criteria in its decisions?
   c. contain no dead ends?
   d. contain only binary decisions?
   e. contain one lead from each step?
   f. include what learner looks for, looks at, does, where he checks, what he checks for; and remedies?

Decision Aid II

Present flow diagram	Procedure
string of decisions— followed by revisions	
Many decisions in a row—with few operations that follow or many decisions in complex combinations for few operations.	

Exercise to Select the Most Appropriate Format for Data Collection

Directions: Identify which of the following formats are most appropriate to collect task data for the following situations

    a.   an outline

    b.   a flowchart

    c.   a table or columnar format contrasting attributes

    d.   a list

    e.   all of the above

Situation 1.   Learning to troubleshoot a photocopy machine. The procedures involve many motor chains.

Situation 2.   Learning to visually classify flying aircraft as "friend" or "foe."

Situation 3.   Learning the radio voice codes for the letters of the alphabet.

Situation 4.   Learning to identify symbols on a weather map.

Situation 5.   Learning which instruments are associated with a wide variety of surgical procedures.

Situation 6.   Learning how to counsel clients with alcohol problems.

Table 6.2   Format Applied to Rule Learning

RULES ABOUT THE USE OF CRITERION VISUALS IN INSTRUCTION

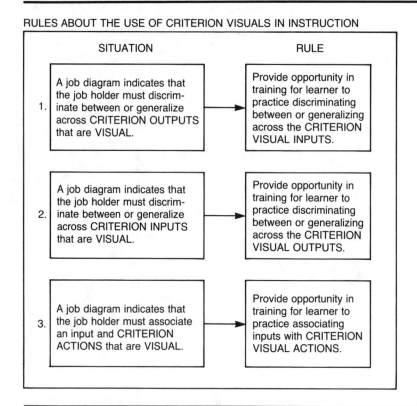

G. L. Gropper/Z. Glasgow, *Criteria for the selection and use of visuals in instruction: A handbook,* (c) 1971. Reprinted by permission of Prentice-Hall, Inc., Englewood Cliffs, New Jersey.

Table 6.3 Outline format for recording a verbal information task: Recall pathological lesions that may be associated with diabetes

1. Pathological Lesions
    A. Retinopathy
        1. Cataract
        2. Microaneurysms
        3. Glycogen in vacuolated iris epithelium
        4. Hemorrhages and exudates
        5. Proliferative retinopathy
    B. Neuropathy
        1. Patchy demyelinization of the peripheral nerves
        2. Hydropic vacuolization of the sympathetic and parasympathetic ganglion cells
    C. Nephropathy (in order of progressive onset)
        1. Basement membrane thickening
        2. Hyalinization of afferent and efferent arterioles
        3. Fibrosis and hyalinization of renal glomeruli
        4. Vacuolization of Henle's Loop
    D. Angiopathy
        1. Micro
            a. Thickening of peripheral basement membrane
            b. Mesangial areas (diabetes of long duration)
        2. Macro
            a. Atherosclerosis
            b. Monckeberg's sclerosis
            c. Arteriosclerosis
    E. Xanthopathy
        1. Xanthochromia
        2. Xanthelasma pelpebrarum
        3. Papular xanthoma
        4. Necrobiosis diabeticorum
        5. Diabetic dermopathy
        6. Bullosis diabeticorum
        7. Mal perforans
        8. Bacterial/fungal infections

INSTRUCTIONAL ANALYSIS

The behavior to be attained at the end of instruction is defined by the task analysis. When the task analysis is completed, a data base exists to answer the question "What will students be doing after instruction?" These learning outcomes are subjected to another type of analysis, called instructional analysis. Instructional analysis is intended to answer the question "What are the learning requirements for achieving the learning outcomes?"

Instructional analysis consists of three steps.

1. Determine whether some tasks should be excluded from instruction and consequently from further analysis. Task analysis activities may have uncovered non-instructional solu-

tions for some tasks. Secondly, limits on time, money, or staff may mean setting priorities for tasks that warrant subsequent development.

2. Make explicit the prerequisites that lead to the learning outcome and have implications for sequencing instruction. As discussed in Chapter 5, prerequisites are subordinate competencies that "enable" the learning of another task. Instructional analysis is the means to identify the prerequisites that enable learning to occur.

3. Finally, assess the capabilities of the "target audience" in light of the outcome of Step 2. The students expected to take the instruction are called the target audience. The purpose of this step is to determine which of the prerequisites were learned previously and which have yet to be learned. The result of this step has implications for how much instruction is needed to achieve the learning outcomes.

Determining What to Include in Instruction

Not all tasks will require the same level or amount of instruction to achieve proficiency. Students may know how to do some tasks, while others will be so easy to learn that merely telling a person what to do or providing a flowchart is all that is needed for successful performance. Some tasks are seldom required and incorrect performance has little serious consequence. On the other hand, other tasks are critical to successful performance, and the complex nature of the tasks makes instruction essential.

Consider the job of an instructional designer whose responsibilities include performing task analysis. The job entails observing videotaped procedures and recording behavioral observations. Obviously, observing and recording accurate and complete task data are the most critical requirements of the job, and these tasks will be the focus of formal classroom instruction. In contrast, knowing how to operate the video playback equipment is necessary to perform the job, but clearly easier to perform and learn. In fact, if time for instruction is limited and someone on the job can demonstrate how to operate the equipment, instruction on this task may be delayed until the person is on the job.

In large-scale educational and instructional organizations, where curricula are planned with career paths in mind, decisions must be made about when instruction on tasks will be most beneficial—when first entering a career field? after some experience in the job? in an advanced course? at the post-graduate level? in a refresher course? Economic and time constraints, which are a part of virtually all design efforts, will also influence decisions about what or what not to teach. When resources are limited, the objective is to emphasize instruction on tasks that are most essential to successful performance. To accomplish this goal, the U. S. Army developed a procedure to help instructional designers set instructional priorities.

The procedures described here are a modified form of a system developed for the U. S. Army Command (Frederickson, Hawley, Whitemore, & Wood, 1980). Ratings for each task are obtained from SMEs on dimensions such as difficulty of the task, frequency of its performance, and seriousness of incorrect performance. Table 6.4 defines seven dimensions and the scale for rating each. The results of these ratings are analyzed in accordance with a set of rules aimed at helping the instructional designer set priorities for instructional development. The rules provide guidance for setting end-of-course performance standards and prescribe which tasks require instruction immediately, which can be taught on the job or delayed, which can be given less emphasis if development time and resources are limited, and which require no instruction at all.

Using the rating scales, ratings for each task are obtained from as many SMEs as practical (ten is a desirable number). A mean rating is calculated for each dimension for each task. If the ratings have been obtained from fewer than three SMEs, then the mode is used as the average. Table 6.5 presents the rules for determining the instructional requirements given the average dimension ratings. The most important consideration is whether the mission will fail if the task is not performed correctly.

Table 6.4   Seven Rating Dimensions for Determining Instructional Requirements

1.   Learning Difficulty: the time, effort, and assistance required to achieve proficiency on a task. Some tasks are so simple or familiar that they can be readily "picked up." Others are so complicated that they are adequately performed only after extensive instruction.

1	2	3	4	5
Easy to learn		Moderately hard		Hard to learn

2.   Consequences of incorrect performance: whether failure to correctly perform the task will result in overall failure of the job or function. What will the effect be on the mission?

1	2	3	4	5
No effect		Will degrade or delay		Mission failure

3.   Frequency: how often a task is performed in a field or job.

1	2	3	4	5
Quarterly		Monthly		Daily

4.   Immediacy of performance: the time gap between completion of instruction and actual task performance. Is the performer expected to be proficient at this task immediately after arrival on the job or start of the function? Or will there be a delay between initial learning and actual performance?

1	2	3	4	5
Three months		One month		One week

5.   Availability of assistance: any help the novice may have during actual performance of the task after instruction. This includes supervisors, peers, and/or references.

1	2	3	4	5
None		Several sources		Many

6.   Decay rate: how quickly the skills associated with a task are forgotten or lost if not performed regularly. How much practice is needed to retain the skill?

1	2	3	4	5
None		Every 3 months		Monthly

7.   Performance difficulty: the time and/or effort required actually to carry out the task once it has been learned. Performance difficulty should not be confused with learning difficulty. A psychomotor task may be very difficult to learn, but once learned, very easy to perform.

1	2	3	4	5
Easy to do		Moderately hard to do		Very hard to do

After *Evaluation of a Training Developer's Decision Aid (TDDA) for Optimizing Performance-Based Training in Marching-Ascendant MOS* (p. II) by E. W. Frederickson, J. Hawley, P. Whitemore, & M. M. Wood, 1980, El Paso, TX: Applied Science Associates. Copyright 1980 by Applied Scientists Associates. Adapted by permission.

The explanations for the instructional recommendations in Table 6.5 are as follows:

Highest Level of Proficiency.   Proficiency level refers to the standard of performance required on the test at the end of instruction, not the amount of instruction required to achieve the objective. Performance on tasks rated high on this dimension means the difference between mission success or failure. Consequently the highest possible performance standards must be set. This may mean a standard that requires all of the students to achieve a perfect score on the test for the task. If the task consists of multiple elements,

Table 6.5   Rules for Interpreting Ratings

If the Average ratings are:	Then the instructional recommendations are:
Dimension 2 rated 4 or better	Highest level of proficiency
Dimension 7 rated 3 or better *AND* *Dimension 4 rated 2 or lower* *AND* *Dimension 5 rated 2 or lower*	Qualified level or proficiency
Dimension 1 rated 3 *AND* *Dimension 4 rated 2 or lower* *AND* *Dimension 5 rated 4 or better*	On-the-job training
Dimension 7 rated 4 or better *AND* *Dimension 2 rated 2 or lower* *AND* *Dimension 3 rated 2 or lower* *AND* *Dimension 6 rated 3 or lower*	Refresher instruction
Dimension 1 rated 2 or lower *AND* *Dimension 7 rated 2 or lower* *AND* *Dimension 2 rated 4 or better* *AND* *Dimension 6 rated 4 or better*	Reduced time
Dimension 1 rated 2 or better *AND* *Dimension 2 rated 2 or lower* *AND* *Dimension 5 rated 4 or better*	Elimination from instruction

After *Evaluation of a Training Developer's Decision Aid (TDDA) for Optimizing Performance-Based Training in Marching-Ascendant MOS* (p. II–8) by E. W. Frederickson, J. Hawley, P. Whitemore & M. M. Wood, 1980, El Paso, TX: Applied Science Associates. Copyright 1980 by Applied Science Associates. Adapted by permission.

each element must be tested, and if the task is performed under a range of conditions, performance should be assessed under all possible conditions. The amount and scope of instruction will consist of whatever it takes to achieve the high performance standard.

Qualified Level of Proficiency.   When incorrect performance only moderately affects mission success and a task is rated low on Dimension 4, Immediacy of performance, and Dimension 5, Availability of assistance, a lower performance standard may be set. Not all task elements need to be tested nor must all conditions be included on the end-of-course test. Again, the amount and scope of instruction will depend on what is needed to achieve the standard of performance.

Refresher Instruction.   Some tasks are performed infrequently and forgotten quickly unless they are practiced often. If practice opportunities are not available on the job, refresher instruction must be introduced from time to time to maintain standards.

On-the-job Training (OJT).   On-the-job training is instruction that can be provided in the workplace rather than under formal conditions. Tasks designated for OJT are rated easier to learn than those covered in formal instruction. Also, conditions on the job allow time and assistance for learning. OJT must be just as carefully planned and controlled as classroom instruction.

Reduced Time. This category refers to those tasks that are easy to learn and perform. Also, because there is a high degree of assistance on the job, the likelihood of a performance failure is reduced. This category alerts the instructional designer to opportunities for reduced teaching time. This outcome has implications for instruction only. High standards on tests are maintained. If reduced instructional time leads to high failure rates in the course, instruction on these tasks should be upgraded accordingly.

Eliminate from Instruction. This is a category for tasks that can be self-taught and where a high degree of assistance is available.

Exercise to Determine the Instructional Requirements Using Ratings on Tasks Criticality Dimensions

Directions: Following are five tasks and a table showing the corresponding mean ratings on the seven criticality dimensions. Use the rules in Table 6.5 to determine which level of instruction is prescribed.

Tasks

1. Clean shop floors or benches. _____
2. Remove or replace air speed indicator. _____
3. Calibrate fuel quantity indicator system. _____
4. Isolate malfunctioning fuel flow system. _____
5. Isolate malfunctioning oil pressure gauge. _____

Dimensions	Mean ratings				
Tasks	**1**	**2**	**3**	**4**	**5**
1. *Learning difficulty*	1.5	3.0	3.1	3.9	4.0
2. *Consequences*	2.0	5.0	3.2	4.1	4.1
3. *Frequency*	5.0	2.2	5.0	2.3	3.1
4. *Immediacy of performance*	5.0	4.1	5.0	3.3	2.9
5. *Assistance*	5.0	3.0	4.4	3.2	5.0
6. *Decay rate*	2.2	4.0	2.0	4.4	3.6
7. *Performance difficulty*	2.7	4.5	3.0	4.1	4.0

Determining Prerequisite Relationships

In order to determine the prerequisite skills and knowledge for a task, the designer asks, "What must the learner know in order to perform this task?" Usually the designer arrives at the answer by constructing hierarchies. As each set level of prerequisites is identified, the designer asks the same question until arriving at a level of performance appropriate for the task and target audience. In Chapter 5 you learned to construct hierarchies to identify prerequisite skills and knowledge.

Intellectual Skills. Gagné's taxonomy of intellectual skills provides the basic structure for constructing hierarchies of such skills. Figure 6.3 illustrates the application of Gagné's

Figure 6.3 Hierarchy for a Concept

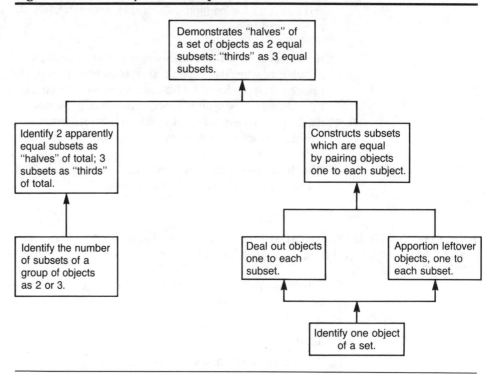

From *Principles of Instructional Design* (2nd Ed.) (p. 48) by R. M. Gagné and L. J. Briggs, 1979, New York: Holt, Rinehart and Winston, Inc. Copyright 1979 by Holt, Rinehart and Winston, Inc. Reprinted by permission. (Adapted by Gagné & Briggs from Resnick & Wang, 1969.)

taxonomy for constructing of a hierarchy for a problem-solving task. The hierarchy dictates the order for learning.

Verbal Information. Simple verbal information tasks such as learning labels or lists usually do not lend themselves to hierarchical analysis. In such cases the most meaningful analysis is to identify major categories of information implied by the task. Dick and Carey (1985) refer to the creation of information categories as cluster analysis. The clusters are lists of related information organized into categories that have no dependency relationships for learning. Thus, learning can proceed in any order.

Verbal information, however, may be a prerequisite for certain complex communication tasks, and in these cases, hierarchies do apply. For example, knowledge of facts about an era in history may be the foundation for performing certain intellectual skills such as writing an essay to compare and contrast the impact of historical events.

Procedural Tasks. Whether the procedural tasks are intellectual or motor skills, they will be in flowchart form. The type of analysis will depend on the type of learning involved in the subtask. Hierarchical analysis should be done for intellectual and motor subtasks; the analysis may reveal that certain subtasks performed later in the procedure are in fact prerequisites for subtasks performed earlier. Therefore, the learning sequence for the procedure will differ from the performance sequence.

Attitude Tasks. Several studies demonstrate the relationship between the cognitive taxonomy and the affective taxonomy (Martin & Briggs, 1986, p. 92). The following relationships between the two domains have been supported: (1) Receiving/awareness is directly prerequisite to knowledge and responding. One must be aware of information and ready to receive it in order to learn it and to respond to it. (2) Knowledge and responding are directly prerequisite to valuing. Attitude tasks are often defined in terms of choosing to en-

Figure 6.4 Diagraming an Attitudinal Task

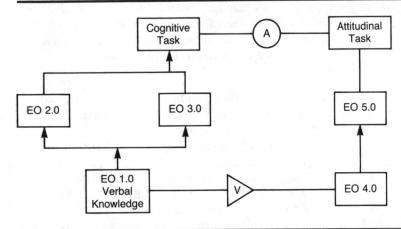

gage in some observable and measurable behavior. The implication is that behaviors have been previously learned. If not, they must be acquired before the attitude can be learned.

Dick and Carey (1985, pp. 55–56) suggest that attitudes also be subjected to a second level of analysis to find out why the learner makes a particular choice. The answer to this question is the verbal information that constitutes the persuasive part of attitude shaping. See Figure 6.4 as an example of the interrelationships of cognitive and affective behavior.

Exercise to Define Prerequisites

Directions: This is a group exercise for three or four students. Doing the exercise in a group emphasizes the fact that in the real world instructional design is carried out by several people. The group should do an analysis of the following goals or two similar goals approved by your instructor.

Your analysis will be judged by the following criteria:

■ The analysis answers the question: "What must the learner know in order to perform this task?" and the answer is clear to a person unfamiliar with the content area.

■ The analysis is carried to the level appropriate for the target audience.

1. For twelfth grade students of U. S. History
   The students should be able to select and list appropriate historical examples of four common sources of conflict (economic, social, political, and religious) during the 1930's (Gow, 1976, p. 74).

2. For elementary school students
   The students should be able to write a complete simple sentence and identify the subject, verb, and object (Gow, 1976, p. 74).

Determining the Entry Level for Instruction. Most people have experienced reading a text or being in a class that is "over their heads." And most people have also had the opposite experience—dealing with subject matter that is too simple. These all too common experiences demonstrate mismatches of instructional material and student abilities. The instructional designer can avoid mismatches by identifying competencies in the target audience—students who will take the course—and then designing the instruction to build on those competencies. What the target audience knows or can do are the entry level behaviors.

"Entry level" is a key concept in instructional design. If entry level is incorrectly set, initial instruction will be either too hard or too easy for the target audience and will therefore be ineffective. Entry levels are often hard to set because the type of data needed for accuracy are often difficult to come by.

Information is collected about what students know and can do with respect to the tasks to be taught. Once this information is known, the instructional designer determines which skills the target audience has already mastered and which must be taught.

Type of Data Needed to Determine the Entry Level. It is important to distinguish between two types of information about the target audience: general characteristics and entry level behaviors. General characteristics describe the educational level, achievement level, socioeconomic background, motivation, interests, and other information about the target audience. Categories such as high school biology majors, eighth-graders, undergraduate psychology majors, and persons with two years' experience on the job give a general idea of the target audience for the instructional materials. Information about the target audience's interests and preferences and about their expectations regarding instruction is helpful when planning strategy for engaging students in learning tasks. However, such information is too general and inclusive for setting entry levels.

When assumptions about what students should be taught are based on general characteristics, the result can be the mismatch previously described. Assume that the target audience for an automotive repair course scores in the upper 25 percentile on a norm-referenced mechanical ability test. What can you conclude about this group's ability to set the timing on a carburetor? Exactly where should the entry level be set? Entry level behaviors define the specific prerequisites for the tasks to be learned. Without knowledge of exactly what the test measures it is impossible to determine with any precision the entry behaviors for the carburetor task. Assumptions can be based only on the instructional designer's preconceived notions about what students with these characteristics should know rather than what they do know.

Here is the recommended procedure to determine entry level behaviors using test results:

1. Examine test items to determine whether any correspond to prerequisite skills.

2. For items that correspond, examine the test results to identify those that were and were not successfully performed by the target audience. Those that nearly everyone performed correctly need not be taught.

3. Where no correspondence is found, obtain other information to define the entry level. If time is available, entry level behaviors should be determined empirically. Construct and administer tests for a representative sample of the target audience to determine the entry level behaviors, or interview members of the target audience to ascertain what they can and cannot do.

What can the designer do if there is no opportunity to collect the task-specific data necessary for accurate determinations of entry level behaviors? If time does not permit verification of assumptions before materials are developed, then verification is delayed until materials are developed and tried out. The dangers of such an approach are obvious, but the instructional designer is often faced with this dilemma.

To reduce the margin of error, assumptions should be based on the best information available. In lieu of test data, you should consult several other sources. Materials and tests from courses the target audience has taken can be examined to find whether prerequisites were covered. Dick and Carey (p. 83) recommend determining whether it would be worthwhile to test for a particular skill before permitting a student to begin instruction. If the answer is yes, you probably have defined an entry-level behavior. This question can be asked of instructors or supervisors with first-hand knowledge of the target audience. They can examine the instructional analysis and answer this question for each of the entry levels. SMEs and/or job incumbents can be asked to respond to the same question based on their own experience.

Figure 6.5   Identifying Entry Behaviors in a Hierarchy

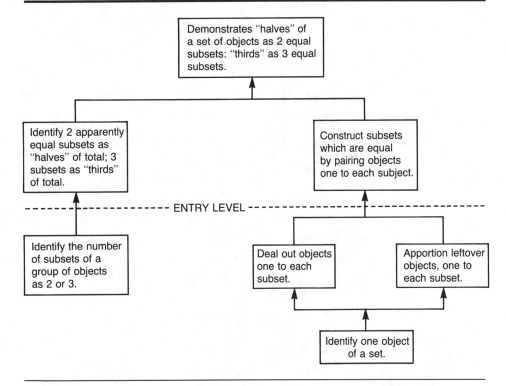

After *Principles of Instructional Design* (2nd ed.) (p. 148) by R. M. Gagné and L. J. Briggs, 1979, New York: Holt, Rinehart and Winston, Inc. Copyright 1979 by Holt, Rinehart and Winston, Inc. Adapted by permission. (Adapted by Gagné & Briggs from Resnick & Wang, 1969).

Setting the Entry Level.   The procedure to identify entry behaviors is fairly straightforward if prerequisite requirements have been fully identified. Evidence about what students know and can do is compared to the prerequisites for performing the tasks to be taught. Most likely, the comparison will show that a majority of the target audience already has some of these skills, so it is not necessary to teach them.

When prerequisites are in hierarchical form, identify the skills that a majority already can do, and draw a line above these skills in the hierarchy. The skills above the line are those you must teach; those below the line are the entry-level behaviors necessary to begin instruction. An example of how entry-level behaviors can be identified for a hierarchy is shown in Figure 6.5.

The same approach can be taken with cluster analysis (outlines) and procedural flowcharts where prerequisites are clear-cut. Figures 6.6 and 6.7 show how entry-level behaviors are identified for a verbal information task and a motor skill. When the target audience has attained the individual skills in a procedure but does not know how they are linked together, the task to be taught is the sequence and should be so noted. Information items in a cluster analysis are reviewed, and those already known by a majority of the target audience are checked and noted as entry-level behaviors.

Exercise to Identify Information Relevant for Determining Entry-Level Behaviors

Directions: Select the information most likely to provide the specific information needed for defining the entry level behaviors for each learning outcome.

1.   Learning outcome: Locate positive and negative numbers on a number line.

_____ **a.** Results from a test of scientific concepts and skills.

_____ **b.** Test results on the same task from students with similar backgrounds.

Figure 6.6   Identifying Entry Behaviors for a Verbal Information Task

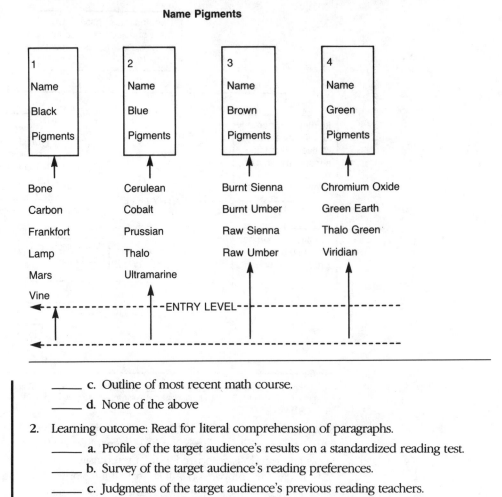

Name Pigments

c. Outline of most recent math course.

d. None of the above

2.   Learning outcome: Read for literal comprehension of paragraphs.

    a. Profile of the target audience's results on a standardized reading test.

    b. Survey of the target audience's reading preferences.

    c. Judgments of the target audience's previous reading teachers.

    d. None of the above.

Figure 6.7   Identifying Entry-Level Behaviors for a Motor Skill

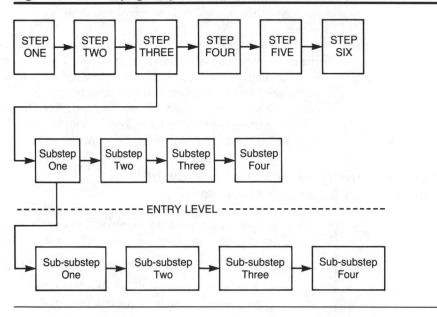

3. Learning outcome: Troubleshoot radio repeater sets.

   _____ a. Previous instructor's assessment of target audience.

   _____ b. Objectives of courses previously taken by the target audience.

   _____ c. Personnel files giving previous experience with radios.

   _____ d. All of the above.

4. Learning outcome: Name the microcomputer and state the function of each component.

   _____ a. Mechanical aptitude scores

   _____ b. Interviews with people in the target audience.

   _____ c. Interviews with supervisors.

   _____ d. All of the above.

5. Learning outcome: Name and define the purpose of each type of test used in an individualized, structured curriculum.

   _____ a. Transcripts showing courses in test construction.

   _____ b. Descriptions of work history in training development.

   _____ c. Judgments by test developers who have no first-hand knowledge of the target audience.

   _____ d. None of the above.

Exercise to Determine Entry-Level Behaviors from Test Results

Directions: Below are six learning outcomes for a lesson on toxoplasmosis. The intended audience is third-year medical students. The percentage of the target audience who successfully answered pretest items associated with each objective appears after each learning outcome. Check which, if any, are entry level behaviors.

_____ 1. State the factors contributing to toxoplasmosis. (81%)

_____ 2. Recognize the characteristics of congenital toxoplasmosis. (40%)

_____ 3. Recognize the signs of acquired toxoplasmosis. (43%)

_____ 4. Describe the potential for differential diagnosis. (45%)

_____ 5. Identify the lab findings associated with toxoplasmosis. (25%)

_____ 6. State the recommended treatments for toxoplasmosis. (46%)

Exercise to Define the Prerequisites and Entry-Level Behaviors for a Procedural Task

Directions: Review an analysis you developed in Chapter 5 for the exercise in flowcharting a procedural task. Define the prerequisite requirements, write a description of the target audience, and identify the entry level behaviors for students. Your product must meet the following criteria:

1. Entry levels are based on behaviors, not general characteristics.

2. Entry level behaviors must be essential prerequisites, not supportive prerequisites.

Exercise to Define Entry-Level Behaviors for Intellectual Tasks

Directions: Review an analysis you developed in Chapter 5 for the exercise in constructing a hierarchy. Define the prerequisite requirements, write a description of the target audience, and identify the entry level behaviors for students. Your product must meet the following criteria:

1. Entry levels are based on behaviors, not general characteristics.
2. Entry behaviors must be essential prerequisites, not supportive prerequisites.

Examples of Task and Instructional Analysis Procedures

There is no one best way to do a task analysis. Kennedy, Esque, and Novak (1983) conducted an exhaustive review of all articles dealing with theory or application of task analysis published between 1979 and 1982. The researchers found that most, if not all, task analysis procedures were generated primarily for idiosyncratic application. They concluded that it is not possible to recommend one best method of task analysis for all problems.

Rarely do procedures used in one set of circumstances apply exactly to another. The designer must consider the nature of the task to determine which analytic procedures are most appropriate. Several examples follow, illustrating how experienced designers have attacked specific problems. Some of the examples focus on task analysis only; others combine task and instructional analysis procedures.

The Extended Task Analysis Procedure (ETAP). ETAP was developed under the auspices of the U. S. Army (Reigeluth 1983). ETAP was designed for analysis of procedural tasks and transfer tasks—"soft skills." Transfer tasks are those for which, depending on certain conditions, the procedure for executing the activities involved varies each time the task is performed. The behaviors are difficult to define because they are undocumented. They are not very easily documented because expert performers may not be consciously aware of how the procedures are performed. Your job as an instructional designer includes many examples of transfer tasks. "Performing a task analysis" is one example.

ETAP's methodology uses information process analysis and interviews to identify underlying knowledge and principles that can generate the right procedure for each situation. The major analysis methods are process analysis, factor transfer analysis, principle transfer analysis, and knowledge analysis. Figure 6.8 shows a flowchart of the ETAP.

Process analysis uses flowcharting techniques to determine the steps in a procedural task. This activity starts with major steps and continues to the lowest level appropriate, given the minimum level of entry. Next ETAP prescribes a knowledge analysis to identify all the facts and concepts that are prerequisites for each step in the flowchart. This is basically a hierarchical analysis of the prerequisite intellectual and verbal information skills needed to perform the step or substep in the procedure.

For analysis of transfer tasks, ETAP describes an interview structure for helping an SME to identify the factors and underlying principles used consciously or unconsciously for each situation.

Factors are the conditions that change the way the task should be performed. Factors are obtained by interviews with SMEs. During the interview, the designer elicits and lists all of the factors that need to be considered in order to perform the task acceptably. Then the SME is asked to provide common rules for deciding which factors are considered and when.

Principles tend to be associated with an entire procedure rather than with specific steps. Therefore, the interview focuses the SME on the most general and inclusive level of the task. Consider again the example of performing a task analysis. An experienced designer would be asked to state important or helpful principles for generating the highest quality task data. The expert might respond, "Work from the general to the specific." As you can see, principles should not be overly detailed, but aimed at the level sufficient for the performer to do the task well. Once necessary factors and principles are identified, the same procedures that were used in the knowledge analysis are applied to identify lower level prerequisite principles, concepts, and facts.

Figure 6.8 Flowchart of the Extended Task Analysis Process

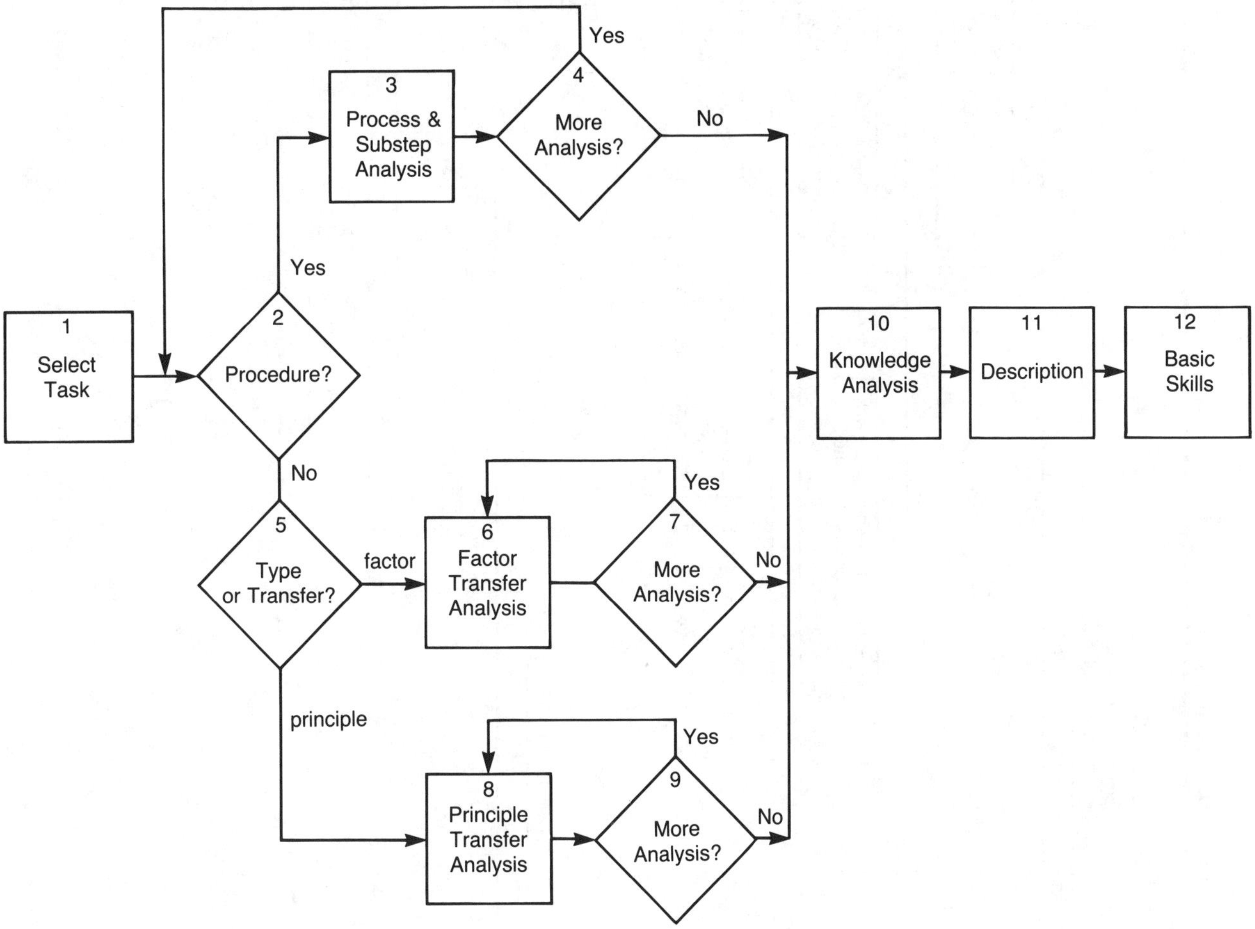

From *Task analysis procedure (ETAP): User's manual* by C. H. Reilgeluth, D. Merrill, R. K. Brandon, R. Begland & R. Tarr, 1980.

Count and Chart Approach. The Count and Chart Approach (Zemke 1979) is a method for recording observations of behavior known or believed to have some relationship to successful performance. The first step in the process is to pinpoint a repeatable job behavior that is easy to observe and validate. Then record the behavior per standard time for the performers. Zemke cites the example of studying sales personnel to document the existence and impact of the specific behavior "asking for the order." Sales representatives were observed during sales interviews. The number of time a sales representative asked for a sale during an interview was recorded. The results were that salespeople with higher ask rates (seven to nine per interview) tended to have more sales than those with low ask rates (two or three per interview). The importance of this behavior was validated. The trainer in question changed her selling program to emphasize this specific behavior.

Concept Elaboration Theory. Concept elaboration theory is a procedure for analyzing a concept that can be taught in a single lesson. Elaboration theory, developed by David Merrill, Charles Riegeluth, and others, is aimed at telling how to instruct and is consistent with research in cognitive psychology suggesting that instruction should be sequenced from the general to specific, and that each part should be related to an overall schema and to other parts of the schema. According to its developers, elaboration theory is a procedure for structuring, sequencing, and determining presentation strategies for complex subject matter within our current understanding of cognition (Merrill, 1977).

Figure 6.9 Comparisons of a Learning Hierarchy and an Elaboration Diagram.

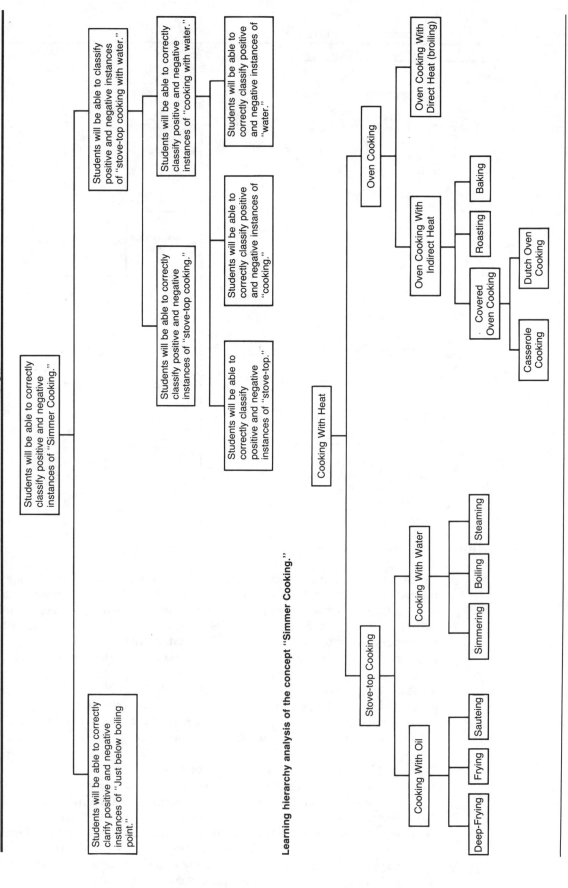

Learning hierarchy analysis of the concept "Simmer Cooking."

From "General-to-Detailed Sequencing of Concepts in a Taxonomy Is in General Agreement with Learning Hierarchy Analysis" by B. G. Wilson and M. D. Merrill, 1980, *NSPI Journal*, p. 13. Copyright 1980 by *NSPI Journal*. Reprinted by permission.

Although it is called a theory, concept elaboration is actually a procedure. The outcomes of elaboration theory procedures are diagrams that look like learning hierarchies but differ in their focus. Learning hierarchies are constructed by asking "What must the student know in order to perform this task?" and are read from the bottom up. Elaboration theory diagrams are read from the top down. They are constructed by formulating a core structure, called an epitome, then elaborating this structure by adding dimensions of complexity. The elaboration diagram starts with a general view of the subject, then divides the subject into parts and elaborates those parts into parts and so on until the desired level of detail is achieved. Figure 6.9 contrasts a learning hierarchy for the concept "simmer cooking" with an elaboration diagram that represents the completion of the first step of elaboration theory procedure for the topic "Types of Cooking" (Wilson & Merrill, 1980).

Elaboration theory is still evolving and there is a great deal of vagueness about how to apply it. Mayer (1981) reached this conclusion after reviewing more than a dozen documents totaling over 500 pages. The developers are sensitive to this criticism; they point out that considerable instruction and practice are needed to learn to use the procedures (Merrill 1977). Mayer also criticizes the lack of empirical tests to support elaboration theory's validity and the focus on content rather than on the learner's processing of content. Elaboration theory is presented here because it is an attempt by leaders in instructional design to build upon developments in cognitive psychology.

Exercise to Develop a Plan to Perform a Task Analysis

Directions: Select a task or function that you would like to analyze and carry out the following steps.

1. Identify the type of criterion behavior to be taught and the type of target audience to whom it will be taught. Review your selection with your instructor before proceeding.

2. Identify methods for obtaining information necessary to describe and analyze criterion behavior.

3. Select information sources needed to describe and analyze criterion behavior.

4. Plan the sequence in which information about criterion behavior will be collected.

5. Develop (or plan to use existing) information-collecting instruments and procedures.

6. Obtain feedback about the adequacy of Steps 2 through 5 from your instructor. Revise the plan as needed before proceeding to the next exercise.

Exercise to Perform a Task Analysis

Directions: Analyze the task you selected according to the plan approved by your instructor. Your analysis should meet the following criteria:

a. All inputs, actions, and outputs are identified

b. Observable and measurable behaviors are described.

c. Sequence and decisions points are shown, if applicable.

Exercise to Perform an Instructional Analysis

Directions: Based on feedback from your instructor, revise the task analysis as appropriate. Then carry out an instructional analysis for the task. Analysis should meet the following criteria:

a. The format and visual representation can be read and understood by others.

b. Prerequisites are essential for task performance.

c. Hierarchical relationships are in accordance with accepted taxonomies or can be defended logically.

d. The level of detail is appropriate for the target audience.

FROM THE READING

Define the following terms.

Directions: Review the definitions in the text and then put them in your own words.

Task analysis   Learner characteristics

Instructional analysis   Target audience

On-the-job training (OJT)   Entry behavior

Refresher instruction

ISSUES FOR DISCUSSION

1. What emphasis should task and instructional analysis be given in the entire instructional design process?

2. What are the implications for the instructional designer regarding tasks designated for OJT?

3. Examine the usefulness of the following student data in determining entry level behavior: Age, sex, socioeconomic background, reading grade level, attitude toward subject, and students' perceived needs for learning.

4. Consider an instructional situation from your own experience. Describe the situation and explain how you would go about determining the students' entry level behavior.

REFERENCES

Dick, W., & Carey, L. (1985). *The systematic design of instruction.* Glenview, IL: Scott, Foresman.

Frederickson, E. W., Hawley, J., Whitemore, P., and Wood, M. M. (1980). *Air defense training development decision aid (TDDA): Model extension and research requirement, final report.* Contract No. MDA 903-80-C-0160. Army Research Institute, Defense Supply Institute. Butler, PA: Applied Science Associates.

Gagné, R. M., & Briggs, L. J. (1979). *Principles of instructional design* (2nd ed.). NY: Holt, Rinehart & Winston.

Gow, D. T. (1976). *Design and development of curricular materials: Self-instructional text* (Vol. 1). Pittsburgh, PA: University Center for International Studies, University of Pittsburgh.

Gropper, G. L. (1971) *A technology for developing instructional materials: Handbook A: Plan study of criterion behavior.* Pittsburgh, PA: American Institutes for Research.

Gropper, G. L., & Glasgow Z. (1971). *Criteria for the selection and use of visuals in instruction: A handbook.* Englewood Cliffs, NJ: Prentice-Hall.

Kennedy, P., Esque, T., and Novak, J. A. (1983). Functional task analysis procedures for instructional design. *Journal of Instructional Development, 6* (4).

Laird, W., Bhatt, S., Bajpayee, T., Glasgow, Z., & Scott, D. (1981). *Development of a training program for fighting small fires in the mining industry: Task analysis report.* Contract No. J0395060. Bruceton, PA: U.S. Department of Interior, Bureau of Mines.

Martin B. L., & Briggs, L. J. (1986). *The affective and cognitive domains: Integration for instruction and research*. Educational Technology Publications, Englewood Cliffs, NJ: Prentice-Hall.

Mayer, R. E., (1981). An evaluation of the elaboration model of instruction. *Journal of Instructional Development, 8* (1), 23–25.

Merrill, M. D. (1977, April). Content analysis via concept elaboration theory. Presentation at Association for Educational and Communication Technology, Miami Beach, FL.

Reilgeluth, C. H., Merrill, D., Brandon, R. K., Begland, R., & Tarr, R. (1980). *Task analysis procedure (ETAP): User's manual*. Fort Monroe, VA: U.S. Army Training Development Institute.

Resnick, L. B., & Wang, M. C. (1969). *Approaches to the Validation of Learning Hierarchies*. Pittsburgh, PA: Learning Research & Development Center, University of Pittsburgh (preprint 50).

Wilson, B. G., & Merrill, M. D. (1980). General-to-detailed sequencing of concepts in a taxonomy is in general agreement with learning hierarchy analysis. *National Society for Performance and Instruction Journal,* 11–14.

Yelon, S. L. (1971). Appendix 8: Task analysis in instructional design and technology. In Thomas E. Harries (Ed.), *The application of general systems theory to instructional development*. University Consortium for Instructional Development & Technology (UCIDT) Instructional Development Institutes; Syracuse, New York: Syracuse University, Instructional Design, Development & Evaluation.

Zemke, R. (1979). Behavioral observations: Why the "chart and count" approach to task analysis pays off. *Training/HRD,* pp. 16–20.

Chapter Seven

Objectives and Tests

Task	Objectives	Criterion

Objectives	■ Given objectives written in different formats, label the component elements of each objective.

Objectives

- Given objectives written in different formats, label the component elements of each objective.
- Given objectives, revise them to fit a specified format.
- Given a topic, write a behavioral objective using the Mager format.
- Given a topic, write a behavioral objective using the IDI format.
- Given a topic, write a behavioral objective using the Gagné and Briggs format.
- Given an instructional analysis, identify tasks that could be written as Enabling Objectives (EOs) and tasks that could be written as Terminal Performance Objectives (TPOs).
- Given TPOs, EOs, and a taxonomy, order the objectives on the basis of that taxonomy.
- Given statements describing tests, identify those that apply to criterion-referenced tests.
- Given descriptions of tests and methods for scoring them, identify the test likely to be done more reliably.
- Given statements of learning outcomes and associated test items, identify the items that reflect the outcomes.
- Given a task, write an objective or criterion item consistent with that task.
- Given an objective, write a task or criterion item consistent with that objective.
- Given a criterion item, write a task or objective consistent with that item.
- Given an objective and type of test item, write a criterion item consistent with test construction rules.

Overview

The use of behavioral or performance objectives can result in problems such as proliferation and fragmentation of objectives, overemphasis on lower-level tasks, and inattention to affective goals. The instructional design approach can prevent these problems. The purpose of an instructional objective is to make clear what evidence of learning is required or how learning will be measured. By translating the tasks and content generated in an instructional analysis into behavioral objectives, you are making design decisions while continuing to analyze. For this reason the step of writing objectives and criterion-referenced items is a bridge between the analysis and design steps of instructional design.

You must choose a format for writing objectives. The formats presented here are Mager's, IDI's, and Gagné and Briggs's (Mager, 1962; UCIDT, 1968; Gagné & Briggs, 1979). After a format is chosen, objectives are written to match the instructional analysis. The objectives clarify enabling objectives (EOs) that lead to terminal performance objectives (TPOs).

You must check to be sure the method of measurement is consistent with the objective's stated intent. For example, you cannot measure problem solving skills with a true/false test, and you cannot judge ability to play the tuba from a paper and pencil exercise. Construct test items consistent with principles of measurement.

Study Questions

1. How do you know when you've achieved the instructional goal?

2. What are the different formats for writing objectives?

3. How does the designer move from instructional analysis to sequenced behavioral objectives?

4. How does the designer use the different theories on sequencing?

5. How can you increase the validity of an achievement test?

6. How can you increase the reliability of an achievement test?

7. How should you proceed when constructing criterion-referenced items?

OBJECTIVES

In education, the term objective connotes something external, extrinsic, and explicit. When you write objectives for instruction you are putting your internal ideas or goals into external form so that you can share them with others. You are going to visualize the goals of instruction by writing them so precisely that all who use them perceive the same meaning. By writing your goals specifically you will later be able to determine whether you reached them.

Previous chapters have dealt with problem, task, and instructional analysis steps. Starting with this chapter, we will deal with the design steps, thereby moving from preparation for planning to planning. To develop an instructional design, start by turning your goal statements into statements of objectives. Then you will develop instruction, media, evaluation, and implementation plans.

The reason the designer must write objectives in order to progress from instructional analysis to design is that objectives put the content goals identified during the analysis into usable form. In order to write objectives, a designer must decide on a means of measurement. This decision puts the goal in concrete form; that is, you now know what will be done. Thus, the means of measurement clarifies the behavior to be developed and how it will be evaluated.

In order to understand how to write objectives, you need to be familiar with types of learning and domains of instruction, concepts introduced in Chapter 2. You also need to know about formats for writing objectives. This chapter will begin, therefore, by introducing these formats. When you are familiar with the basic terminology of formats, we will proceed with an in-depth discussion of the process for writing objectives.

Formats

Formats are simply different ways of making the desired behavior explicit. There are many formats for writing objectives (Popham & Baker, 1970; Popham, 1979). The Mager format, the IDI format, and the Gagné and Briggs format are three formats that are recommended for the instructional designer. You may even find it desirable to develop your own format by modifying one of these approaches. The formats can all be described as behavioral objectives because they make the expected behavior explicit. Mager's instructional objectives and comparable formats are called behavioral objectives or performance objectives. "A behavioral objective is a statement of certain behaviors that indicate a student has some skill, attitude, or knowledge" (Morris & Fitz-Gibbon, 1978, p. 19).

Mager Format. Robert Mager published *Preparing Instructional Objectives* in 1962. Few books have had as wide an impact on education and training. James Popham (1979, p. 10) has said that "without question the most important advance in education during the 1960s was the widespread advocacy and increased use of behavioral objectives." Mager prepared a programmed instruction text in branching or scrambled book form. In this branching text, a multiple-choice question is asked. Depending on the student's answer, he or she is directed to another page that provides the instruction appropriate for that answer. This classic, easy-to-read text teaches you how to write behavioral objectives in a short time.

Here are Mager's requirements for a behavioral objective:

1. Identify the terminal behavior or performance by name.

2. Decide under which conditions the behavior will occur.

3. Specify the criteria of acceptable performance.

In other words, what must the learner do, under what conditions, and how well? Mager offers this correct example:

> Given a list of thirty-five chemical elements (condition), the learner must be able to recall and write the valences (behavior) of at least thirty (criterion) (Mager, 1962, p. 30).

Mager describes the audience only as the student or the learner, or uses the "you will be able to" form.

ABCD Format. The ABCD format was used in the IDI institutes described in Chapter 3. It is a mnemonic device that helps the designer remember to include four elements: audience, behavior, condition, and degree. It is similar to Mager's format but adds a requirement for identification of the audience. Here is an example:

> **Given a ten-item matching question (C), a seventh grader in the Social Studies 101 section (A) will match each general with his battle (B) with no errors (D).**

Note that the audience is described more specifically here than in the Mager format.

Gagné and Briggs Format. Gagné and Briggs present a five-component performance objective: (1) Situation, (2) Learned Capability, (3) Object, (4) Action, and (5) Tools and Other Constraints (Gagné & Briggs, 1979). Thus to the condition, behavior, and criteria components of Mager, Gagné and Briggs add the object (content), thereby returning to the two aspects of an objective specified by Ralph Tyler (1964): behavior and content. This emphasis on specifying content is consistent with the cognitive approach to design that emphasizes domains or content areas.

Briggs and Wager (1981, p. 55) give these two examples of an objective written in the Gagné and Briggs format:

A. Situation–Given the request "Recite Old Ironsides."
   Learned Capability–The student will recite. [verbal information—poem]
   Object–That poem.
   Action–Orally.
   Tools/Constraints–Within five minutes with no errors, prompting, or pauses.

B. Situation–On a written test in the classroom.
   Learned Capability–The student will summarize. [verbal information—organized knowledge]
   Object–Four protections mentioned in the Bill of Rights.
   Action–In writing.
   Tools/Constraints–Within ten minutes, using no references.

Table 7.1 compares three formats for writing objectives.

By capability Gagné and Briggs mean the behavior as described by one of the five categories of learning outcomes introduced in Chapter 2: intellectual skills, cognitive strategies, verbal information, motor skills, or attitudes. The intellectual skills category is subdivided into five capabilities with a verb to describe each: discriminates (discrimination), identifies (concrete concept), classifies (defined concept), demonstrates (rule), and generates (problem solving). The verb for cognitive strategy capability is "originates." One capability verb for verbal information is "states," for motor skill is "executes," and for

Table 7.1 Comparison of Formats

Component	Mager	Gagne and Briggs	ABCD
Behavior (What will be done)	Behavior (Doing verb)	Learned capability, object, and action	Behavior
Condition (Under What)	Condition	Situation	Condition
Criteria(How well)	Criterion	Tools/Constraints	Degree
Learner (By whom)	(Implied)	(Implied)	Audience

attitude is "chooses." The designer can clearly designate the type of learning with these nine verbs: discriminates, identifies, classifies, demonstrates, generates, originates, states, executes, chooses.

Each capability verb has to be paired with a gerund—an "ing" form—that tells what the learner will do. Examples of action verbs are matching (discriminates), naming (identifies), defining (classifies), solving (demonstrates), synthesizing (generates), applying (originates), stating (states), executing (executes), and choosing (chooses). This list suggests the semantic difficulties that may arise from trying to limit a verb to a category. Does "generate" connote synthesizing exclusively? Does "solving" suggest only rule learning? Although Gagné and Briggs establish a theoretical basis for use of terminology, broader connotations can cause confusion. When you write an objective in Gagné and Briggs format, you can first select the learned capability verb (type of learning) from the list of verbs and then add an "ing" form that describes what the learner will do, e.g., discriminate by matching.

As a beginning instructional designer, use the format approach that functions best for your project. There is general agreement that conditions, behavior, and criterion are essential components of any format.

Writing the Objective

Whatever the format, the written expression should meet the standards for good writing. The behavioral objective must be clear and specific. The techniques introduced in Chapter 5 will make your writing more precise.

You will often change the order so that you start with the condition or situation and end with the criterion or degree statement. The behavior usually appears in the middle of the sentence. The format may be ABCD but it is usually written C, ABD, or C, B, D. This procedure helps prevent the indefinite antecedents and misplaced phrases that tend to occur

as you string modifying phrases out at the end. Also avoid run-on phrases and sentences. Be as specific as possible. For example, what's wrong with this objective?

> The nurse will administer an intravenous solution from the steps of gathering the supplies to monitoring the patient when given an inventory of supplies and a patient and then will be evaluated on a checklist.

It reads more clearly as:

> When given an inventory of supplies and a patient in a bed, the nurse will administer an intravenous solution from the step of gathering supplies through monitoring the patient. She must receive 100 points on an evaluation checklist.

You need to communicate how the behavior will be measured, not how it will be taught. In your condition statement, describe the situation the student will encounter when making the response. Do not describe the instruction which leads to the response. For example, here are two objectives: which expresses the measurable behavior best?

1. Given two weeks of instruction in emergency childbirth, you will answer ninety percent of the questions on procedures to use during the four stages of labor to birth correctly.

2. Given a forty-item objective test containing true/false, matching, and completion questions on procedures to use during the four stages of labor and birth, you will answer at least thirty-six of the questions correctly.

Example 1 is wrong because the condition describes the instruction, not the test. It should read "Given a forty-item multiple-choice test, etc."

The degree part of an objective is often the most difficult to write. Under no circumstances write "to the teacher's satisfaction" as a criterion because this is simply not a replicable or reliable method. It does not communicate well because it has a different meaning for each reader or teacher.

With affective objectives, there are times when you want to make the degree component flexible to allow for personal variation. In this case, your criterion might be "a positive change"—without specifying the amount of change. You will have to think clearly about whether it is desirable simply to allow for a change in reported information processing or whether you need to be more specific.

An Exercise to Identify the Comparability of Objectives Written in Different Formats

Directions: Bracket, then label above the brackets, the component parts of each objective. For objectives written in the Gagné and Briggs format use situation, capability, object, action, and tools/constraints as components. For objectives written in Mager format use condition, behavior, and criteria as components. For objectives written in ABCD format use audience, behavior, condition, and degree as formats.

1. (Gagné and Briggs)

   Given a battery, light bulb, socket, and pieces of wire, demonstrate the making of an electronic circuit by connecting wires to battery and socket and testing the lighting of the bulb.

2. (Mager)

   Given a list of thirty-five chemical elements, the learner must be able to recall and write the valences of at least thirty.

3. (ABCD)

   Given all the basic shapes—cone, cylinder, cube, and sphere—each second-semester geometry student will identify orally each shape.

4. (Mager)

   Given a meter scale, the learner is to be able to identify the value indicated by the position of the pointer as accurately as the construction of the meter will allow.

5. (ABCD)

   Using tape recorded readings of the tryout sessions for the school play, students in the drama class will select the proper voice for each character as indicated in the drama text.

6. (Gagné and Briggs)

   In response to a question, the learner will state orally three technological trends that will affect the future capabilities of navies. The answer is to be completed in three minutes.

An Exercise in Revising Objectives to Fit Behavioral Formats

Rewrite each of these objectives so that it fits another behavioral format: ABCD, Mager, or Gagné—Briggs.

1. Given an essay test, the student will state four causes of the Civil War within fifteen minutes using no references (Gagné and Briggs).
   Revision in _____ Format:

2. Given a properly functioning camcorder unit (any model), the student will make the adjustments and control setting necessary prior to on-location shooting (Mager).
   Revision in _____ Format:

3. Given the names and pictures of four prescription drugs, the second-year medical student will identify orally which one is inappropriate for the treatment of high blood pressure in patients with no other health problems (ABCD).
   Revision in _____ Format:

4. Given a videotaped role playing situation, the sales trainee will identify which steps in the proposal selling procedure were not properly demonstrated by writing them on the response sheets provided (ABCD).
   Revision in _____ Format:

5. In informal conversations with other students the student will choose to speak positively about the teaching and grading in Sociology 101 Section C when he or she is observed unobtrusively (Gagné and Briggs).
   Revision in _____ Format:

An Exercise in Writing Behavioral Objectives In Three Different Formats

Write an objective on the topic specified. Vary the objective in three different formats.

1. Topic: Use the dummy Resuscitation Annie (with sensors) to demonstrate proficiency in CPR.

   Mager Format:
   ABCD Format:
   Gagné and Briggs Format:

2. Topic: Use nutritional principles in planning a well-balanced daily menu.

   Mager Format:
   ABCD Format:
   Gagné and Briggs Format:

3. Topic: Write a short article suitable for publication in a business newsletter.

   Mager Format:
   ABCD Format:
   Gagné and Briggs Format:

4. Topic: Demonstrate counting one to ten on an abacus.

   Mager Format:
   ABCD Format:
   Gagné and Briggs Format:

5. Topic: Identify the paintings of Van Gogh.

   Mager Format:
   ABCD Format:
   Gagné and Briggs Format:

Expressive Objectives

There are formats for writing objectives that are not behavioral. The constructivist instructional design paradigm, for example, holds that behavioral objectives are detrimental to learning that involves problem solving. Design based on constructivist theory requires an autotelic environment (intrinsic motivation rather than praise or punishment), an instructional strategy that allows a unique, personal response through play and discovery, content that permits development of new solutions through creative use of past knowledge, and a situation that permits role-taking and exploration of perspectives. These principles of constructivism all protect the openness of the learning system in terms of objectives, strategy, and content. While constructivists do not advocate behavioral objectives, neither do they insist on total freedom. They believe instruction should always be based on specified goals and values.

Though the exclusive use of predetermined behavioral objectives makes instruction too confining for this paradigm, constructivists can use objectives. Formats appropriate for the constructivist approach are the problem solving or expressive objectives proposed by Elliot Eisner (1969, 1979).

In a problem solving objective a definite problem is presented to the learner, but there are many means by which the problem can be solved. The ends are closed and definite, but the means are an open system.

With expressive objectives both the means and the ends are open-ended. The learner is provided with a rich experience by an instructor who has a hope in mind. There are no preformulated behavioral and sub-objectives. For example, an expressive objective for early readers may be that given a mentor they will develop and publish a newspaper. Through this newspaper project they will develop new skills by being engaged with relevant material of intrinsic concern. Expressive objectives usually require a tutor or mentor to provide feedback and advice for the student.

The problems with using this approach for instructional design are evident. How do you determine to what extent you have achieved the goal? Will you be satisfied no matter what kind of newspaper the student produces? If this is a group project, what is expected of the individual student? According to constructivist theory, there must be allowances for individual differences in achievement.

The expressive objectives format needs more theoretical and practical development. For example, innovative ways to measure achievement need to be identified.

The Arts Propel Project (Gitoner & Drew, 1987) has had some success with a portfolio used in conjunction with a tutorial as a way of measuring growth in aesthetic ability and as a way of following Eisner's recommendation to measure process instead of product.

Using an Instructional Analysis

Suppose you are at the stage of using an instructional analysis as a basis for writing objectives. How should you proceed? You could start by consolidating tasks to reduce the number of subtasks that must be taught and tested separately. Then you could identify goals and sub-objectives by writing final performance objectives and identifying sub-objectives. Next, using your learning classification theory as a guide, you could write sub-objectives to match each task. Finally, you would check the appropriateness of the criterion-referenced items against test construction principles.

These four steps will take you from instructional analysis to objectives and tests:

1. Consolidate tasks in instructional analyses by determining common elements.
2. Write major goals in behavioral objective format.
3. Write sub-objectives in behavioral objectives format.
4. Write criterion-referenced items and check them against criteria for constructing tests.

The output of this procedure is a diagram of TPOs and EOs consistent with your instructional analysis but in observable, measurable format.

Consolidating

Let's take an example. The needs assessment you perform reveals that city school students who must use transportation authority buses to reach school are absent because they do not understand the schedules, routes, and pay options offered by the authority. Your task analysis reveals that a competent bus rider knows how to read published literature on schedules, tours, and costs, how to obtain information about buses by telephone, and how to determine and choose the best alternative tours, schedules, and pay options. How would you consolidate the prerequisite tasks in order to plan for efficient instruction? You would look for like tasks—in this case, knowledge necessary to understand many pieces of transit authority literature. For example, instead of teaching each route and pay schedule, you might consolidate tasks and teach how to read a bus schedule and how to choose a payment option.

The Air Force manuals for instructional designers call for the consolidation procedure of deriving common elements in order to make specific objectives more efficient and to simplify sequencing of objectives (Department of the Air Force, 1978). Table 7.2 is an example of the common elements approach used by Air Force instructional designers.

In the Air Force example, behavioral objectives to match each task were written first; then the designer looked at other tasks involving the XYZ calculator and determined that setting up for multiplication was a common element.

TPOs and EOs

The terms TPO and EO were used by the IDI project. They stand for Terminal Performance Objective and Enabling Objective. A TPO is a final performance goal stated in behavioral format; it represents the most complex behavior to be demonstrated. EOs are sub-objectives; they are the prerequisite learning stated in behavioral format. This is a TPO: "Given an extemporaneous topic, speak for five minutes on that topic following the principles of rhetoric summarized in a ten-point checklist. You must score an average of eight or more on the checklist of three trained observers." Either of these could be an EO:

> **Given a topic for a ten-minute speech, orally outline what you would say about the topic, including introduction, major points, and conclusion.**

> **Given a rule of extemporaneous speech, orally provide one illustration of following that rule in a speech.**

In both cases the implied criterion is mastery; the learner either performs the task completely and correctly or he doesn't.

Both TPOs and EOs should be written in behavioral objectives format. If EOs are not written as measurable observable behaviors, the designer may be unable to determine whether all the objectives were achieved through instruction and whether all of the ob-

Table 7.2   Sample Objectives for the Job "Use of Electronic Calculator"

Objective (Task 8)	(1)	
Condition(s)	**Performance**	**Standard(s)**
Given an XYZ calculator and a list of 25 three-digit number with decimals,	student will enter number and multiply each by a constant	All 25 products calculated and corded within 1 minute, without error (timing begins after setup of calculator is completed).

Subobjective (Activity 8.78)	(2)	
Condition(s)	**Performance**	**Standard(s)**
Given lists of three-digit numbers and XYZ calculator,	student will enter numbers and press ± key after each number is entered	without looking at keyboard touch rate of 40 numbers in 1 minute with less than 5% error.

Common-Element Objective (Activity 8.1)		
Condition(s)	**Performance (3)**	**Standard(s) (4)**
Given an XYZ calculator,	student will demonstrate steps of the procedure for setting up a calculator to perform multiplication.	No more than one error of sequence.

From *Handbook For Designers of Instructional Sytems*: Vol. III. Objectives and Tests (pp. 3–6), 1978, Department of the Air Force, AF Pamphlet 50–58.

jectives were necessary for instruction. And if the TPO is not achieved, measuring EO's makes it clearer where instruction fell short. When you have written the TPOs and EOs, develop a visual representation of the objectives and their relationship that parallels the visual representation of the instructional analysis.

Basis for Sequencing

Before developing criterion-referenced items, examine the TPOs and EOs. Do they follow an accepted learning classification such as Gagné's outcomes or a cognitive taxonomy? If so, how? Is the visual convention, e.g., hierarchy or flowchart, used appropriately? Is it logically consistent with the relationship among objectives?

One technique for checking logical consistency is to use the curriculum structure concept. In curriculum structure, discrete units not needed as prerequisites for transfer of learning are handled horizontally, and units that are necessary for transfer of learning are handled vertically. A curriculum can also be a combination of discrete and prerequisite units. Figure 7.1 compares flat, vertical, and hierarchical curriculum structure. A flat curriculum has discrete components that can be presented in any order. With vertical and hierarchical structure, the order is fixed as in a learning hierarchy. A spiral curriculum introduces a concept and then returns to it and expands on it as the student progresses through developmental levels.

The proposed relationship of EOs and TPOs will resemble a curriculum structure. Be sure that structure is consistent with the basis for sequencing in the instructional analysis. In other words, if you are using Gagné's outcomes you can correctly have

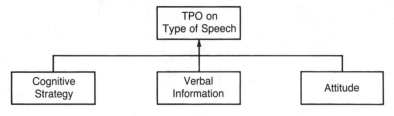

but not

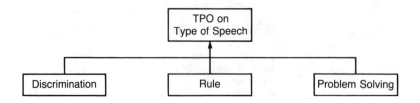

because intellectual skill outcomes should have a vertical or hierarchical sequencing.

Figure 7.1   Comparison of Flat, Vertical, Hierarchical, and Spiral Curriculum Structure

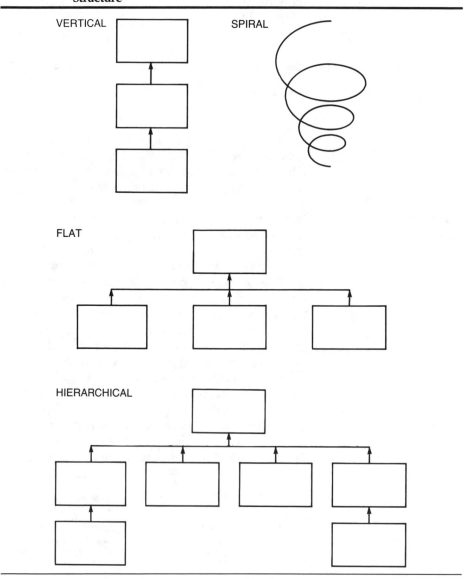

Here's another example. The theoretical basis for sequencing is Bloom's taxonomy. Can you have

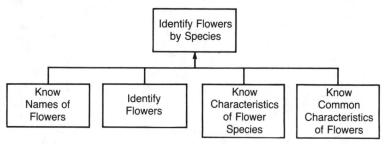

No, you cannot, because the taxonomy is a hierarchical basis for sequencing. But you could have

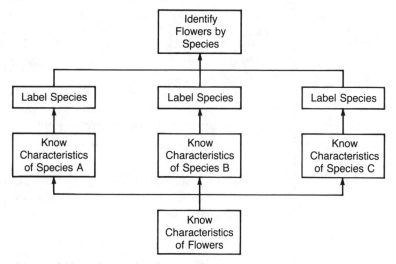

because this would be a hierarchical curriculum structure based on taxonomic levels.

An Exercise in Using an Instructional Analysis When Writing Objectives

1. Study the instructional analysis on French restaurant words.
2. Identify:
   a. Tasks that should be written as terminal performance objectives.
   b. Tasks that should be written as enabling objectives.
3. Use the instructional analysis to practice writing objectives. Develop one area of the analysis by writing enabling objectives.

Instructional Analysis for French Restaurant Words

When children learn French, they are often immersed in French conversation. After many dialogues to help them learn French words and sentences and their English equivalents, students are led to discover rules for French pronunciation and to use the vocabulary they have learned to create their own dialogues.

This situation is an example of learning which involves verbal information plus intellectual skills. This learning problem is broad in scope, yet specific. It is an excellent topic for instructional analysis because it is complex and realistic, yet is narrow enough to be accomplished within the constraints of this exercise.

To start this instructional analysis, you need to analyze the tasks involved in this learning problem. Let us assume that we have interviewed some French teachers and reviewed several French textbooks. As a result, the two major components of this learning problem

Figure 7.2   Association Analysis for French Restaurant Words

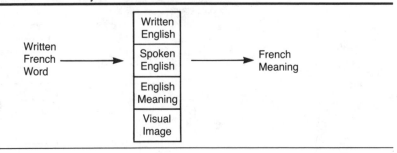

are identified. The first component is memorizing English/French equivalents and their meaning. The second component is applying rules for pronunciation that enable the student to see new French words on a menu and pronounce them. A separate task and instructional analysis is needed for each component, and the types of learning must be identified more specifically. Then, there must be an analysis of how the two major components relate.

Let's start with the verbal information component. The task analysis reveals associations that must occur during information processing. These tasks can be shown in a diagram of the association process, as shown in Figure 7.2.

Next, the types of verbal information that must be learned are translated into more specific goals:

> **Be able to state the English equivalent of a French word for food and to describe the meaning of the word. (Verbal Information—names, labels and organized knowledge)**

The instructional analysis for this verbal information goal takes the form of a cluster analysis:

French Words for Food

Entrée	Principal	Desserts	Boissons
Avocat	Quiche	Dessert	Thé
Vinaigrette	Carotte	Fruit	Café
Concombre	Boeuf	Abricot	Chocolat
Crème	Lentilles	Banane	Limonade
Radis	Porc	Figues	Perrier
Salade	Mayonnaise	Poire	Jus D'Orange
Tomate	Saumon	Orange	Vin
Paté	Crabe	Peche	Bière
Escargot	Soufflé	Raisin	Champagne
Oignon	Mouton	Chocolat	
Céleri	Sauce	Crêpes	
Soupe	Olives	Pruneau	
	Moutarde		

Now let's turn to the task analysis for the demonstrate pronunciation component. The tasks identified are visualized in a hierarchy in Figure 7.3.

These tasks must be clearly identified in goal statements as levels of intellectual skills. Robert Gagné (1977) says that declarative knowledge is a synonym for verbal information, and procedural knowledge is a synonym for intellectual skills. With declarative knowledge, you can state information without being able to apply or demonstrate it. With procedural knowledge, you may not be able to state the information, but you can use it. The goal statements for the intellectual skills component are:

Figure 7.3 Learning Hierarchy for Pronouncing French Words

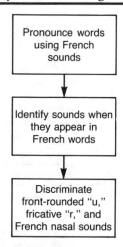

Be able to distinguish among sounds for (1) French front-rounded "u", (2) a French fricative "r" and (3) French nasal vowels (a, e, i, o) followed by "n" or "m". Be able to distinguish among either printed or spoken sounds. (Discrimination)

Be able to identify instances of French sounds for front-rounded "u", fricative "r" or nasal vowels when they appear in spoken or written French words. (Concrete Concept)

Be able to pronounce in French new or familiar words for foods. (Rule Using)

When more than one type of learning outcome must be shown in an instructional analysis, a line is drawn to the related outcome in a different domain and a symbol is inserted in the middle of the line to show learning that occurs concurrently. The symbol for motor skills is an M in a square, for attitudes is an A in a circle, for verbal information is a V in a triangle pointed as a cursor and for intellectual skills is a dotted line. (Briggs and Wager, 1981) The instructional analysis for the intellectual skills component can be combined with the verbal information tasks. The visual form of the completed instructional analysis (Figure 7.4) would be a hierarchy showing the intellectrual skills and associated verbal information learning.

This is one way to do an instructional analysis on learning French restaurant words.

An Exercise in Using a Basis for Sequencing

There are four objectives for each learning taxonomy. Label each objective as TPO or as EO1, EO2, or EO3 (EO1 is the most basic objective). Use the levels of the taxonomy (see Chapter 2) to determine the order of EOs.

Cognitive Domain

    a. Given a list of questions, the student will write next to each question the type of "PROBE" it represents. Accuracy should be at least 75 percent.

    b. Given a resume and a job description, the student will conduct a simulated employment interview segment in which he or she successfully demonstrates ap-

Figure 7.4   Instructional Analysis: French Restaurant Words

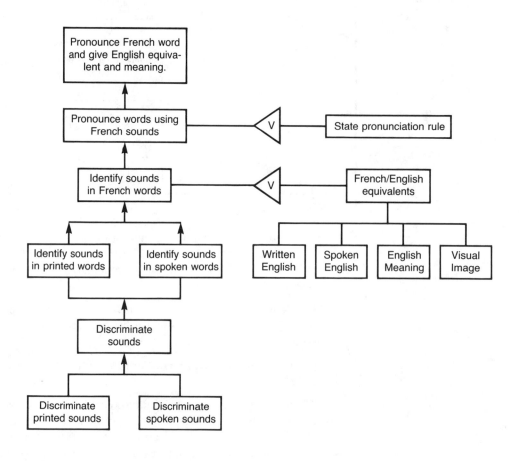

plication of the PROBE interviewing technique by asking appropriate questions to identify an event, role, or outcome.

c.   Given a list of PROBE terms and a list of definitions, the student will match the terms to the definition. The terms will be primary/secondary, open/closed, leading/neutral, redirective, mirror, and nudging.

d.   Given a definition of the PROBE interview technique, the student will label that definition as true or false.

Affective Domain

a.   Given information on events, the student will voluntarily attend three events sponsored by extracurricular organizations.

b.   Given an orientation session on extracurricular activities, the student will listen attentively as evidenced on a checklist of nonverbal behaviors completed by an observer.

c. Given time and transportation after school, the student will join an extracurricular activity and participate in preparation for one of that organization's events.

d. Given the opportunity to elect an extracurricular activity-related course rather than another academic course, the student will elect the extracurricular-related course.

Learning Outcomes, Intellectual Skills

a. Given a song, the clarinet student will identify characteristics of the song by reading symbols such as the clef sign, the measures, the values of notes and the musical terms and marks.

b. Given fingering positions for different notes, the clarinet student will distinguish among correct and incorrect finger positions.

c. Given an arrangement of a song, the clarinet student will play the arrangement with correct interpretation.

d. Given printed music for beginners, the clarinet student will play the notes using correct fingering.

Psychomotor Domain

a. Given a dance partner and a simple routine, the dance student will perform the routine and make adjustments in movements as necessary to maintain balance and extension.

b. Given a musical sequence, the dance student will develop and perform an interpretive dance that includes skilled movement and utilizes the whole body.

c. Given a series of exercises, the dance student will perform them by stretching, bending, and twisting so that the body is extended in all movements.

d. Given a solo ballet sequence requiring strenuous effort and highly skilled movement, the dance student will perform the complete sequence without stopping.

TESTS

Before you develop tests it is essential that you understand some basic measurement concepts. You need to know about types of tests and criteria for test construction. This section will introduce several measurement concepts.

Achievement Tests

Instruction is designed to bring about learning, and tests are used to determine whether learning occurred. Tests that measure what a person has learned to do are called achievement tests. There are two types of achievement tests: criterion-referenced tests (CRTs) and norm-referenced tests (NRTs).

Criterion-referenced Tests. CRTs are sometimes called content-referenced or objective-referenced tests. A test is criterion-referenced when its score can be translated into a statement about what a person has learned relative to a standard; a CRT score provides information about a person's mastery of a behavior relative to the objective and reflects that person's mastery of one specific skill. A person who passes a state's automobile driving test can be said to have the competencies set as a standard for driving in that state. Success on a CRT means being able to perform specific competencies. Usually a cut-off score is established, and everyone reaching or exceeding the score passes the test. There is no limit to the number of test takers who can pass a CRT.

Norm-referenced Tests. On an NRT the score tells where the person stands relative to other persons who have taken the test. The Scholastic Aptitude Test (SAT) is an NRT; its score tells where a person stands relative to other potential college entrants. Success on an NRT is defined as being ahead of most of the other test takers. NRTs are designed to "reliably" select the best performers. NRTs seldom provide specific information about mastery of a specific skill because they are designed to measure a person's relative standing in a group with respect to some broadly defined capabilities.

Purposes of CRTs

CRT scores let everyone (students, parents, administrators, and teachers) know exactly how well students stand relative to a standard. CRTs can be constructed to measure the separate prerequisites in learning hierarchies. The hierarchical analysis serves as a blueprint to enable the test developer to plan testing systematically.

When instruction begins, tests are administered to determine which competencies in the hierarchy students have mastered. The test results help the teacher decide where to place the student based on how much instruction is needed to achieve the desired competency level. As instruction on each level is completed, end-of-lesson tests (post-tests) reveal whether mastery has occurred and whether the student can move on to the next lesson.

Also, CRTs are used to evaluate the instruction itself. If an acceptable number of students are achieving mastery, then the instruction is obviously working. If there are too many failures, test results can be analyzed to determine where the instruction failed and to plan the necessary revisions.

Exercise to Distinguish CRTs and NRTs

Directions: Read the following statements and check the ones that apply to CRTs.

_____ 1. At the end of instruction, test scores showed that eighty percent of the students achieved a score of at least ninety percent correct.

_____ 2. Mary's math score showed that she was in the eightieth percentile for students in the tenth grade.

_____ 3. Betty's test score showed that she needs tutoring in how to multiply fractions.

_____ 4. After studying test results of a group of fifteen people who completed a course on using a computer program, an instructional designer concluded the instruction would have to be revised because ten people did not achieve mastery on two of the objectives.

_____ 5. Harry's test score showed that he was below average in abstract reasoning.

_____ 6. On the basis of her score on a French test, Ann was placed in the advanced French class.

_____ 7. The teacher gave John an A because he had the highest test score in the class.

Characteristics Desired in Tests: Reliability and Validity

Reliability means that a test yields a dependable measure. Reliable tests have consistency and temporal dependability.

Consistency. A student may correctly answer a question by guessing, or answer a question incorrectly because it was phrased misleadingly. A single item is not sufficient evidence to conclude that a student has or has not mastered an objective. To draw a conclusion confidently from a test, it is necessary to determine whether the student's performance is consistent on other items aimed at the same objective.

A student who answers several test questions correctly is more likely to have mastered the objective than a student who can answer only one or two questions. To increase the internal consistency of an NRT, developers simply increase the number of items on the test. This is not always a practical solution for CRT developers who must strive to assess each separate competency a test covers. If this rule were rigidly followed, tests might last longer than the course. These are factors that affect the number of items developed:

1. Consequences of misclassification: What is the cost of judging a master a non-master, and vice versa? The greater the cost, the greater the need for multiple items.

2. Specificity of the competency: The more specific the competency, the smaller the number of test items needed to assess competency. This is especially true in performance tests of simple motor skills. Once is usually enough.

3. Resources available for testing: When it is impossible to allot long periods of time to testing or when the costs of extensive testing are prohibitive, a strategy will have to be devised for selecting competencies for testing to make maximum use of time or money (Shrock et al., 1986, 3–7).

Temporal Dependency. Each time the test is administered, it should produce similar results. The student's demonstration of mastery should be the same on Tuesday as it is on Friday. Temporal dependency is usually determined by administering the tests on two occasions to the same group of students. A high degree of correspondence between scores suggests good reliability. Statistics employed for traditional norm-referenced reliability are not appropriate here. The comparison can be done by a simple percentage.

Test-retest reliability is enhanced by constructing unambiguous items and by making scoring as objective as possible. The most objective tests are those that can be scored by machine or by anyone with a scoring key. By contrast, subjective items must depend upon the judgment of experts who may have varying opinions about correctness. Subjective tests get varying results from the same students on different days. Table 7.3 illustrates types of written tests and their degree of objectivity.

Validity means that a test measures what it is supposed to measure. (There can be no validity without reliability.) The performance on a CRT must be exactly the same as the performance specified by the objective. Consider this example: If the test item says that an automotive repair student must remove a brake drum, then to be valid, the test must be designed to provide an automobile and the equipment to actually remove the drum. A multiple-choice test requiring students to recognize the correct procedure for removing the drum is not a valid test of the objective, nor would the test be valid if it required the student to recite from memory the procedures for removal. Neither test provides evidence of the student's ability to use the actual equipment. Responses to such a test may be interpreted as a memorized verbal chain. Only when the test and the objective are congruent is the test valid.

Achieving validity is not always straightforward. Frequently, it is not possible to test the actual performance of a task because it is difficult to obtain the resources to develop and administer the test. For example, consider the problem of obtaining equipment for the test on automotive repair. Practical considerations may necessitate a scaled-down version of

Table 7.3 Types of written tests and degree of objectivity

Objective	Less Objective	Subjective
Multiple choice	Production items (case studies or problems) when answers are specific and not open to interpretation	Essay in which a student is required to discuss a topic
Completion when answers are short requiring a specific phrase		Completion answers when answers can phrased in various ways
True-false when indisputably factual or not factual		True-false when dependent on context

From *Handbook of procedures for the design of instruction* by Leslie Briggs and Walter W. Wager, 1981, Englewood Cliffs, NJ: Educational Technology Publications. Copyright 1981 by Educational Technology Publications. Reprinted by permission.

the actual performance. Therefore, the objective must be written to take these constraints into consideration while still obtaining a valid measure. In cases such as these, it is a good idea to obtain the judgment of others about whether the objective and the test truly reflect the purposes of the lesson.

The best approach to establishing a test's validity is to empirically demonstrate that a test correctly distinguishes between masters and non-masters. One acceptable method is to administer the test to approximately thirty persons rated as masters and thirty rated as non-masters. If the test is valid, most of the masters should be able to answer each item on the test and most of the non-masters should not. Items that do not distinguish between masters and non-masters should be dropped from the test or revised.

Exercise to Recognize Ways to Achieve Greater Reliability in a Test

Directions: For each learning outcome below, two types of scoring are described. Check the type of scoring which is likely to be more objective.

1. Learning outcome: Student must identify a major theme in *The Scarlet Letter*. The scorer checks to see whether

   a. the correct answer in a multiple choice item is endorsed.

   b. ideas involved in the major theme are present in an essay.

2. Learning outcome: Student must correctly punctuate an unpunctuated paragraph. The scorer

   a. rates the student on a scale of 1 to 5 for each type of punctuation. The score is the total of the rankings.

   b. works from a correctly punctuated paragraph and compares the student's paragraph with it. The score is the number of correspondences.

3. Learning outcome: Student must compare and contrast "criterion-referenced testing" and "norm-referenced testing." The scorer

   a. assigns points to the student's essay depending on the student's estimate of adequacy of coverage.

   b. has a list of characteristics the essay must cover for each type of test and adds up the number cited.

4. Learning outcome: Student mechanic must set spark plug gap to correct width. The scorer

   a. passes instrument through gap and checks for snugness of fit.

   b. visually inspects gap and accepts or rejects.

5. Learning outcome: Student must comply with lunchroom rules of conduct. The scorer

   a. checks to see whether the correct answer in a multiple-choice item is endorsed.

   b. observes the student in the lunchroom and rates the adequacy of the student's behavior against a list of the rules of conduct.

6. Learning outcome: Student must subtract four-digit numbers. The scorer

   a. checks to see whether the student can correctly subtract his or her birth year from the current year.

   b. checks whether the student can solve ten subtraction problems involving four-digit numbers.

Exercise to Recognize Test Items Likely to Lend Greater Validity to a Test

Directions: For each statement of a learning outcome, two test items have been developed. Check the one that better reflects the behavior in the statement.

1. Objective: Given specific travel needs, the student travel agent will prepare a travel itinerary which includes the traveler's name, date, destination, and credit card number; names of airlines, flight numbers, departures, and arrivals arranged chronologically; and the amount charged to the traveler's account.

   _____ Test A presents hypothetical travel information. The student must write a travel itinerary that conforms to the criteria in the objective.

   _____ Test B asks "What items should be included in a travel itinerary?"

2. Given a politician's speech, the student will identify the known facts contained in the speech and separate facts from inferences.

   _____ Test A presents an entire speech and directs the student to "Underline one statement of fact. Double-underline one inference contained in the speech."

   _____ Test B presents an entire speech and directs the student to "Underline all of the known facts. Double-underline the inferential portions of the speech."

3. Given a drawing of a Hopi residential structure, the student will identify the description that best characterizes the structure.

   _____ Test A shows a picture and directs the student to "Study this picture and read the four sentences below it. Put a check mark in front of the one sentence that is appropriate for the structure."

   _____ Test B shows a picture and directs the student to "Study this picture and read the sentence below it. Indicate by a true or false answer whether the sentence is appropriate for the structure."

4. Given a specific geographical location and a specific month, the student will name the season.

   _____ Test A asks "What season would it be in Bogotá during June?"

   _____ Test B directs the student to "Fill in the following chart by identifying the season for each city."

City	Month	Season
Montevideo	June	
Miami	January	
Montreal	January	
Seattle	September	
Bogotá	September	

5. Given an instance in which man has altered his environment, the student will name the positive and negative effects of the alteration on the ecosystem.

   _____ Test A states, "A dam is a man-made alteration of the environment. Give a negative and a positive effect on the ecosystem."

   _____ Test B states, "The following are man-made alterations to the environment: dam, oil drilling, freeway, solid-waste disposal system, gravel pit, park. Provide one positive and one negative effect resulting from each."

6. Given a moving van, the student will load the van with household items so that they will not shift during movement.

   _____ Test A requires the student to load a scale model of a truck with scaled-down furniture.

   _____ Test B requires the student to describe the placement of the furniture in the truck.

Evidence of Mastery   What information is collected as evidence of mastery will depend on the competency being measured.

Cognitive Tests. For learning requiring acquisition of knowledge, the test is fairly self-evident. Verbal chains may be measured by recitation. Knowledge of facts and other types of information may be assessed by test questions that require the student to make mastery explicit. Intellectual skills are assessed by having a student solve problems, apply rules, or classify objects.

Unobservable cognitive tasks are usually made visible by some form of a written test. There are six types of tests that apply to cognitive tasks: multiple-choice, true-false, fill-in, matching, short answer, and essay.

Performance Tests. In contrast to tests which measure cognitive abilities, performance tests measure a student's ability to do something. For example, a student's ability to perform a motor task is evaluated by observing and judging his behavior. In the test, the student is directed to perform a task and his performance is evaluated against some predetermined standard. If the output is a process, performance is evaluated as it occurs. Tasks evaluated this way include, for example, actions performed by athletes, performing artists, and equipment operators.

If the specific output is a product, the student produces the product and it is evaluated against a standard. Products may take many forms. A sample of the student's handwriting may be compared to an ideal sample of correct penmanship, or an apprentice cabinetmaker's work may be evaluated against certain workmanship standards.

On a performance test, an examiner using either a rating scale checklist or frequency count measures the student on the actual output defined in the objective. Because performance tests directly measure capability, they are inherently more valid than written tests. But because performance tests usually require judgment by the examiner, they tend to be less reliable than most cognitive tests.

Evidence of Attitude Change. Ways to assess attitudes include interviews, surveys and polls, questionnaires, and rating scales. You can also use logs, journals, and diaries. Sociometric procedures, observation reports, and examination of records are also valid techniques for measuring attitudes. If affective objectives are the major point of a design project, you will probably want to use several of these methods.

When you are assessing attitudes it is essential to place the learner in a voluntary situation in order to collect data. Otherwise the learner may indicate a preference just to please the examiner rather than be honest. This means that you measure preference for reading indirectly by counting books signed out in the library, not by collecting a book report done to fulfill an assignment.

The following objective is an example of attitude assessment through a journal or diary kept on a voluntary basis:

> **Given a budget and the opportunity to participate in a research study, the teenage volunteer will show preference for a balanced diet in reports on a five-day eating period in restaurants. The balanced diet will be judged on a five-day rather than a meal-by-meal basis.**

Criterion Measures   Each objective must be examined for a correct match between means of evaluation and the type of learning or behavior. Criterion-referenced measures define achievement on the basis of a pre-established standard stated in an objective. Students either reach this standard or they don't. Criterion items are those on which the student must demonstrate mastery by performance.

Table 7.4 shows a good way to check the validity of your objectives by matching the task on your instructional analysis with its objective and criterion item. If the chart indicates discrepancies across columns, then rewrite the objective.

Table 7.4 Task/Objective/Criterion Chart

Task	Objective	Criterion
Identify data. *Identify editing.* *Identify saving.* *Identify printing.* *Identify on-screen help.*	Given an oral example of a procedure, the student will identify the procedure by naming it correctly as data entry, editing, saving, printing, or on-screen help.	When you direct the computer to save, you are using a procedure called.
Determine distance and travel.	Given two locations on a map and a rate of travel, the student will determine the distance and time of travel.	Determine the distance from Syracuse, New York to Washington, D.C. and the time of travel at an average of 50 mph.
Identify/trace routes on the map using the correct legend.	Given a bus schedule, circle 3 route stops on the schedule map.	Select a bus route and circle 3 stops on the schedule map for that route.
Pay correct bus fare.	Given a predetermined location, select the appropriate payment.	What is the designated fare in the downtown area?
Recognize the order of events in the first stage of labor.	Given events in the first stage of labor, the student will list the order of events as they occur in labor.	Put numbers in front of these events to indicate the order in which they occur in labor. Make the first event #1.
Distinguish rhythm through syllabification.	Given 5 poems, the student will write at the end of each line the number of syllables in that line.	At the end of each line in the poem "The Road Not Taken," write the number of syllables in that line.

How do you go about writing valid criterion items? You use your classification guides to select appropriate verbs and evidence for a level. Then you write an objective that meets the criteria for a good objective. Finally, you write a criterion item consistent with the objective and test construction rules. A good reference on constructing criterion items is Mager's (1973) *Measuring Instructional Intent or Got a Match?* The taxonomies of objectives include sample test items that can be used as models (Committee of College & University Examiners, 1956; Krathwohl, Masia, & Bloom, 1964; Harrow, 1972).

Appropriateness of Items

Each of the types of test or non-test criterion items is more appropriate for some learning outcomes than others. This is not to say that multiple-choice items cannot be used for knowledge and attitude assessment. However, it is difficult to measure psychomotor skill with multiple choice. Items can be constructed to be suitable aims of several learning outcomes. Still, there are domains an item is most suitable for, as shown in Table 7.5, Type of Item Most Appropriate for Each Type of Learning.

It is also important to remember that items can be test or non-test in nature. Test items are required and used to determine mastery. Affective objectives are measured by criterion items that are always voluntary, often indirect, and have a flexible rather than a mastery level for success. An objective test's criterion items are standards set for mastery. An attitude inventory has non-test criterion items—standards the designer sets for success.

Test Construction Rules

Test developers must also consider guidelines for writing items. There are some general and specific rules for writing items; they are derived from several sources and are summarized in Table 7.6 on p. 156 (Remmers, Gage, & Rummerl, 1965; Payne, 1968; Gay, 1980; Nitko, 1983).

An Exercise in Using a Task/Objective/Criterion Chart

Directions: Where a column is blank, complete it so that the row across is logically consistent.

Task	Objective	Criterion
	Given a blank 5.25 floppy disk and a flow chart, the student will generate an initialized disk within 15 minutes.	
Load DOS.	Given DOS software and a microcomputer, the student will follow the recommended procedure to load DOS.	
Estimate distance to locations.		What is the distance in miles between Indianapolis and New Orleans? Select a bus route and trace the route on the schedule map.
	Given a predetermined location, determine charges for travel within and between zones.	How much fare would be paid for a ride from Zone 1 to Zone 2?
Describe the events in the second stage of labor.		There are at least four events in the second stage of labor. Write a paragraph about each event.
Use phonetics to distinguish rhyme.		After each line in "The Raven" write the phonetic ending.

An Exercise in Applying Test Construction Rules

Directions: For each of the behavioral objectives listed, an appropriate type of test item is identified. Use Table 7.6, Rules for Writing Test Items, as a guide in developing criterion items for these objectives.

1. Essay: Given an essay question, explain the causes of diabetic shock and the predicted effects of several modes of treatment.

2. Matching: Given illustrations of five inventions, match them with their inventor and name, e.g., Alexander Graham Bell's telephone.

3. True/False: Given ten statements about the mechanical properties of a V-8 gasoline engine, identify all ten correctly as true or false.

4. Multiple-choice: Given four multiple-choice questions about the requirements to become president of the United States, identify the constitutional requirement presented in each question.

5. Short Answer: Given a completion question, give the definition of each of the parts of speech, e.g., verbs.

Table 7.5 Type of Item Most Appropriate for Each Type of Learning

Type of Item	Domain Most Associated With	Motor Skill	Verbal Information	Discrimination	Concrete Concept	Rules	Problem Solving	Cognitive Strategy	Attitudes	COMMENTS
OBJECTIVE										
True/False	C		o	o	o					Efficient for items with only two logical responses
Completion	C		o			o				Natural for brief responses
Multiple-Choice	C		o	o	o					Use when answer is long, reduces effect of guessing, so can have fewer items
Matching	C		o	o	o	o				Efficient but not for higher level learning tasks
ESSAY										
Essay	C					o	o	o	o	Score systematically
Extended Report	C					o	o	o	o	Clarify required components
ACTIVITY										
Lab Reports	C					o	o	o		Type of learning used for depends on content and structure
Exercises	C, P	o				o	o			Separate use for testing from use for instruction
Projects	C,P,A	o					o	o		Good for interactive domain learning
OBSERVATION										
Checklists	P, A	o						o	o	Excellent for procedural knowledge and practice
Rating Scales	P, A	o						o	o	Self or observational, degrees of subjectivity
Anecdotes	A								o	Subjective
Interviews	A							o	o	Revealing, can have degree of objectivity
APPLICATION										
Problem Solving	C,A					o	o		o	For higher level of learning
Product	C,P,A	o				o	o	o	o	Especially for interactive domain learning

KEY
o Very Appropriate For

C Cognitive
P Psychomotor
A Affective

Table 7.6 Rules for Writing Test Items

General Rules

Be careful not to provide cues to the correct answer.

Avoid dependent items where one item cues the answer in another item.

Avoid negatives.

Avoid unnecessary difficulty, such as use of obscure vocabulary.

Avoid direct quotations.

Do not call for trivial, obvious, ambiguous, or meaningless answers.

Each item should have only one correct answer.

Use illustrations appropriately and accurately and make them clear.

Follow the rules of grammar and syntax.

Avoid items that give away the answer.

Avoid complex sentence structure.

Multiple-Choice Items

Make the stem a direct question.

Ask one definite question.

Avoid making correct alternatives obviously different.

Present alternatives in logical order.

Avoid making correct alternatives systematically different.

Present alternatives in logical order.

Make response alternatives mutually exclusive and of similar length.

Make response alternatives plausible but not equally plausible.

Use "none of the above" seldom and with caution.

Make options and the stem grammatically parallel and consistent.

Present the term in the stem and definitions as options when testing knowledge of terminology.

Avoid requiring personal opinion unless on attitude survey.

Avoid redundancy in alternatives by stating once in the stem.

Avoid a collection of true/false alternatives.

Use "all of the above" option when there are several correct answers, not a best answer.

Put as much of the problem as possible into the stem.

Matching Items

Use response categories that are related but mutually exclusive.

Keep the number of stimuli small and have the number of responses exceed stimuli by 2 or 3.

Present response in logical order (e.g., alphabetically, chronologically).

Use longer phrases in the response list, shorter in the stimuli list.

Identify stimuli with numbers and responses with letters.

Keep everything relating to an item on a single page.

FROM THE READING

Define the following terms.

Behavioral Objective

Terminal Performance Objective

Enabling Objective

Curriculum Structure

Criterion-referenced Test

Norm-referenced Test

Criterion Item

Reliability

Validity

Table 7.6   Rules for Writing Test Items (continued)

Matching Items

Explain the basis for matching; give clear directions.	Make stimuli and response columns similar in level of difficulty.
Avoid "perfect" matching by including one or more inplausible responses.	Avoid using complete sentences in stimuli column; use phrases or words instead.

True/False, Constant Alternative Items

Be sure the item is definitely true or false.	Use quantitative language when possible.
Avoid determiners such as always, often.	Place crucial elements at the end of the sentence.
Use approximately the same number of words in each statement.	Instead of true/false, you can use yes/no, right/wrong, true/false, depends, correct/incorrect, same/opposite.
Avoid quotations or stereotypes.	
Don't present items in a pattern.	Phrase items unambiguously.

Short Answer, Completion, or Supply items

Word items specifically and clearly.	Provide the terms and require the definition rather than vice versa.
Put the blank towards the end of the sentence.	Specify the terms in which the response is to be given, e.g., word, phrase, sentence, inches, feet.
Use only one blank.	
Avoid quoted or stereotyped statements.	Use direct questions rather than incomplete declarative sentences.
Require short, definite, explicit answers.	

Essay Items

Focus the type of response you wish the student to make.	Word question so experts can agree on correct response.
Clarify limits and purposes of questions.	Use more than one essay question.
Avoid optional questions.	Set up a systematic scoring procedure.

Application or Problem Solving Items

Use new or novel test materials.	Test ability to use materials.
Use introductory materials followed by item dependent on that material.	Use pictures or diagrams for testing.
Call for identifying or producing examples.	Use reading material for testing.
Call for identifying components or relationships.	Allow for creativity.

ISSUES FOR DISCUSSION

1. What are some of the problems and issues associated with behavioral objectives?

2. How feasible is the expressive objectives format?

3. How would a norm-referenced test be used by an instructional designer?

4. Why should you be concerned about the reliability of a criterion-referenced test used as a diagnostic tool?

5. How can affective goals be stated as behavioral objectives?

6. How do criterion-referenced tests relate to the affective domain?

7. How does validity relate to criterion-referenced tests for the affective domain?

REFERENCES

Committee of College & University Examiners, (1956). *Taxonomy of educational objectives: Handbook I: Cognitive domain*. Bloom, B. S. (Ed.). NY: David McKay.

Briggs, L. J., & Wager, W. W. (1981). *Handbook of procedures for the design of instruction*. Englewood Cliffs, NJ: Educational Technology Publications.

Department of the Air Force. (1978). *Handbook for designers of instructional systems: Volume III, Objectives and tests*. AF Pamphlet 50–58. Washington, DC.

Department of the Air Force. (1978). *Handbook for designers of instructional systems: Volume IV, Planning, developing and validating instruction*. AF Pamphlet 50–58. Washington, DC.

Eisner, E. (1969). Instructional and expressive objectives: Their formulation and use in curriculum. In W. J. W. Popham (Ed.), *Instructional objectives: An analysis of emerging issues* (pp. 13–18). Chicago, IL: Rand McNally.

Eisner, E. (1979). The educational imagination: On the design and evaluation of school programs. NY: MacMillan.

Gagné, R. M. (1977). *The conditions of learning*. NY: Holt, Rinehart & Winston.

Gagné, R. M., & Briggs, L. J. (1979). *Principles of instructional design*. NY: Holt, Rinehart & Winston.

Gay, L. R. (1980). *Educational evaluation & measurement*. Columbus, OH: Merrill Publishing.

Gitoner, D. (1987). Team develops exercise and portfolio to help teachers assess learning in the arts. *ETS Developments, 33* (1).

Harrow, A. J. (1972). *A taxonomy of the psychomotor domain*. NY: David McKay.

Krathwohl, D. R., Bloom, B. S., & Masia, B. B. (1964). *Taxonomy of educational objectives. Handbook II: Affective domain*. NY: Longman.

Lindvall, C., & Nitko, A. J. (1975). *Measuring pupil achievement and aptitude*. NY: Harcourt Brace Jovanovich.

Mager, R. F. (1962). *Preparing instructional objectives*. Palo Alto, CA: Fearon.

Mager, R. F. (1973). *Measuring instructional intent or got a match?* Belmont, CA: Fearon.

Mager, R. F. (1976). Why I wrote . . . . *National Society for Performance and Instruction Journal, 15* (8).

Morris, L. L., & Fitz-Gibbon, C. T. (1978). *How to deal with goals and objectives*. Beverly Hills, CA: Sage Publications.

Payne, D. A. (1968). *The specification and measurement of learning outcomes*. Waltham, MA: Blaisdell.

Popham, J. (1979). Instructional objectives 1960–1970. *National Society for Performance and Instruction Journal, 18* (10).

Popham, J., and Baker, E. L. (1970). *Establishing instructional goals*. Englewood Cliffs, NJ: Prentice-Hall.

Remmers, H. H., Gage, N. L., & Rummerl, J. F. (1965). *A practical introduction to measurement and evaluation*. NY: Harper and Row.

Shrock, S., Mansukhani, R. H., Coscarelli, W., & Palmer, S. (1986). An overview of criterion-referenced test development. *Performance and Instruction Journal*, 3–7.

Tyler, R. (1964). Some persistent questions on defining of objectives. In C. M. Lindvall (Ed.), *Defining educational objectives* (pp. 77–83). Pittsburgh, PA: University of Pittsburgh Press.

University Consortium for Instructional Development and Technology. (1968). *Objective marketplace game*. Syracuse, NY: Instructional Development Institutes, Syracuse University, IDDE.

Chapter Eight
Instructional Strategies

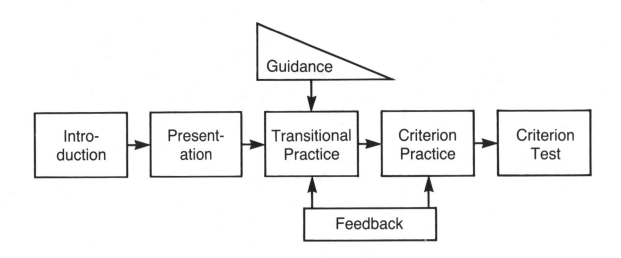

Objectives	- Given learning situations, identify effective introductions of what is to be learned.

Objectives

- Given learning situations, identify effective introductions of what is to be learned.
- Given ineffective introductions, revise them to make them more effective.
- Given instructional objectives, develop introductions to the new material.
- Given learning situations, identify effective presentations of what is to be learned.
- Given ineffective presentations, revise them to make them more effective.
- Given instructional objectives, develop presentations to present the new material.
- Given learning situations, identify practice schedules that will facilitate learning.
- Given learning situations, identify transitional practice that will facilitate learning.
- Given inadequate practice situations, revise them to make them more effective.
- Given practice conditions, identify effective feedback for the situation.
- Given ineffective feedback, revise the feedback to make it more effective.
- Given instructional objectives, produce transitional practice and feedback.
- Given research abstracts, identify those that are examples of comparative experiments.
- Given a model of the variables necessary for effective instruction, choose an article, make a presentation on the variable studied, and state the implication of the research for instructional design.

Overview

Once you have written and sequenced the objectives and constructed tests, you are ready to develop your strategy for designing the learning events that will accomplish the objectives. Whatever the size of the instructional segment, there is a set of events generally prescribed for all learning situations. The diagram by Virginia Johnson at the beginning of this chapter shows the basic instructional events of a simple instructional segment. The same events should be included in any type of instruction, whether it is self-paced or group-paced, and no matter what medium or methods of instruction are employed (e.g., computer-assisted instruction, films, simulations, etc.).

The introduction directs students' attention to the learning task, motivates them by explaining the benefits of achieving the objectives, and relates the new learning to previous learning.

The presentation is the point during which the information, facts, concepts, principles, or procedures are introduced to the student. Presentation requirements will vary depending on the type of learning to be accomplished and the students' entry-level behavior.

The criterion test measures the students' accomplishment of the terminal objective(s).

The criterion practice occurs under the same conditions as the final test. The purpose is to determine whether a student is ready to take the final test, or whether remediation is necessary.

Transitional practice is designed to help the students bridge the gap between entry-level behavior and behavior required by the terminal objective(s). Less difficult situations are presented at the beginning of instruction, and gradually practice becomes more difficult. The important thing to remember about transitional practice is that it prepares students to perform the criterion practice.

Guidance is the coaching and prompting that helps students perform correctly. The shape of the figure representing guidance shows that more assistance is present at the beginning of practice, and that it is gradually reduced until the students can perform unassisted. As the diagram shows, assistance is provided only during transition practice, not during criterion practice.

Feedback, an integral part of practice, tells students whether they are right or wrong, and how they can improve performance. Feedback is provided during transitional and criterion practice. Practice alone is not sufficient for effective learning.

How much practice is needed? What form of feedback is best? How should new information be presented? Research on instructional design variables that facilitate learning provides many of the answers. The body of research on instructional design variables is quite large, however, and beyond the scope of a single text. Therefore, this chapter will concentrate on some of the basic principles of learning—practice, feedback, and presentation—that apply in most circumstances. A discussion follows of how these principles apply to different types of learning. Finally, you will have an opportunity to review research studies and define their implications for instructional design.

Study Questions

1. What forms can practice take?

2. What forms can feedback take?

3. What are the ingredients of an effective introduction?

4. What variables affect how information will be presented to the learner?

5. What are the criteria for evaluating the quality of research that asks "What instructional condition leads to what learning outcome?"

6. How would you review the research on a topic of interest to you?

PRINCIPLES OF LEARNING

Introducing the Lesson

The first activity in the teaching/learning process is to direct the students's attention and prepare them to practice. As noted earlier, an introduction should explain the objectives of instruction, describe the benefits of achieving the objectives, and relate the new learning to previously learned material.

Students accomplish objectives more effectively if they know, when instruction begins, exactly what is expected of them. They then can focus on those activities that lead to achievement of the objectives. If nutrition is being studied, for example, it may not be obvious to a student whether the objective is to identify foods in each food group, or plan a menu with foods in each food group—two quite different outcomes. Students should not have to guess what is expected of them.

It is important to communicate objectives in a language students understand. For older students, it may be sufficient simply to give them the actual objectives devised by the instructor. For younger students, the objectives must be restated at a level they comprehend. This may entail providing an example or demonstration of the performance expected at the end of the lesson or samples of the types of questions asked on the final exam.

Many teachers erroneously assume that students understand the value of what is being taught. In fact, students may not understand how what they are being asked to learn fits into a larger goal. Yet considerable evidence suggests that students who see a real purpose to the learning task will learn it better. The instructional designer should include a statement in each lesson about why the material or task is of value. Sometimes a straightforward statement about the benefits of instruction is enough, but other times it takes ingenuity to convey the long-term benefits to students. If you cannot devise a good reason for learning the topic or task, perhaps you should reassess your task analysis and instructional analysis data to determine whether the instruction is really necessary.

Learning is more effective when it can be related to previously learned information for instance, by a brief recall of previous lessons to show how the current lesson relates to them. Or, you can compare the concepts to be learned to concepts already known to the students. For example, electrical current is often explained by comparing the flow of electricity to the flow of water.

An Exercise to Recognize Effective Introductions to Lessons

Directions: Below are examples of instructional objectives and an introduction for each. Evaluate each introduction by the following criteria.

Describes the objective of the lesson and how students will be evaluated.

Describes the benefits of learning.

Relates the new learning to previous learning.

1. Objective for mail room clerk: Determine how much postage is required for different classes of mail.

   Introduction: The amount of postage needed for a package will depend on its weight, content, destination, and the mailing class selected. Mailing classes include parcel post, first class, second class, and third class. Packages with too much postage waste money. Those with too little postage are returned to the sender and are late reaching their destination. In this lesson you will learn how to determine the right amount of postage to use.

   Check those that apply:

   _____ Describes the objective of the lesson and how students will be evaluated.

   _____ Describes the benefits of learning.

   _____ Relates the new learning to previous learning.

2. Objective for coal miners: Follow procedures for putting out fire in underground coal mines.

   Introduction: It is important that miners be trained in firefighting—for their own safety and because they are the ones who can attack a fire while it is still small and while the chance of putting it out is greatest.

   In this lesson you will learn the procedures to follow in fighting small mine fires. At the end of the lesson, you will review written descriptions of miners' actions when fighting fires and determine whether they followed the correct procedures.

   Check those that apply:

   _____ Describes the objective of the lesson and how students will be evaluated.

   _____ Describes the benefits of learning.

   _____ Relates the new learning to previous learning.

3. Objective for first lesson of a fitness program for beginners: Take a 45-minute walk, do three to five modified pushups, abdominal curls, and leg raises.

   Introduction by Stockton (1989) for a series of articles on fitness: This is a ten-week fitness program for people who have yet to incorporate exercise into their life and want to start it. It is based on four workouts a week. At the end of the ten weeks, you will be able to walk eight miles a week at three miles an hour, burning 650 calories a week. . . . From simple beginnings like this, totally sedentary people have permanently altered their lives, discovering new energy, losing weight, stopping smoking, and boring family and friends with incessant talk about their new obsession.

Check those that apply:

_____ Describes the objective of the lesson and how students will be evaluated.

_____ Describes the benefits of learning.

_____ Relates the new learning to previous learning.

An Exercise to Edit Ineffective Introductions to Make Them More Effective

Directions: Select one of the deficient introductions from the previous exercise and rewrite it to satisfy all of the criteria.

An Exercise to Produce Effective Introductions

Directions: Select three objectives from a course of study with which you are familiar. Prepare introductions for each objective. The introduction must meet all of the following criteria. When you have completed the exercise, write a brief statement describing how you met each criterion.

Describes the objective of the lesson and how students will be evaluated.

Describes the benefits of learning.

Relates the new learning to previous learning.

Presenting New Content

When new content is to be learned, the lesson should present the facts, concepts, and rules, and/or describe and demonstrate the skill. New material is easier to remember when it is presented in an orderly, highly structured form that is meaningful to the student, reduces extraneous information and confusing stimuli, and contains a great deal of redundancy.

When planning presentations, avoid information overload. Substantial research evidence suggests that information chunked into limited bits (seven bits plus or minus two is ideal) is more easily stored in memory. The appropriate number of chunks depends on the students's previous experience with similar material and the rate of delivery. Rapid delivery increases information load.

The presentation should include cues such as the following to help the student learn.

Calling attention to important characteristics of the material.

Providing examples (and non-examples) of concepts.

Providing verbal or pictorial cues to call attention to critical elements of the new material. Visual presentations are more effective for difficult or even meaningless concepts, while aural presentations facilitate reception of familiar, fairly simple, and very meaningful material.

Using mnemonic devices to help students learn arbitrary associations.

An Exercise to Recognize Effective Presentations

Directions: Below are examples of instructional objectives and presentations prepared for each. Evaluate each presentation against the following criteria:

Logical structure.

Information is chunked to prevent memory overload.

Cues direct attention to relevant aspects of the learning.

1. Objective: Recall a list of words.

   Presentation: During the introduction, the instructor says: "Here are a list of words that you are expected to learn. On the test, you may recall the words in any order." Then the instructor writes the following list on the board and tells the class to copy them.

Summer	Noon
Blue	Red
Night	Winter
White	Spring
Fall	Night
Morning	

   Check the criteria that apply:

   _____ Logical structure.

   _____ Information is chunked to prevent memory overload.

   _____ Cues direct attention to relevant aspects of the learning.

2. Objective for infantry soldier: Ignite smoke pots using manual ignition, electric ignition, and manual chain firing.

   Presentation: The instructor distributes a checklist of the steps for each procedure. There are four steps in the manual ignition procedures:

   1. Strip off waterproof tape and the metal clamp.
   2. Remove the outer cover to expose the matchhead.
   3. Remove the scratcher block from its envelope.
   4. Draw the scratcher block rapidly across the matchhead.

   The eleven steps in the electric ignition procedure and three steps in the chain firing procedure are similarly detailed on the checklists.

   The instructor starts with the manual ignition because it is easy and most familiar to the students. As he demonstrates the procedure, he describes what he is doing and why.

   He demonstrates the chain firing procedure next because it is also a manual procedure. During the demonstration, he describes what he is doing and why.

   Finally he demonstrates the electric ignition procedure using the same instructional strategy. The entire presentation takes fifty minutes.

   Check the criteria that apply:

   _____ Logical structure.

   _____ Information is chunked to prevent memory overload.

   _____ Cues direct attention to relevant aspects of the learning.

3. Objective for a salesperson: Identify a customer's style in risk taking, decision making, and communicating. The styles are Active Positive, Active Negative, Active Neutral, and Dominant Negative.

   Presentation: The instructor presents a definition of the four styles and discusses how to negotiate with each. He then distributes scripts of how each type might respond to a salesperson's call. Key phrases that signal the prospect's type are underlined. The instructor reviews and elaborates on each underlined segment.

   Check the criteria that apply:

   _____ Logical structure.

   _____ Information is chunked to prevent memory overload.

   _____ Cues direct attention to relevant aspects of the learning.

An Exercise to Edit Ineffective Presentations to Make Them More Effective

Directions: Select one of the deficient presentations from the previous exercise and revise it to satisfy all of the criteria.

An Exercise to Produce Effective Presentations

Directions: Prepare presentations that follow the introductions you prepared in the last exercise. The introduction must meet all of the following criteria. When you have completed the exercise, write a brief statement describing how you met each criterion.

Logical structure.

Information is chunked to prevent memory overload.

Cues direct attention to relevant aspects of the learning.

Practice

Learning is an active process. It is more effective when students produce, practice, or try their hand at the task to be learned. Practice is the single most important ingredient of effective instruction; it speeds up learning, aids long-term retention, and facilitates recall.

Instruction is less effective when there is no opportunity to perform the task or when practice is delayed until after the instruction has been completed. Unfortunately, much of the instruction in our classrooms provides little or no opportunity for practice. Too often, instruction is designed so that students passively receive information; they listen to lectures, read texts, or watch demonstrations.

Cognitive psychologists believe effective practice creates cognitive structures for efficient storage and retrieval of information from long-term memory. Behaviorists are less concerned with what goes on inside the student's head than with the conditions that make practice more effective. Regardless of their theoretical orientation, however, all scientists agree on three aspects of practice:

1. Practice opportunities must allow students to perform the task actively.

2. Practice is most effective when it occurs immediately after the presentation of new material, while information is still fresh in the students' minds.

3. There must be multiple opportunities for practice. Learning very seldom occurs after only one try at a task.

Overt or Covert. Practice may be either overt or covert. An overt response, such as writing an answer, performing a procedure, or repeating a word or phrase, is observable. A covert response, such as thinking of an answer, mentally practicing a verbal chain for later recital, or silently selecting the correct answer from a series of options, is not observable.

Experiments that address whether covert or overt responding facilitates learning have mainly dealt with verbal learning. The findings show that students who respond covertly learn and retain verbal material as well as students who respond overtly. Learning from films, lectures, or similar presentations can be increased by using techniques to elicit covert responses. For example, the lecturer can strategically pause to pose a direct question or to allow the students to complete a sentence.

During the past several years, an increasing number of studies have examined how learning from written materials takes place. A related issue is the use of questions embedded in textual material. Questions designed to evoke higher-level cognitive processing (e.g., compare, synthesize, evaluate, problem solve, etc.) are preferable to questions that require lower-level learning, such as recall of facts. Presumably, the higher-level questions cause the student to study the written material more thoroughly to get the correct answer. When the questions require only simple recall, however, students study only those parts of the text specific to the questions.

Under certain circumstances overt responding is preferable because it allows the teacher to verify the accuracy of students's responses, especially with less able students who require more assistance. In addition, overt responding facilitates rote memorization. Overt responding is also preferred for psychomotor skills and for procedural tasks that have not been well established.

Schedule of Practice. In general, the more opportunities the student has to respond, the more learning occurs. Practice opportunities should not be massed into one session. Cramming for an exam is an example of massed practice. Cramming may result in high performance on the test, but it is subject to rapid forgetting. For long-term retention of material, practice should be distributed over a period of time with short rest periods between each practice opportunity. "Distributed" practice is preferable for all learning, but it is needed more for less able students and it is essential for learning long, difficult tasks and skills.

Shortening the rest period is better than lengthening the work period. Rest periods should not be too long, because after a certain point they fail to pay off. Intervals between practice should be shorter when error tendency is high than when it is low. There are no hard and fast rules. For example, if students forget between sessions much of what was learned, it may be because weekly practice sessions are spread too far apart. Daily sessions may be more effective for some situations, but two or more brief sessions per day may be necessary for others.

Transitional Practice   Transitional practice bridges the gap between entry-level behavior and criterion performance. It is intended to provide students early in learning with situations they can handle. Gradually, practice becomes more difficult until students can perform at the criterion level. In other words, practice starts easy and ends hard.

Transitional practice may take several forms. One way is to break down the task into its component parts and have students practice solving part of a problem before the whole problem, or practice the separate steps in a procedure before combining them in the proper sequence. (The component subtasks or substeps were identified earlier—during the task analysis phase of the instructional design process.)

Another common way of making practice less difficult is by starting with easier responses and building to harder ones. Gropper (1971) recommends providing recognition practice, then editing practice, and finally production practice. In recognition practice, students merely select a correct answer from two or more options. In editing practice, students are shown an incorrect performance and asked to correct it. Production practice is the closest to criterion performance (assuming the criterion performance requires students to produce rather than merely recognize a correct performance). Unlike criterion practice, during production practice students may receive guidance. Table 8.1 shows examples of recognition, editing, and production practice. Notice the guidance in both examples of production practice.

Practice may be made easier by lowering the standards for performance (such as speed, accuracy, completeness, quality, etc.) during the early stages of learning. As learning proceeds, students are brought progressively closer to criterion standards. For example, a timed task may have no time limits at first. Gradually, time limits are applied and shortened to what the criterion performance will require.

Another important principle of learning is that practice should be as error-free as possible. Once made, a correct response is likely to recur. But the same is true for an incorrect response. Therefore, it is up to the designer to provide guidance and prompts during the early stages of practice in order to reduce guesswork and make sure the student's initial response is correct. Having to "discover" the correct response by trial-and-error wastes time; it confuses and frustrates the learner. There may be a place for discovery learning in some educational settings, but the method is difficult to implement when instructional time is limited. Error-free learning is especially important in learning motor skills. (Ask any skier or golfer who has tried to correct a bad technique.)

Table 8.1   Examples of Transitional Practice

Recognition practice

- Which of these two carburetors is assembled correctly?
- Is this a nimbus or cumulus cloud?

Editing practice

- This carburetor has been assembled incorrectly. Assemble it correctly.
- This cloud was incorrectly labeled a nimbus cloud. What kind is it?

Production practice

- Assemble this carburetor. Don't forget that the choke must be completely assembled first.
- Look at the shape and color of this cloud. What kind of cloud is it?

From *Module 13. Principles of learning: Student resource book* by V. Johnson, 1985.

Since it is impossible to ensure that every student will always respond correctly the first time, the designer should plan cues. Cues help guide students to the correct response, but they should not be so obvious as to reveal the response. Cues may, for example, tell the form of the response (e.g., "your answer should be a fraction"), depend on meaningful associations or past knowledge, or draw attention to key properties (by means of arrows, charts, diagrams, etc.).

An Exercise to Recognize Effective Practice Schedules

Directions: Below are examples of instructional objectives and two practice schedules prepared for each. Indicate which is the better schedule and tell why.

1. Objective. Given a distribution curve, select the appropriate average (i.e., mean, median, or mode) and calculate it.

   _____ Practice Schedule A
   Statistics teacher will lecture on the topics and conclude with a series of thirty exercises on all averages.

   _____ Practice Schedule B
   Statistics teacher will lecture on the topics. After each topic is presented, it will be followed by ten exercises.

   Explain your choice.

2. Objective. Classify food items into four food categories: milk, grain, meat, and vegetable.

   _____ Practice Schedule A
   Instructor will assign reading as homework, directing students to think of two examples of each food group. The next day students will be asked to write them on the board.

   _____ Practice Schedule B
   Instructor will assign reading as homework assignment. The next morning, students will be asked to think of two examples of each food group and write them on the board.

   Explain your choice.

An Exercise to Recognize Effective Transitional Practice

Directions: Below are examples of instructional objectives and two transitional practice strategies prepared for each objective. Indicate which is the better strategy and tell why.

1. Objective. Packs grocery bag so that fragile items are on top.

   _____ Practice A
   Student is given a list of fragile items. He discusses the items on the list. He is directed to pack three orders.

   _____ Practice B
   Student is given a list of fragile items. He critiques a videotape of a clerk packing fragile items. He is directed to pack three orders.

   Explain your choice.

2. Objective. Associate colors on resistors with resistance values.

   _____ Practice A
   Directions: Column A shows the resistance values and associated colors. Write the correct value in Column B.

A	B
black-0	red _____
brown-1	green _____

   and so on for 10 colors.

   _____ Practice B
   Directions: Write in the proper resistance values for the following colors.

   brown _____
   black _____
   red _____
   green _____

   and so on for 10 colors.

   Explain your choice.

3. Objective. Distinguish between examples of term and revolving loans.

   _____ Practice A
   (1) With the aid of a written definition *and* verbal cues, select examples of each type of loan. (2) With only the definition, select examples of each. (3) Select examples unassisted.

   _____ Practice B
   (1) With the aid of verbal cues, select examples of each type of loan. (2) With the aid of only a definition, select examples. (3) Select examples unassisted.

   Explain your choice.

An Exercise to Edit Ineffective Practice to Make It More Effective

Directions: Below are examples of practice devised by instructional designers. Revise each to improve it.

1. Objective: Inspect tires for defects. No more than five percent of the defects are missed.

   Practice: Using a checklist of defects to look for, the student inspects four tires. Then practice is unassisted.

   Revision:

2. Objective: Produce a design by (1) drawing a design with water soluble paint on a watercolor board, (2) covering the entire board with non-soluble ink, and (3) washing off the soluble paint to reveal the design delineated by the ink. Practice: After a demonstration of the process, students use the technique. The instructor circulates around the room offering help as needed.

   Revision:

3. Objective: Plan seating arrangement to facilitate discussion and consensus among participants. Practice: Distinguish among several proper and improper seating arrangements, then develop a seating plan for a room of own choosing.

   Revision:

Feedback

Another way to minimize errors is to let the student know immediately when a response is incorrect. Knowing when they are right or wrong helps students correct their actions during subsequent trials and focus on parts of the task that require refinement.

Feedback may take two forms. It may arise naturally out of the task environment—during learning and later during the criterion performance on the job or on a test. Target practice is one example of a task where feedback is natural. But often feedback does not arise naturally from the task itself, and in these cases the instructional designer must devise methods for providing it. "Artificial" feedback is present only during learning.

Feedback devised by the instructional designer should be as follows:

Complete. Provide the entire correct answer. Simply telling students they are wrong doesn't tell them how to be right.

Specific. Identify errors in the performance and provide information about the magnitude and direction of the error. This information allows students to make the appropriate correction.

Corrective. Explain the logic of the correct answer. Students who are told why their answers are right or wrong learn more effectively than students who receive no feedback until they get the right answer.

Immediate. Give the correct answers after each practice trial.

Reinforcing. Reward correct responses with praise, recognition, or something else you know to be reinforcing. A student who is reinforced for doing something is more likely to do the same thing again. Often, simply knowing that one has performed correctly is in itself rewarding.

An Exercise to Recognize Effective Feedback

Directions: Below are examples of instructional events. Indicate which feedback option is better and tell why.

1. Instructional event. A man is learning to develop black and white film.

   _____ Feedback A. Stop him after a mistake, and demonstrate what he should have done.

   _____ Feedback B. After he completes the procedure, summarize what he did wrong. Explain your choice.

2. Instructional event. A woman is undergoing on-the-job training to be a supervisor.

   _____ Feedback A. Comment about effective and ineffective performance at the end of each day.

   _____ Feedback B. Comment about effective and ineffective performance each Friday.

   Explain your choice.

3. Instructional event. A man is learning to complete income tax forms. He is given several problems using the short form.

    _____ Feedback A. A model of a correctly completed short form using another exercise.

    _____ Feedback B. A model of a correctly completed short form using the same exercise.

    Explain your choice.

An Exercise to Edit Ineffective Feedback to Make It More Effective

Directions: Below are examples of feedback devised by instructional designers. Revise each to improve it.

1. Practice: A woman learning tennis is practicing her backhand.

    Feedback: After practice, she watches a video replay of herself.

    Revision:

2. Practice: A woman is learning to recognize clinical signs of depression. Using a checklist, she observes several dramatizations on video tape of interviews with clients and checks off the signs she observes.

    Feedback: After she completes the task, she verifies her answer against a completed checklist in the back of her workbook.

    Revision:

3. Practice: A trainer is learning how to use questions to draw students into discussion groups. In response to an exercise he prepares three questions.

    Feedback: The instructor reviewing his questions says, "Those will never do. Try again."

    Revision:

An Exercise to Produce Effective Practice and Feedback

Directions: Select three objectives from a course or field of study with which you are familiar. Devise practice and feedback opportunities for each. The practice must meet all of the following criteria. When you have completed the exercise, write a brief statement describing how you met each criterion.

Scheduled immediately after presentation of the task to be learned.

Multiple practice opportunities.

Practice is distributed.

Practice progresses from easy to hard.

Practice opportunities are designed to be as error-free as possible.

The feedback must meet all of the following criteria:

Complete

Specific

Corrective

Immediate

Reinforcing

RESEARCH ON LEARNING

Instructional designers look to research to determine what conditions have increased learning in situations similar to the ones they face. Behavioral scientists use a number of methods to study behavior. They observe people in various situations, they question people in-depth about their experiences, they survey large groups of people to determine their likes and dislikes, they construct and administer tests for many human capabilities and characteristics. But the most important and productive method of studying learning is the experiment in which the researcher makes a careful and controlled study of cause and effect.

Experimentation

Experimentation on learning involves the introduction of some new or untried element and evaluating its effects. The experiment is designed to determine whether a direct relationship exists between the introduction of the new element and the learning outcome. This determination is accomplished by comparing groups that differ with respect to the element being evaluated but are similar in all other relevant dimensions.

Assume, for example, that a researcher wishes to evaluate a new method for teaching spelling to third graders. If the method is effective, the curriculum committee will introduce it into the entire school system. To evaluate the new method, the researcher constructs two matched groups of third graders typical of the school system. At the beginning of instruction, the groups are equal in spelling ability, intelligence, background, and attitudes toward school. The researcher uses the new method with Group A, the experimental group. The method currently employed in the school system is used with Group B, the control group. The researcher strives to ensure that, in terms of all factors that affect performance, administration of both methods is the same. (Class schedule and teaching staff, for example, may affect performance.) After a period of time judged reasonable to evaluate the teaching methods, the researcher tests both groups on the same spelling test, or a battery of tests may be used. Results are compared to determine whether there is a difference in the groups's spelling competencies. Given the outcome, the curriculum committee has a sound basis for deciding whether the expenditure of time and resources required to make the change is warranted. If the research is published, other school systems will look to it and to findings from related research to guide them in making curricular decisions.

Because there are so many variables that can affect learning, controlled experimental designs are difficult to implement. Results frequently are not consistent from one study to the next, and often no significant differences appear. Part of the difficulty can be explained by problems in the research design. Wilkinson (1980) cites minimal acceptable standards for comparative studies. These are the acceptance criteria:

1. Experimental and control groups must have at least twenty-five subjects.
2. Experimental and control groups are equal on all relevant dimensions. This is accomplished best by randomly selecting and assigning subjects from the same population to the experimental and control groups.
3. Both groups are taught by the same instructor.
4. Performance is measured by a testing instrument that is valid and reliable.
5. Test results are evaluated by acceptable statistical procedures.

Exercise to Distinguish Controlled Experiments from Other Types of Research

Directions: Read the following research abstracts and check those that are examples of experiments. For each item checked, name the variables being compared and the groups used in the experiment.

_____ 1. Three spatial tasks were created in two forms, as video and as computer graphics. Both forms of each task were presented to third graders, middle schoolers, and university students. Middle schoolers and adults preferred working with the video but were more accurate working with computer graphics. Third graders preferred the computer but were equally successful working with both displays. The study suggests that the expectations with which students approach an instructional technology may determine the effectiveness of that technology more than characteristics of the technology in question (Acker & Klein, 1986).

Variables compared:

Groups used:

_____ 2. College students wrote compositions that elicited their technical knowledge of three topics. Then they completed a questionnaire that assessed which of four informational sources had contributed to their knowledge of the topics—formal education, mass media, social interaction, and direct experience (Graesser, Hopkinson, Lewis & Bruflodt, 1984).

Variables compared:

Groups used:

_____ 3. Varying approaches to mathematics were explored in a philosophy of mathematics course. Students were asked which foundational schools they preferred and their preferences were compared with scores on hemispheric tests. The results indicate that preferences may be related to the brain's hemispheres (Fidelman, 1985).

Variables compared:

Groups used:

_____ 4. The purpose of this study was to determine the effects of various mastery criteria on student performance and attitude in a course in which mastery strategies were employed. Undergraduates in an introductory course in educational psychology were randomly assigned to one of three treatments— one in which mastery criteria were gradually increased from 70% to 90%, a second in which mastery criteria gradually decreased from 70% to 90%, or a third in which mastery criteria remained constant at 80%. Results indicated that although the high mastery criterion (90%) had a positive effect on some aspects of quiz performance, it had no effect on final examination performance. Results also indicated that students preferred mastery criteria to remain constant during a semester. When examined in light of previous research, these findings call into question some prior notions regarding the levels at which mastery criteria should be set (Reiser, Driscoll, Farland, Vengara, & Tessmer, 1986).

Variables compared:

Groups used:

_____ 5. Ideas on teaching-learning theory of ratio are presented. Views of children and of members of an international panel are presented, and five questions and their responses are compared with real classroom experience (Streefland, 1984).

Variables compared:

Groups used:

Table 8.2   A Summary of Two Research Designs

Study 1: Krendl and Watkins (1983)

Summary: "This article examines the claim that television is a 'passive' medium, one that does not actively involve the viewer cognitively in ways usually associated with mature information processing" (p. 201).

Learner: demographics—children, fifth grade, male and female; Cultural Background—Rural, Midwest

Content: Learning task—cognitive, verbal information

Environment: setting—educational vs. entertainment

Delivery: strategy—media, video (videotape) Presentation—Form (sender control), no stopping vs. receiver control, stopping); Sequencing—Schedule, Pacing

Study 2: McCombs and McDaniel (1983)

Summary: "The effects of various alternative treatments (modules), designed to compensate for student differences in pre-course memory abilities (processing and retrieval skills) and motivation (anxiety, curiosity), were investigated for lessons differing in content and task requirements" (p. 213).

Learner: Demographics—Adult (ages 18–26, male and female: Competence—Prerequisite skills, information; Attitudes—Motivation (anxiety, curiosity)

Content: Learning task—Cognitive, Intellectual Skills; Mental Operations—Retention; Subject Matter—Vocational/Professional, Technical

Environment: Setting—Military

Delivery: Scope—Course (6 months); Strategy—Media, Non-projected; Process—Individualized Instruction; Presentation—Tactics: Secure Attention, Provide Reinforcement, Maintain Interest, Facilitate Retention: Form, Receiver Control

---

A Conceptual Model of Research on Instructional Design

The enormous body of research on instructional design variables can be unwieldy without a scheme for organizing it. Richey (1986) has clustered the research on instructional design variables into four major groups: the learner, the content, the environment, and the delivery system. Instructional design can vary depending on the specific nature of each group.

Learner variables that may affect instructional design are demographics, capacity, competence, and attitudes. Content refers to three major areas: type of learning, subject matter, and mental operations required. The environment has two aspects: setting and climate. The delivery system is limited to the actual conducting of the instruction. It excludes all design activities; decisions made during design, however, obviously have an impact on delivery. Delivery variables are scope, strategy, presentation, and sequencing.

Table 8.2 shows how this conceptual model can be used to describe research.

Exercise on Application of Research to Learning

Directions: Select two experimental studies from the following journals or other journals that publish research reports relevant to instructional design.

Educational Technology Research and Development

Journal of Applied Behavior Analysis

Journal of Educational Psychology

Journal of Educational Research

Journal of Educational Technology Systems

Journal of Personalized Instruction

Using the outline below, write a report using Richey's model. Attach a copy of the journal article to your report. Then join a small group of other class members and compose an oral presentation with them. The report must cover the following points:

1. What is the research question?
2. Summarize how the research was conducted (i.e., the subjects, the research methods, the learning task, and the dependent variable) and relate it to Richey's model.
3. What are the authors' conclusions?
4. What do the results mean for designing instruction?

Outline to Describe Research

Summary of the Study

Description of the learner variables

Description of the environmental setting and climate

Description of the system for delivery of the instruction

Evaluation Criteria:

Your performance will be judged on whether the studies selected are comparative experiments and on the accuracy with which your presentation reflects the information and conclusions in the research reports.

FROM THE READING

Define the following terms.

Criterion practice	Covert
Transitional practice	Cues
Guidance	Structure
Feedback	Experimentation
Overt	

ISSUES FOR DISCUSSION

1. Describe the instructional strategy used in a recent course in which you were a student. Discuss its adequacy in terms of the presentation methods used, the practice opportunities, and the feedback given.
2. Discuss the pros and cons of discovery learning.
3. Think of a formal learning experience that you have participated in or observed. Describe it in terms of Richey's four major grouping of instructional design variables.

REFERENCES

Acker, S. R., & Klein, E. L. (1980). Visualizing spatial tasks: A comparison of computer graphic and full-band video. *Educational Communications and Technology Journal 34* (1), 21–30.

Fidelman, U. (1985). Hemispheric basis for school in mathematics. *Educational Studies in Mathematics, 16,* 59–74.

Graesser, A. C., Hopkinson, P. L., Lewis, E. W., & Bruflodt, H.A. (1984). The impact of different information sources on idea generation: Writing off the top of our heads. *Written Communication, 1,* 341–364.

Gropper, G. L. (1971). *A technology for developing instructional materials: Handbook*. Pittsburgh, PA: American Institutes for Research.

Johnson, V. (1985). *Module 13. Principles of learning: Student resource book.* Contract No. F41689-83-C-0048. Randolph AFB, TX: USAF Occupational Measurement Center (ATC).

Krendl, K. A., & Watkins, B. (1983). Understanding television: An exploratory inquiry into the reconstruction of narrative content. *Educational Communication and Technology, 31,* 201–212.

McCombs, B. L., & McDaniel, M. A. (1983). Individualizing through treatment matching: A necessary but not sufficient approach. *Educational Communication and Technology, 31,* 213–225.

Reiser, R. A., Driscoll, M. P., Farland, D. S., Vergara, A., Tessmer, M. C. (1986). The effects of mastery criteria on student performance and attitude in a mastery-oriented course. *Educational Communications and Technology Journal, 34,* (1), 31–38.

Richey, R. (1986). *The theoretical and conceptual basis of instructional design.* NY: Nicols.

Stockton, W. (1989, January 23). A slow but sure way to get in shape. *The New York Times,* p. 19.

Streefland, L. (1984). Search for the roots of ratio: Some thoughts on long term learning process (towards . . . a theory). Part I: Reflections on a teaching experiment. *Educational Studies in Mathematics, 15,* 327–348.

Wilkinsen, G. L. (1980). *Media in instruction: 60 years of research.* Washington, DC: Association for Educational Communications and Technology.

Chapter Nine
Media Decisions

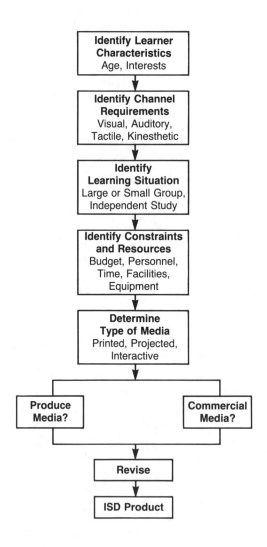

Objectives	■ Given a category of method/media options, list three of the options (alternate forms) in that category.
	■ Given a description, identify the learner characteristics in the description.
	■ Given an objective, identify the type of learning involved.
	■ Given a media chart, learner characteristics, and an objective, identify several appropriate media.
	■ Given a written description of a media design problem including learner characteristics, objectives, instructional plan, constraints, and resources, select appropriate method/media and write a brief rationale to justify your decisions.
	■ Given a topic, write a treatment.
	■ Given a topic, write a one-page script.
	■ Given a topic, develop a ten-frame storyboard.

Overview

The instructional designer determines method/media options, selects methods or materials, identifies commercially available materials, and initiates and monitors the production process. The designer does not produce audiovisual materials. In the case of the new interactive technologies, the designer may do all the conceptual planning and scripting, but seldom produces the software for distribution. The limits for the designer's role in method/media decisions vary from situation to situation.

Although there are many ways to classify media into categories, no satisfactory taxonomy of media has been developed. This chapter proposes three categories: methods, traditional media, and newer technologies. Within each category are many options and forms. For example, methods can include lecture, role play, discussion, or laboratory. There are many traditional media options, such as graphics and film or television. And graphics take a variety of forms: charts, cartoons, and illustrations.

Methods/media choices are based on methods/media selection criteria. The criteria are appropriateness for the learner, objective, and constraints. Learner characteristics, objectives, learning situation, and constraints must be identified before methods or media are selected.

After appropriate methods/media are identified, the designer searches media indexes for available commercial materials that can be adapted or adopted. If materials are not available, they must be produced.

The designer must decide who will produce the materials and who will constitute the production team. The designer must initiate and monitor the production process. To do this it is important to be familiar with the production process. It is the designer's responsibility to ensure the integrity of the design and quality of materials by monitoring production.

Study Questions

1. What is an instructional designer's role in method/media decisions?
2. What are major categories of methods/media options?
3. What are some of the options or forms in those categories?

4. How do you make methods/media choices?

5. What procedures should you follow to identify appropriate commercially prepared materials?

6. What is the designer's role in the media production process?

7. How can the designer monitor media production to ensure the integrity of the design and the quality of the materials?

THE DESIGNER'S ROLE

The instructional designer has many functions to fulfill during the media decisions step. At this stage the designer can function as a decision-maker who selects methods/media options, as a policeman who sees that instructional design recommendations are implemented, or as a manager who initiates and evaluates production. In this chapter you will read about the designer's role in the realization of the design, the choices or options available for methods/media, how you make the choice, how you obtain commercial materials, and how you initiate and monitor the production process.

You must consciously limit your role to the functions you can perform and finish effectively. Beware of also becoming the media producer, the photographer, or the programmer. It is challenging to try to make others understand that you will not be able to do all the production or that it may be more advisable for you to coordinate with a production team than to lead one. Your essential responsibilities are to determine method/media options, select the method or media, determine how the materials necessary for implementation will be obtained or produced, and as either a team member or leader, initiate and guide the production process. You cannot do all this well if you also serve as photo researcher, scriptwriter, photographer, and editor. This does not mean that you never produce or help edit. It means that you are aware of your guidance function and your skill limitations. You know, for example, that your group process skills are more developed and will be more useful than your photographic skills.

DECISIONS ABOUT METHODS

Method and media decisions are sometimes made concurrently. At other times, the method is chosen first and decisions about media necessary to implement the method follow. Dugan Laird (1985, p. 129) compares methods to highways that lead to your destination (objective), and media (training materials) to the highway "accessories," such as signs and maps, that make travel easier.

Methods are instructional strategies at a more specific level than the strategies developed in Chapter 8; they are approaches to instruction that determine the nature of the lessons. Joyce and Weil (1977) call them models for teaching. A method is a way to structure the learning experience at the lesson level rather than the curriculum unit level.

Ausubel (1968) distinguishes between two major methods—discovery learning and reception learning. Reception learning is learning from lectures or audiovisual material that present information. Discovery learning is creating a situation where the learner is free to explore and the ends of learning are not predetermined. Guided discovery learning has elements of both discovery and reception. Rather than being told exactly what they are to learn, the learners are given cues that lead them to discovery. Ausubel believes either method can become rote or meaningful. You can have rote guided discovery and meaningful reception learning and vice versa.

The designer can choose from methods such as lecture, laboratory, discussion, readings, field trips, note-taking, demonstrations, programmed instruction, case studies, role play, exercises, independent study, and simulations. Each of these methods takes several alternative forms (Laird, 1985). A lecture can be a dramatization, an audiovisual presentation, an exposition, or a combination of these. Discussion can take several forms, such as panels, open forum, and brainstorming. Case studies can vary from case history to a problem to solve. Similarly, role plays, which are also a type of simulation, vary from dyads to small plays.

Programmed instruction requires frequent responding and immediate feedback and can be presented through a scrambled book, exercises, or a computer. The style of programming can be linear or branching, or in the case of the computer approaches, drill and practice, tutorial, or simulation. Demonstration can be an audiovisual presentation, a performance, or an interactive presentation and discussion. Independent study can be done with modules, media kits, or the audio-tutorial approach.

An Exercise about Successful Use of Methods

Directions: In a small group discuss your experiences as a student in a variety of class formats, e.g., lecture, discussion, independent study, simulation. Discuss instances in which you felt the approach to instruction was effective and explain why. Discuss instances in which you felt the instructional method was ineffective and say why.

DECISIONS ABOUT MEDIA

Media are the means by which information is presented and experiences are shared. While media is the term used to refer to modes of delivery, it is necessary to have material to send through those modes. An analogy would be the necessity for both hardware and software for computer-based learning; similarly the medium of television requires programming.

Media decisions can precede, follow, or accompany methods decisions. Generally, they follow, or occur concurrently. A lecture may need media components or it may be in the form of a television program. Audiovisual materials are media, as are the more traditional print materials.

In this chapter, we divide methods/media options into three categories: methods, traditional media, and newer technologies. Methods are general curriculum approaches that may incorporate but are not synonymous with media. Traditional media include print and audiovisual media. The newer technologies are telecommunications and microprocessor-based.

Media options are extensive and complex. Many good references are available on each type (Heinich, Molenda, & Russell, 1982; Gross, 1986; Seels & Kanyarusoke, 1983; Allessi & Trollip, 1985). It is the designer's responsibility to be familiar with such references and with media alternatives. We can only summarize these media options and encourage you to gain first-hand experience with each. A word of caution—although we point out the best known characteristics of a medium, do not assume it can be used in only one way. An audiotape, for example, can be used to evoke images as well as present information, and a game can be open-ended but so can a film.

Media can be grouped as print materials, nonprojected visuals, projected visuals, audio media, multimedia systems, film, and television (Heinich, Molenda, and Russell, 1972). Each of these media breaks down into several alternate forms as shown in Table 9.1, Traditional Media Options.

Table 9.1 Traditional Media Options

Projected Visuals: Static	Nonprojected Visuals	
opaque projection	pictures	
overhead projection	photographs	
slides	charts, graphs, diagrams	
filmstrips	displays–exhibits, feltboards, bulletin boards	

Audio Media	Multimedia Presentations	
records	sound slide	
tapes–reel, cassette, cartridge	multi-image	
audio cards	film–cassette	
	multimedia kit	

Print	Projected Visuals: Dynamic	
text book	FILM	TELEVISION
programmed text	8mm	8mm
workbook	super 8mm	1/2 inch
job aid	16mm	3/4 inch
	35mm	1 inch

Games	Realia	
board games	models	
simulation games	manipulatives	
puzzles	specimens	

DECISIONS ABOUT NEWER TECHNOLOGIES

Newer technologies include computer-based instruction and telecommunications-based distance learning technologies. Distance learning occurs when the learner is in one location and the source of instruction in another. Newer technology options take a variety of forms, as shown in Table 9.2. Definitions of media or technology terms that may be unfamiliar are given in Table 9.3, Newer Technologies of Instruction Defined.

Table 9.2 Newer Technology Options

Telecommunications-based
    Teleconferencing
    Telelectures

Microprocessor-based
    Computer-assisted Instruction
        Computer Games
        Expert Tutoring Systems
        Hypermedia
        Interactive Video
    Computer-managed Instruction
    Compact Disc

Table 9.3 Newer Technologies of Instruction Defined

Compact Audio Disc (CD ROM):
  5 1/2″ laser discs which hold several hours of digitally recorded sound. (Gross, p. 152)

Computer-Assisted Instruction:
  Microprocessor-based system for delivering instruction directly to students by allowing them to interact with lessons programmed into the system. (Heinich, Russell, and Molenda, p. 319)

Computer-managed Instruction:
  A microprocessor-based system is used to administer and score tests, prescribe appropriate next steps, and monitor student progress. (Heinich, Russell, and Molenda, p. 319)

Hypermedia:
  An extension of hypertext that incorporates other media in addition to text. With a hypermedia system authors can create a linked corpus of material that includes text, static graphics, animated graphics, video, sound, music, etc. (Ambron and Hopper, p. 37)

Hypertext:
  Nonsequential writing. An authoring system that allows authors to link information together, create paths through a corpus of related material, annotate existing texts, and create notes that link text. (Ambron and Hooper, p. 37)

Intelligent Tutoring Systems:
  Computer-assisted instruction with the capability to carry on a dialog with the student and through that dialog allow the student to direct the course of instruction. (Jonassen, pp. 297–395)

Interactive Video:
  An instructional delivery system in which recorded video material is presented under computer control to viewers who not only see and hear the pictures and sound, but also make active responses, with those responses affecting the pace and sequence of the presentation. The equipment configuration includes a micro-computer, a laser videodisc player, and a high-resolution monitor. (Heinich, Molenda, and Russell, 1985)

Teleconference:
  A communications technique in which groups of separate geographic locations use microphones and special amplifiers that are tied together to allow everyone to participate actively in one large meeting. (Heinich, Molenda, and Russell, 1985)

Telelecture:
  An instructional technique in which an individual, typically a content specialist or well known authority, addresses a group listening by means of a telephone amplifier. The listeners may ask questions of the resource person with the entire group able to hear the response. (Heinich, Molenda, and Russell, 1985)

Videodisc:
  A video recording and storage system in which audio-visual signals are recorded on plastic discs rather than on magnetic tape. (Heinich, Molenda, and Russell, 1985)

An Exercise in Recalling Methods/Media Options

For each category list three options the designer can consider.

Methods	Traditional Media	Newer Technologies
1.	1.	1.
2.	2.	2.
3.	3.	3.

Circle one method or medium from each category above and list two alternative forms of that method or medium.

Methods	Traditional Media	Newer Technologies
1.	1.	1.
2.	2.	2.
3.	3.	3.

MEDIA SELECTION MODELS

There are ID models for the selection of media (Heinich, Molenda, and Russell, 1985; Kemp, 1985). These models are simpler versions of instructional systems design models. Two media selection models will be explained: Gerlach and Ely's, and Reiser and Gagné's. Each model was developed to aid in the selection and utilization of material.

Gerlach and Ely (1980)

The Gerlach and Ely model was first introduced in 1971 in their text *Teaching and Media*. It was reintroduced in 1980 with the second edition. As the title suggests, the text is intended for teachers at all levels and is to be used in education courses, especially in introductory instructional technology courses required by most teacher preparation programs. The Gerlach and Ely model, shown in Figure 9.1, is not intended for professional instructional designers; it is meant to help novices and teachers use instructional design concepts.

This model is most useful in an educational setting such as public schools or colleges. The reason is that the model starts with content and stresses constraints common to schools. Most schools start design with consideration of curriculum or content areas. Schools are bound by scheduling, space, and resource constraints that can be difficult to overcome.

Figure 9.1   Gerlach and Ely Model

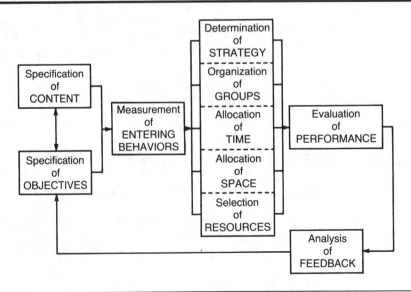

Vernon S. Gerlach/Donald P. Ely, *TEACHING & MEDIA: A Systematic Approach*, 2e, (c) 1980, p. 28. Reprinted by permission of Prentice-Hall, Inc., Englewood Cliffs, New Jersey.

A major contribution of this model is the ladder specifying variables that must be taken into account in the design. The authors recommend procedures such as flexible scheduling and differentiated staffing as ways to deal with the constraints of variables such as group size and time allocation.

Although the ladder of variables integrates constraints and resources with design, some major questions dealing with curriculum design are not addressed. When information on writing objectives is presented, psychological specifications for conditions of learning are discussed, but only at a basic level. For this reason, though the model is useful for teachers using design skills, it can be used by an instructional designer only in conjunction with another model, such as Briggs's, which specifies the ID steps in more detail.

Nevertheless, the systematic approach to media selection represented by the Gerlach and Ely model works. It is especially useful for helping beginning teachers and designers deal with constraints and resources.

Reiser and Gagné (1983)

The Reiser and Gagné Model (1983) has a psychological base. It starts with gathering information on the objectives, the domains of learning to be taught, the setting, and the learner's reading level. The designer then proceeds through a series of questions on a flowchart to determine the feasibility of each general category of presentation: job competence, central broadcast, self-instruction with leaders, self-instruction with non-readers, instructor with readers, instructor with non-readers. Only after a category of presentation modes is determined does the designer narrow the selection to a medium within that category. In the category "job competence decision," which deals with training the student to perform a task without error, media include equipment, simulator, radio or TV broadcast, training device, computer, programmed text, interactive video, motion picture, slide-tape, videocassette, filmstrip, text, audio, chart, overhead projection, slides, and instructor. In the branching loops on the flowchart, Reiser and Gagné provide questions to help narrow the selection of media.

The Reiser and Gagné method for media selection is complex. The model uses two forms: the media selection flowchart, which guides you through decisions on media selection and utilization, and a media selection work sheet. Figure 9.2 reproduces a flowchart panel.

The learning factors given prominence in this model are the instructional situation, the scope of the instruction, the objectives of the instruction, the domains of learning outcomes, and critical events of instruction (Reiser and Gagné, 1983, p. 45).

After using the flowchart to determine factors and media favorable to learning, the designer selects media by also considering practical factors such as cost and availability. Thus instructional effectiveness and feasibility are both taken into account. To guide you, Reiser and Gagné provide questions about practicality, such as "Can the media be produced in the time needed?" and "Can each medium meet your estimated requirements for change and updating?"

Selection Criteria

There is great merit in the models, such as that of Gerlach and Ely, that use grouping as a criterion for selection. The feasibility of media depends very much on whether instruction is to be by a large group, small group, or independent study method. A television tape prepared for a large group lecture can differ from one prepared for a small discussion group. A filmstrip can be suitable for independent study, but generally not for a large group lecture.

Another critical criterion is the symbolic code used in media. The importance of this criterion is emphasized in the model by Tosti and Ball (1969) and the writings of Gaviel Salomon. According to Salomon (1976, 1979), different media, e.g., film or graphics, require different codes and thus different mental skills or processes. For a medium to be effective it must match the symbolic requirements of the learning task and the learner's mental capability. Television, for example, is suited to showing transformations and processes that require spatial manipulation.

Figure 9.2   Central Broadcast Decision

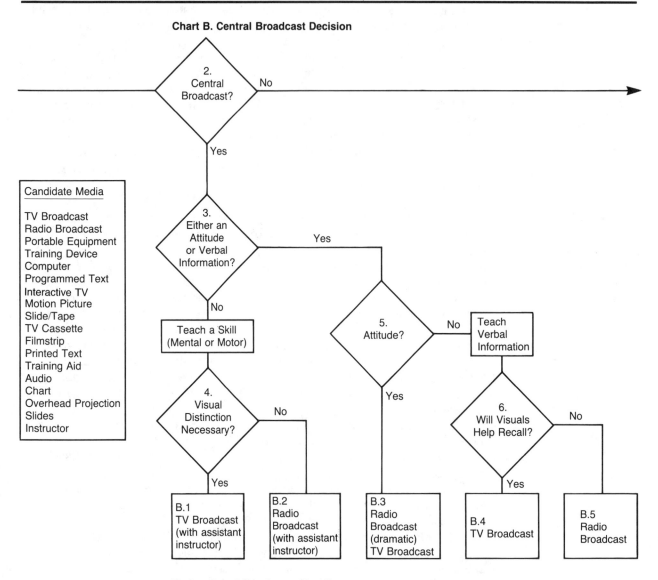

Chart B. Central Broadcast Decision

Candidate Media

TV Broadcast
Radio Broadcast
Portable Equipment
Training Device
Computer
Programmed Text
Interactive TV
Motion Picture
Slide/Tape
TV Cassette
Filmstrip
Printed Text
Training Aid
Audio
Chart
Overhead Projection
Slides
Instructor

Explanation of Questions - Chart B

2. Central Broadcast? Is the instructional system designed to serve students who are dispersed over a wide geographic area and who are able to receive centrally broadcast instruction at scheduled times?
3. Either an Attitude or Verbal Information? Is the aim either to influence the student's values (attitudes) or to have the student learn to 'state' (rather than 'do') something?
4. Visual Distinction Necessary? Is the visual presentation of task features necessary or will it aid in learning the task?
5. Attitude? Does instruction aim to influence the student's values or opinions?
6. Will Visuals Help Recall? Is it likely that the use of visuals will help the student establish images that will aid recall of verbal information?

After *Selecting Media for Instruction* (p. 73) by R. A. Reiser and R. M. Gagné, 1983, Englewood Cliffs, NJ: Educational Technology Publications. Copyright 1983 by Educational Technology Publications. Reprinted by permission.

A third critical criterion is the learner's characteristics; motivation or preferences can affect attention and learning. The more novel the medium, the more likely it is to have an increased effect for a while, but this is because of the novelty, not the medium itself (Clark & Clark, 1984). Furthermore, learners who find a medium frustrating will learn less. Materials must be appropriate for the audience's level.

Similarly, there seems to be value in looking at the psychological characteristics of the task, as in Reiser and Gagné's model (Higgins and Reiser, 1985). The task requires a specific type of learning. You don't teach discrimination of objects with a textbook chapter—not if you teach it well. Nor, as a rule, do you change attitudes through text readings. It can happen, but there are more powerful media for attitude change.

A final critical consideration is practicality. If there is no time for production or no resources to produce a medium, do not select it. The most expensive or time-consuming medium is not always the best (Clark and Clark, 1984).

A Model for Beginners

We recommend a simple approach that is consistent with other models but easier to use. This approach is shown in Figure 9.3, Media Selection Model for Beginners. It is important to understand why each step is essential to the process of media selection.

In the model, step 1 is to identify relevant learner characteristics: age, attention span, language ability, learning style, preferences, interests, etc. Learner characteristics may be physical or sociological. Each characteristic has implications for media selection. Psychological characteristics, such as ability, motivation, and learning style, should be used to determine the desired difficulty and appeal of the material. Physical characteristics, such as need for mobility, can influence the decision about which media will be most effective. Sociological characteristics, such as ability to work in groups, may have a bearing on whether a game or group work is appropriate. Learning style refers to traits that characterize how

Figure 9.3   Media Selection Model for Beginners

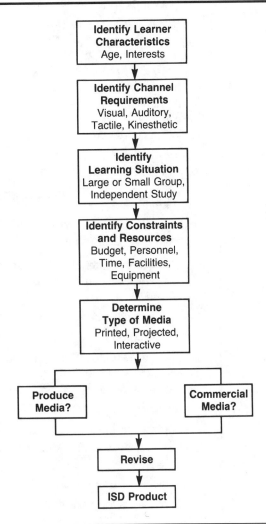

a learner prefers to learn. A student may find one perceptual channel more comfortable than another. Generally, we speak of tactile learners, visual learners, and auditory learners.

Step 2 is identify channel requirements. Channel means the perceptual modes needed for presentation, practice, and feedback. Perceptual mode requirements come from objectives and learning style. If the task is to discriminate visually, use the visual channel. If the learner prefers to learn visually, that is another reason for using the visual channel through a medium that offers pictures. (National Association of Secondary School Principals, 1982; Fleming and Levie, 1978).

Step 3 is identify the learning situation based on whether instruction will be large or small, group or independent study. A filmstrip may be effective in independent study, but not in large group presentation where group pacing is required (Kemp, 1985).

Step 4 is identify constraints and resources. Constraints are limitations or parameters that must be taken into account in the design specifications. Resources give you flexibility by allowing you to manipulate the project.

Step 5 is identify the media options appropriate for the learner characteristics, channel requirements, learning situation, and constraints.

Steps 6 through 8 require determining whether commercial materials are available in the chosen medium and, if so, whether they need revising. If not, you must determine what materials will be produced. The information yielded by steps 6 through 8 may lead you to choose another medium.

Step 9 requires completing the media selection process by incorporating the final media decisions in an ID product.

The following exercises help you identify factors that should influence media selection. The factors are useful only when you can connect them to media characteristics. The ability to do this comes from broad experience with using media, so an instructional designer should try to obtain such experience. A lengthy discussion of this topic, however, is beyond the scope of this book.

In summary, a media selection model provides a rationale for media selection; the rationale explains how a systematic process was followed to determine appropriate media. The connections between variables and media need to be made logically, and it is the systematic process the model provides that ensures the logic will be complete and consistent.

An Exercise in Inferring Learner Characteristics

Directions: In the space provided after each audience description, write at least two characteristics of the learners in that audience.

1. The twelve preschoolers at ABC Day Care Center range in age from three to five years. Each week they study two different letters from the alphabet. This week the letters are "l" and "u."

    Audience characteristics:

    Implications for media:

2. The director of the Westmont High School Marching Band is concerned about poorly executed routines. This week he will work with the band on more precision of movement.

    Audience characteristics:

    Implications for media:

3. The 10 sixth graders in Mrs. Rowe's gifted class are interested in studying how a bank works.

    Audience characteristics:

    Implications for media:

4. Some of the eleventh grade chemistry students who are starting a unit on the metric system have had difficulty in mathematics classes. They have no previous experience with the metric system.

Audience characteristics:

Implications for media:

5. Homebound elementary students are required to achieve the same objectives as other students. Their tutors have identified two areas where many of the homebound students have difficulty: math problems and phonics.

Audience characteristics:

Implications for media:

An Exercise in Identifying Channel Requirements

Directions: Below are six learning objectives. The channel requirements for instruction and for the student's response can be inferred from each objective. After the objective, write the implied channel requirements. The channel might be audio, visual, audiovisual, or other (tactile, kinesthetic, olfactory).

1. Given pictures of signs of the Zodiac, the student will identify each sign orally.

Instruction channel(s):

Response channel(s):

2. Given a standard transmission automobile, the student will use the clutch while operating the car.

Instruction channel(s):

Response channel(s):

3. Given the choice of classical or popular music, the student will listen to classical music.

Instruction channel(s):

Response channel(s):

4. Given an aquarium with fish, the student will orally identify five types of fish in the aquarium.

Instruction channel(s):

Response channel(s):

5. Given an outline of a human face, the child will locate and label parts of the face.

Instruction channel(s):

Response channel(s):

6. Given an egg, the student chef will separate the yolk from the white using the shell as a tool.

Instruction channel(s):

Response channel(s):

An Exercise in Identifying Learning Situations

Directions: Here are five situations in which one of the following is more desirable: large group, small group, or independent study. In the blank after the situation write which type of instruction is most appropriate—LG, SG, IS—and then give the reason why in the space provided.

1. An expert will be available as a guest speaker for one presentation in whatever format is desirable.

   Learning situation:

   Reason:

2. Students have done individual research on a topic and are now ready to share their findings and establish further directions for research.

   Learning situation:

   Reason:

3. Before students can practice in a field setting, they must build a base of knowledge and skills. An excellent textbook, a workbook, and demonstration videotapes are available.

   Learning situation:

   Reason:

4. Some students enter without prerequisite knowledge. But all students must achieve the same objectives in fifteen weeks.

   Learning situation:

   Reason:

5. The instructor feels it is important to discuss problems and issues related to the topic.

   Learning situation:

   Reason:

An Exercise in Writing a Rationale for Method/Media Selection

Directions: Here is an instructional problem. Use the Media Selection Model for Beginners in Figure 9.3 to write a rationale justifying your media recommendations. Your rationale should be in essay form.

A Spelling Problem

Goal: To improve students's spelling achievement.

Objective: To correctly differentiate to, too, two; their, they're; its, it's.

Learner Characteristics: Ungraded classroom of fourth and fifth graders ranging in age from eight to twelve years. Some have no understanding, some partial understanding, and some full understanding of topic.

Instructional Plan: Independent study.

Setting: Two large classrooms with moveable divider between them. Forty-eight students. Independent study and display areas are available. Desks are movable.

Resources: Four cassette tape players, Two Apple IIe computers, and duplicating facilities.

Schedule: Start study of this area in two weeks, then continue for two weeks.

Commercial Media

It is desirable to determine whether useful commercial materials are available. If you do decide to use commercial materials, be sure you follow any provisions of the copyright law that affect your use of them. This means you must obtain permission to include the materials or to include adapted materials in the final product. Do not worry about commercial materials used for in-class student projects. The copyright law permits this use.

Table 9.4, Selected Materials and Equipment Indexes, compares five of the most important indexes for non-print materials and equipment.

Table 9.4 Selected Materials and Equipment Indexes

Resources/Tools	Scope/Contents	Arrangement	Special Features/Comments
Educational Film/Video Locator: of the Consortium of University Film Centers and the R. R. Bowker Co.	Moving pictures and videotapes in education.	Subject, title, and audience level index; Title descriptions	Producer/distributor list; series index; subject headings and cross index to subject.
The Educational Software Selector. (T.E.S.S.)	Educational software for use on microcomputer equipment.	Subject	Index by product name; software suppliers.
The Equipment Directory of audio-visual computer video products.	Audiovisual, video, and computer equipment.	Classified equipment —company name —model name	An illustrated catalog; list of membership and dealers; software suppliers.
Media Resource Catalog: from the National Audio-visual Center.	Videotapes, films, and multimedia kits in slide/sound program.	Subject; title	U.S. Government produced or distributed media; about the Center's services.
Film & Video Finder. (NICEM)	Moving pictures and videotapes for education.	Subject; title	Introduction to new publication of the Center.
Index to Educational Slides. (NICEM)	Educational slides in twenty-six subjects.	Subject; title	Index to subject headings; directory of producers

Table 9.5 lists a few of the non-print materials and equipment indexes the designer will find useful.

THE PRODUCTION PROCESS

If you cannot adopt or adapt commercial materials, then you must arrange for the materials to be produced. Although it is unlikely you will produce the materials, you could be a member of the production team. Your best chance of being able to function effectively on that team is to understand the production process intimately. Every designer should have experience scripting, shooting, and editing in order to communicate with producers. To insure the integrity of the design, you need to monitor each stage of production to make sure that design guidelines are followed, that consistency is maintained from step to step, and that quality is evident.

The production process, which you initiate by contract and agreement, starts with conceptualizing by scripting and storyboarding. You may be involved creatively at this stage or you may be monitoring the work of others. In either case, it is important that you understand the process that leads to the visual (or audio) instructional material.

The process follows three steps if the end product is to be visual material. The first step is a treatment, then a script is based on the treatment, and finally a storyboard is based on the script. Each step becomes a more concrete plan for the final product.

Let's start with a treatment. A treatment is a one-to-two-page (usually less) description of how the material will be organized, the approach to be taken, and the content. Table 9.6,

Table 9.5   Non-print Materials and Equipment Indexes

1. *Audio Video Market Place: a multimedia guide*. (AVMP) (Annual; 1969–) New York, NY: R. R. Bowker Co. (Old title: *Audio Visual Market Place*).
2. *Educational Film/Video Locator: of the Consortium of University Film Centers and R. R. Bowker Co.* (Irregular; 1978–) New York, NY: R. R. Bowker Co. (Old title: *Educational Film Locator of the C.U.F.C.*)
3. *The Educational Software Selector*. (T.E.S.S.) (19??–1986) Southampton, NY: EPIE Institutes & Teachers College Press.
4. *The Equipment Director: of audio-visual computer and video products*. (Annual; 1954–) Fairfax, VA: International Communications Industries Association. (Old title: *Audio-Visual Equipment*)
5. *The Guide to Simulations/Games for Education & Training*. (1980) Newbury Park, CA: Sage.
6. *International Index to Multi-Media Information*. (Quarterly; 1970–). Pasadena, CA: Audio-Visual Associates. (Old title: *Film Review Index*)
7. *Landers Film Reviews*. (3 Quarterly with annual and quinquennial cumulations; 1956–) Escondido, CA: Landers Associates. (Old title: *Bertha Landers Film Reviews*).
8. *Library of Congress Catalogs: Audiovisual Materials*. (Annual; 1951–) Washington, D.C. Library of Congress. (Old titles: *Library of Congress Catalogs: Motion pictures and Filmstrips* then continued by *Films and Other Materials for Projection* as part of the National Union Catalog).
9. *Media Resource Catalog: from the National Audiovisual Center*. (Annual; 1969–) Capitol Heights, MD: National Audiovisual Center.
10. *Media Review Digest: The Only Complete Guide to Reviews of Non-Book Media*. (Annual; 1970–) Ann Arbor, MI: Pierian Press. (Old title: *Multi-Media Review Index*).
11. *The New York Times Film Reviews*. (1970–) New York, NY: The New York Times Book Co., Inc.
12. NICEM (National Information Center for Educational Media) Publications Los Angeles, CA: NICEM, University of Southern California. (1964–).
    A. *Film & Video Finder* (Annual; 1987–) Albuquerque, NM: Access Innovations. (A merger of the *Index to 16mm Educational Films* and the *Index to Educational Videotapes*).
    B. *Index to Educational Audio Tapes*. (Irregular)
    C. *Index to Educational Overhead Transparencies*. (Irregular)
    D. *Index to Educational Records*. (Irregular)
    E. *Index to Educational Slides*. (Irregular)
    F. *Index to 8mm Motion Cartridges*. (Irregular)
    G. *Index to Producers and Distributors*. (Annual; 1971–)
    H. *Index to 35mm Educational Filmstrips*. (Irregular)
    I. *NICEM Update of Nonbook Media*. (Quarterly in every other year; 1981–)
13. Universities/Colleges AV Center Catalogs
14. *Videodiscs for Education: A Directory*. (1988, Third Edition). St. Paul, MN: Minnesota Educational Computing Consortium.
15. *The Video Source Book*. (Annual; 1979–) Sycosset, NY: The National Video Clearinghouse, Inc.

Table 9.6   Example of a Treatment

Project Treatment
Recreational Parks and Our Township

After titles and a series of slides of signs at park entrances in neighboring townships, the narrator explains that the purpose of the presentation is to stimulate discussion on recreation planning in our township by presenting comparisons with similar townships.

The presentation will be organized as a series of visits to parks in neighboring townships. Facts about their recreation program, e.g., per capita expenditure, will be interspersed with the narration of their parks. The presentation will conclude with a history of our township's recreation planning and investment in parks. Graphics will be used at the end to summarize per capita investment and proportion of land. The presentation will conclude with text slides that stimulate open-ended discussion by posing questions.

Example of a Treatment, is a description of a sound slide presentation proposed for a township.

A treatment should describe the content of the visual presentation and the approach to that content. For example, a presentation can have a dramatic, humorous, factual, historical, or how-to treatment. The treatment should also specify any special aesthetic elements such as music or artwork or artwork style. You may wish to prepare for a treatment by preparing your storyline. How will your story be presented or your storylines interweave (Simonson & Volker, 1984)?

After a treatment is proposed and accepted, work can begin on a script. The script will make the idea even more specific by detailing the audio and visual material for each frame. At this point the visual material can be described in phrases, using abbreviations for technical terminology, rather than in sketches.

LS, MS, CU, and ES, for example, stand for long shot, medium shot, close-up, and establishing shot. Table 9.7, Example from a Script, was written for adults who have been ordered to undergo a Nuclear Magnetic Resonance (MRI) body or head scan to aid diagnosis of their medical problem. These people will range from grade school to college educated, will range in age from adolescent to geriatric, and for the most part will possess little knowledge of MRI (also called Nuclear Magnetic Resonance) technology. The goal of the slide presentation will be to educate these people about what it is they will undergo in order to make them as emotionally comfortable going into the procedure as possible.

The final step in the conceptualization process is a storyboard. The storyboard is a script translated into still pictures. Each shows a successive frame or segment of the proposed presentation. A storyboard can take many forms—thumbnail sketches on index cards, stick figures on a page with frames on one side and a column for narration on the other, or photographs, with comments below.

Whatever form it takes, the storyboard makes the visual part of the script more specific so that the producer knows the camera angles and distances and the graphics that will be required. From a storyboard a producer can prepare a shooting script in which all the shots at one location and one camera set-up are grouped. These shots can then be made out of order for greater efficiency. Table 9.8, Example of a Storyboard, illustrates one storyboard format.

Scripts and storyboards for interactive technologies such as videodisc are more complex. Table 9.9, Example of a Script/Storyboard Page for Interactive Video, illustrates this. In this case the script and storyboard are combined.

To take shortcuts with any of this treatment/script/storyboard process means to risk misunderstandings, greater costs, and less efficiency. Production often takes longer than design activities, and while time passes, original intent may be misinterpreted or forgotten. It is the designer's responsibility to see that specified objectives are met consistently in development. Production changes may negatively affect the project. Aesthetic changes, for example, must be consistent with instructional intent. Suppose you have approved a storyboard for a slide-tape presentation on "What Are Non-Print Materials?" The storyboard shows a character looking at pictures on a screen. In an attempt to add interest the artist pictures voluptuous women on the screen. The design has been compromised; the materials need to be exemplars without stereotypes, because one criterion for media selection is that the medium should not reinforce stereotypes.

Aesthetic changes are often improvements, but they should be made only for instructional reasons or if consistent with instructional reasons. An audiovisual producer should not be expected to know the goals of instructional analysis in depth. His job is to see that the script is shot. The designer's job is to oversee script changes or interpretations.

An Exercise in Writing a Treatment and Script

You have been asked to prepare a treatment and script on a topic related to nutrition. Prepare a treatment of one page or less and then develop a ten-frame script based on part of that treatment.

Table 9.7 Example of a Script

Audio	Getting an MRI Scan	Visual (Slides)
Flute music over		
Narrator: Your doctor has scheduled you for magnetic resonance imaging, or MRI. We would like you to feel as comfortable as possible during the procedure, so we have put together this program on MRI for your information.		Front of MRI Center with sign as seen from driveway
Flute music down		
MRI, also called NMR, for "nuclear magnetic resonance," is used as a diagnostic tool by your physician. This technology is something like X-rays in that it produces pictures, or IMAGES, of the inside of the body. However, these images are more informative than regular X-rays. In addition, the MRI procedure exposes you to NO radiation. In fact, in extensive research with animals and in clinical trials with human beings, MRI has been shown to be a virtually harmless procedure.		Several shots of different MRI scans: head/abd/chest/spine "NO RADIATION" slide
MRI will allow your doctor to see more clearly the difference between healthy and diseased tissue, and he will thus be able to develop the most appropriate treatment plan for you.		Physician looking at scan
How does magnetic resonance imaging work? Your body is made up of millions of atoms. Under normal conditions, the protons in these atoms spin randomly. But when the strong magnetic fields of the MRI scanner are passed through your body, these protons line up in the field's direction.		Figure 1 Figure 2
Then the radio wave is transmitted to the magnetic field. This causes the protons to change direction 90° and spin together.		Figure 3
When the radio waves are turned off, the protons return to the alignment they had in the magnetic field. During this realignment, they give off a signal that is measured by a receiver antenna. This antenna is connected to a computer that compiles the information and produces an image.		Figure 4
Flute music over		
Narrator: When you come to the MRI Institute for your scan, you should plan to spend 2 to 3 hours with us.		Close-up of MRI Center entranceway with patient coming in.
First, you will be asked to complete some medical insurance information.		
Then a technician or a nurse will question you about your medical history and will answer any questions you might have.		Tech and patient talking (MS)
Flute music down		
You will not be able to have an MRI scan if any of the following applies to you: if you have a cardiac pacemaker in place if you have had an operation for aneurysm of the brain if you have any metal implants or shrapnel anywhere in your body if you are in the first trimester of pregnancy if you weigh over three hundred pounds		Text slide of list
If you have extreme claustrophobia, please tell the technician before the start of the test. You will be administered a mild tranquilizer to help you cope with the confined quarters of the scanning tube.		Tech giving patient tranquilizer

Table 9.8   Example of a Storyboard

Hold the hamster, Fiona. (MS)	I have to clean the cage. (MS)	It smells! (MS)
You better not do it here, Jody (LS)	Take it to the laundry, Jody (LS)	OK. (MS)
(LS—Taking lid off)	(LS—Dumping drawer in bag)	(LS—Dump bottom of box)
(CU—putting chips in cage)	You can put the hamster back, Fiona. (LS)	You forgot the water, Jody. (CU)

An Exercise in Developing a "How To" Storyboard

Create a storyboard on "how to" do something. Break the process into understandable steps and use stick figures or thumbnail sketches in the frames. Make some narration notes under each frame. Be sure to indicate camera distance and angle in each frame. Use this form.

Table 9.9   Example of a Script/Storyboard for Interactive Video

FUNCTION KEY	INSTRUCTIONAL UNIT	TYPE	CONDITION	AUDIO NARRATION
NEXT BACK SHIFT BACK HELP AUTO-ADV		QUESTION INDEX PAGE REMEDIATION HELP PAGE REINFORCEMENT TESTING OBJECTIVE LESSON OTHER Title		☐ Track 1 ☐ Track 2

COURSE   MODULE/FILE   INST'L UNIT   VIDEODISC   TO   RAME#   D 3.112

COMPUTER DISPLAY

VIDEODISC DISPLAY

☐ MOTION   ☐ CONCEPTUALLY
☐ STILL   LINKED TO
☐ LOCATION
☐ STUDIO
☐ 16mm
☐ 35mm
☐ GRAPHIC
☐ VIDEOGRAPHIC
☐ OTHER

After *The Videodisc Book* by R. Daynes and B. Butler, 1984, NY: John Wiley & Sons, Inc. Copyright 1984 by John Wiley & Sons, Inc. Reprinted by permission.

FROM THE READING

Define the following terms.

Methods   Media Indexes

Media   Treatment

Newer Technologies   Storyboard

Learner Characteristics   Script

Task Characteristics

ISSUES FOR DISCUSSION

1. How can the designer clarify roles in relation to method/media decisions?
2. Is there one factor that is more critical than others in media selection?
3. To what extent is it important for an instructional designer to be familiar with production processes?
4. How can one make a rationale for media selection?
5. How and why should the designer monitor the production process?

REFERENCES

Alessi, S. M., & Trollip, S. R. (1985). *Computer-based instruction: Materials and development.* Englewood Cliffs, NJ: Prentice-Hall.

Ambron, S., & Hooper, K. (1988). *Interactive media.* Redmond, WA: Microsoft Press.

Ausubel, D. P. (1968). *Educational psychology: A cognitive view.* NY: Holt, Rinehart & Winston.

Clark, R. C., & Clark, R. E. (1984). Instructional media vs. instructional methods. *National Society for Performance and Instruction Journal, 23,* 1–3.

Daynes, R., & Butler, B. (1984). *The Videodisc Book.* NY: John Wiley.

Fleming, M., & Levie, W. H. (1978). *Instructional message design.* Englewood Cliffs, NJ: Educational Technology Publications.

Gerlach, V. S., & Ely, D. P. (1980). *Teaching and media: A systematic approach.* Englewood Cliffs, NJ: Prentice-Hall.

Gross, L. S. (1986). *The new television technologies.* Dubuque, IA: Wm C. Brown.

Heinich, R., Molenda, M., & Russell, J. D. (1985). *Instructional media and the new technologies in education.* NY: John Wiley & Sons.

Higgins, N., & Reiser, R. A. (1985). Selecting media for instruction: An exploratory study. *Journal of Instructional Development, 8*(2), 6–9.

Jonassen, D. H. (1988). *Instructional designs for microcomputer software.* NJ: Lawrence Erlbaum Associates.

Joyce, B., & Weil, M. (1980). *Models of teaching* (2d ed.). Englewood Cliffs, NJ: Prentice-Hall.

Kemp, J. (1985). *The instructional design process.* NY: Harper & Row.

Laird, D. (1985). *Approaches to training and development.* NY: Addison-Wesley.

National Association of Secondary School Principals. (1982). *Student learning styles and brain behavior, 16,* Reston, VA: NASSP.

Reiser, R. A., & Gagné, R. M. (1983). *Selecting media for instruction.* Englewood Cliffs, NJ: Educational Technology Publications.

Salomon, G. (1976). A cognitive approach to media. *Educational Technology, 16,* 25–28.

Salomon, G. (1979). *Interaction of media, cognition and learning.* San Francisco, CA: Jossey Bass.

Seels, B., & Kanyarusoke, C. (1983). *Introduction to educational communications.* Pittsburgh, PA: External Studies Program, University of Pittsburgh.

Simonson, M. R., & Volker, R. P. (1984). *Media planning and production.* Columbus, OH: Merrill Publishing.

Tosti, D., & Ball, J. (1969). A behavioral approach to instructional design and media selection. *Audiovisual Communication, 11,* 5–27.

Chapter Ten
Evaluation

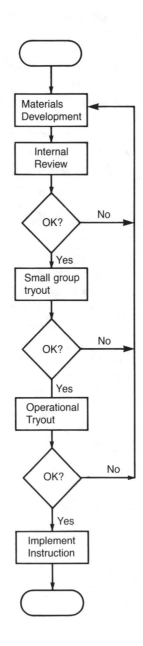

Objectives	■ Given descriptions of instructional design projects, state which experts should review the materials and at what stage they should do the review.

Objectives   ■ Given descriptions of instructional design projects, state which experts should review the materials and at what stage they should do the review.

■ Given examples of how designers collected information during small-group tryouts, identify the one who used the better method.

■ Given descriptions of individual tryouts, select one that demonstrates a better application of the tryout guidelines presented in this chapter.

■ Given the results from a formative evaluation, identify acquisition, retention, and transfer failures.

■ Given an instructional design project, sequence the steps in the formative evaluation and specify the resources and procedures you would use.

■ Given an example of a formative evaluation plan, evaluate its adequacy.

Overview   One of the tenets of a systems approach to instructional design is that the instruction is submitted to an evaluation during its development. That is, the instruction is tried and revised until objectives are met. The term "formative evaluation" was coined by Michael Scriven (1967) to describe the kind of evaluation performed during the developmental or "formative" stage of the instructional design process. Formative evaluation provides feedback that is used for improvement of the product being developed.

Scriven uses the term "summative" for the evaluation that is carried out after the instructional design process is completed. Summative evaluation is aimed at obtaining evidence about the "summed" effects of the instruction. The effects of the new instruction are compared with instruction currently in place. Findings from a summative evaluation might be used by a school to determine whether to adopt a new curriculum package or to stick with what they have. Summative evaluation is seldom carried out by the designers responsible for developing the original instruction and is not an integral part of our systems model.

Formative evaluation typically involves three phases (Dick, 1977). A description of them follows.

Internal Review Phase. The instructional designer enlists the assistance of other instructional designers or a supervisor, SMEs, sponsors, and other knowledgeable people who review the instruction and provide comments and criticism. The internal review may be done by one person or a team. Internal reviews should start with the problem definition and task analysis phases of the process and continue until the final product is turned over to the organization responsible for accepting and implementing the program.

Tutorial and Small-group Tryout Phase. The materials are tried out on naive learners to determine to what extent the instructional objectives are met. The designer responsible for developing the instruction administers the materials and collects information about where the instruction worked and where it did not. When instruction fails, the designer questions students to obtain as much evidence as possible about why the material failed; this evidence is the basis for revision.

Operational Tryout. The materials are tried out under conditions that simulate those of the actual instructional environment. The operational tryout provides an opportunity to work out administrative, equipment, facility, or any other implementation problems.

Formative evaluation techniques and procedures have been used for nearly thirty years and are included in nearly every systems model, yet there is little research on the topic. Dick (1980) cites as barriers to research the lack of funding, the complex problems associated with conducting research on a component of the systems approach to instructional design, the difficulty in obtaining a sufficient pool of equally skilled designers available to work on the same instruction in a comparative research study, and the fact that in large organizations where systematic design is taking place, there is no time for or interest in such research.

Study Questions

1. What is the purpose of formative evaluation?

2. What are the steps in the formative evaluation process?

3. How should each step in the tryout be conducted?

4. What kind of evidence is gathered during each step of a formative evaluation?

5. What evidence is symptomatic of specific learning failures?

INTERNAL REVIEWS

Internal reviews can serve two functions; they provide an opportunity to spot and correct technical inadequacies and flaws early, and they serve as a mechanism for gaining acceptance of and commitment to the new materials.

Geis (1987) suggests a number of different experts who might be involved in an internal review. Table 10.1 summarizes the areas of expertise and the functions performed. Internal reviews should include potential users and sponsors who have a stake in the outcome of the project as well as people who, because they have no involvement in the specific program, provide a disinterested review. They should also be concise and constructive critics.

Depending on when the particular area of expertise is needed, expert reviews may occur at any point in the instructional design process. Sponsors and SMEs, for example, may be involved in every stage of the process, while others, such as media consultants, will be brought in during the design and development phases only.

Different types of reviewers provide different types of information. It is often helpful to structure the review to focus the reviewer on what it is you want evaluated. Geis suggests at least three questions for reviewers of draft materials:

1. Where does something appear to need fixing?

2. What appears to be the cause of the problem?

3. What might be done about it?

Product review guidelines from an instructional design viewpoint have been developed by Merrill and his associates (1979) for the Navy Personnel Research and Development Center (NPRDC). The Instructional Strategy Diagnostic Profile was designed to evaluate cognitive and psychomotor instructional materials for consistency and adequacy. (Consistency refers to the correspondence of the objectives, test items, and instructional presentation; adequacy means how well the instructional presentation communicates the information to be learned.) Subsequently, the NPRDC performed extensive revision and field testing, and the procedures evolved into what the Center calls the Instructional Quality Inventory.

Research results on the relationship of test performance to ratings are mixed. Choi, Merrill, Callahan, Hawkins, and Norton (1979) reported no relationship between the In-

Table 10.1.   Expert Reviewers and the Functions Served

Subject Matter Expert	A master performer who supplies the content for instruction. SMEs attend to questions of accuracy, emphasis, timeliness. They indicate whether the knowledge and skills to be taught are the ones used on the job and whether the examples are representative. They are most critical in the analysis and development phases.
Instructional Designers	Peers or supervisors who evaluate the prototype material for formal features (e.g., Is there an introduction?) and functional features (e.g., Is there adequate opportunity for practice?)
Media Specialists	Graphic artists and specialists in audiovisual presentation who can comment on the physical features of the message design (e.g., layout, color, clarity of display, and aesthetic elements).
Audience Specialists	Instructors or teachers experienced with teaching the content to the intended audience can comment on suitability of the chosen strategy for the target audience. Additionally, materials that are to be instructor-delivered can be reviewed for acceptability, practicality, ease of use, and likelihood of adoption by teachers.
Gatekeepers	Representatives of the community or organization regarding acceptability on social, ethical, legal, and moral grounds. In educational settings, they might include parents, religious leaders, ethnic leaders; in work settings, they would include decision makers and/or those responsible for insuring adherence to policy. Input would come during the analysis, design, and development phases.
Sponsor	The sponsor reviews often serve all of the functions listed in this table. In addition, sponsor review may be directed toward matters of cost, implementation, and deadlines.
Former Students	Those who have already taken the course in another form may provide special insights about the new version, having had to learn roughly the same content in another environment.

After "Formative Evaluation: Developmental Testing and Expert Review" by G. L. Geis, 1987, *National Society for Performance and Instruction Journal, 26*(4), pp. 1–8. Copyright 1987 by NSPI. Adapted by permission.

structional Strategy Diagnostic Profile and ratings of materials on complex content (college chemistry texts). But Montague, Ellis, and Wulfeck (1983) found significant differences in favor of the Instructional Quality Index on job-relevant instruction for Navy radio operators. It appears that the index is less effective when complex subject matter is the object of revision rather than simpler tasks such as those performed by the radio operators.

Montague, Ellis and Wulfeck point out that the concepts underlying the index are sound. Also, they note that it is more cost effective for identifying deficiencies than existing formative evaluation methods, although they do not recommend the inventory be used in lieu of an actual tryout.

Even though the results of internal reviews do not provide conclusive proof of the adequacy of the instructional system, at least they identify some of the problem areas and suggest where improvements may be made.

An Exercise Designed to Identify Who Should Conduct an Internal Review and When

Directions: Below are descriptions of instructional design projects. For each project name an expert who should review the materials and the step in the instructional systems design process where the review should take place.

Steps: Analysis, Design, Development, Evaluation, Implementation.

1. Project: Develop a slide-tape to explain to parents and employees the school board's plans for asbestos removal from the high school.

2. Project: Revise an instructor-delivered course on the documentation requirements for commercial loans. Students are new employees in the commercial loan departments of banks.

3. Project: Develop a videotape for elementary school children on safe street-crossing behavior. The videotape will employ a nationally known host of a children's television show.

4. Develop a two-hour course for emergency medical technicians on how to deal with the emotional trauma of parents whose infant dies as a result of sudden infant death syndrome (SIDS). The sponsor is the U. S. Department of Health and Human Services. The training is mandated under a law enacted as a result of the efforts of parents who have experienced SIDS.

TUTORIAL TRYOUTS

At the beginning of tryouts students individually go through the materials in the presence of the instructional designer. After a handful of students have worked through the materials, the instruction is revised and an additional group of two to five students work through the revised material. Revisions are seldom made on the basis of one student's idiosyncratic problems. Instead, the instructional designer looks for trouble spots and errors that consistently crop up. The tryout-and-revision cycle continues as long as necessary to achieve the standard specified in the objectives.

Sources of Feedback. The instructional designer determines the adequacy of the instruction through feedback obtained from three sources:

1. Diagnostic tests. Pretests identify the entering behavior. Posttests assess learning due to instruction. Analysis of the posttest will identify errors and help interpret learner difficulties.

2. Student performance during learning. As students work through each exercise or task, the instructional designer notes difficulties and probes for the source of any failure.

3. Student comments. After students complete the posttest, reactions to the instructions and suggestions for improvement are obtained.

Student Sample. Students participating in the tryouts should fall within the range of prerequisite abilities defined as the entry-level behavior of the target audience. Research using ninth graders as tryout subjects for math materials suggests that different aptitude groups in the one-to-one stage of formative evaluation provide different types of feedback (Wager, 1983). High-aptitude students can help analyze weak spots in the instruction and provide information about the strategies they use to overcome them. Low-aptitude students are able to identify more basic problems, but are unable to suggest revisions. Groups with mixed aptitudes provide a greater variety of feedback than either high- or low-aptitude groups. Wager reports that materials revised on the basis of the mixed aptitude group produced higher posttest scores and were more favorably received than materials revised solely on the basis of either high- or low-aptitude students.

Media Requirements. The medium used during the tryout will depend on what is available and economically feasible. One of the purposes of the tryout is to uncover problems before expensive production has begun. Therefore, unless the medium of choice can be inexpensively produced in a rough version, the tryout uses storyboards, scripts, drawings, or mock-ups of the instructional materials. Thiagarajan (1978) suggests that tryouts of complex multimedia instruction be done in successive stages. For example, if the finished product is to be a videotape, formative evaluation might begin with a storyboard, then use a "rough cut" of the video before final editing.

Tryout Practices. Lowe, Thurston, and Brown's (1983) guidelines for conducting one-to-one tryouts are based on their experience developing vocational technology courses for students in Saudi Arabia.

- Conduct the tryout early in the development process to allow designers time to improve materials while still in development, thereby saving time and money.

- Put the student at ease by explaining that it is the instructional system and not the student that is being evaluated. Make the student feel that he or she is a part of the development team.

- Prepare for the tryout in advance by reviewing all material and setting up any equipment or media before the student arrives.

- Select a quiet place with no distractions for the tryout.

- Use a checklist to ensure that all necessary materials are available and procedures are correctly followed.

- Sit close enough to the student to see what he or she is working on, but not so close as to crowd the student.

- Do not help answer questions until the student has sought the answers in the materials. Question the student to locate the difficulty only when he or she is frustrated by a problem.

An Exercise Designed to Help You Recognize Appropriate and Inappropriate Tryout Practices

Directions: Below are descriptions of an instructional designer's behavior during a small-group tryout. Indicate whether the designer's behavior is correct or incorrect. If incorrect, state what the designer should have done.

1. Materials being tried out: Self-instructional slide-tape art appreciation course. Target audience is ninth graders.

   Instructional designer set up the equipment before a ninth grader arrived for the tryout. The designer had already determined that the tryout subject's aptitude was average. When the tryout began, the designer gave the directions on what to do and left the student alone to work.

   _____ Correct?   _____ Incorrect?

   Explain your answer.

2. Materials being tried out: Self-instructional science materials for seventh grade.

   Instructional designer asks a seventh grade teacher to provide subjects for the tryout. The teacher, wanting to make a good impression, sends the three best pupils.

   _____ Correct?   _____ Incorrect?

   Explain your answer.

3. Material being tried out: Course to teach bank employees which forms are required to document commercial loans.

   A bank employee agrees to try out the material. The instructional designer explains to the employee that assistance is needed to find out how well the materials work. The designer points out that on the basis of the employee's comments, the materials will be revised, and that thereby the employee will contribute to the effectiveness of the training eventually to be offered to other bank workers. The designer leads the bank employee through the materials, noting difficulties and discussing possible improvements. They work as a team throughout the tryout.

_____ Correct?   _____ Incorrect?

Explain your answer.

4. Materials being tried out: Management training presented on videodisc.

    The scriptwriter and instructional designer try out the materials in storyboard form on typical management trainees.

    _____ Correct?   _____ Incorrect?

    Explain your answer.

5. Materials being tried out: Correspondence course for soldiers in the reserves who are being trained to do maintenance and repair radios.

    Instructional designer sends out draft materials to several reserve units after selecting subjects based on their aptitude test scores. A person assigned to each unit will administer the materials and mail them back to the designer.

    _____ Correct?   _____ Incorrect?

    Explain your answer.

Revision. Stolovitch (1982) compares twelve systems models, all of which prescribe formative evaluation. None of them, however, is among the models he cites that prescribe specific revisions to counteract learning failures. He also points out that fewer than one percent of the instructional materials in the U.S. market and in Canadian school systems have undergone student testing.

Typically the revision step in a systems approach is largely a process that draws on the designer's knowledge of the principles of learning. The designer uses posttest information as well as other subjective and objective data. If the materials have been subjected to an internal review and are the product of an experienced designer, decisions about how to revise them are usually straight forward. For a skilled and experienced designer, usually the "fix" is obvious. Practice and feedback requirements may be insufficient, or step size may be too large, and so on. That is, the materials must be broken down into smaller parts with additional guidance and practice added. But with less able designers or with complex subject matter, a number of tryouts may be necessary before learner outcomes are affected.

Under a contract with the U.S. Air Force, Glasgow (1974) developed guidelines for translating tryout data to revisions. Three types of student failures are identified:

Failure in retention. The student correctly performed during learning, but on the posttest failed to remember what he had learned.

Failure in transfer. The student correctly performed during training, but on a posttest failed to apply what he had learned to a similar situation not encountered in training.

Failure in acquisition. The student failed to learn the material during instruction and demonstrated that failure by errors during training and on the corresponding posttest items.

Diagnostic checks and revision treatments are spelled out for conditions that create difficulty for learners. These conditions should have been identified first by the task and instructional analysis steps. The failure occurs either because the initial analysis was deficient or the conditions were not adequately addressed during the design step. These learning difficulties include the following:

Parts of task are complex

Interference from previous learning

Many steps in procedure

Large number of inputs/outputs

Similarity of inputs/outputs

Dissimilarity of inputs/outputs

Large number of attributes for each input/output

Revisions are specified for these learning difficulties as they apply to motor skills, verbal associations, verbal chains, discriminations, concepts, rule-using, and problem-solving. Although the guidelines have been a part of an official Air Force document (AFP 50-58. July 15, 1978) for many years, they have never been formally tested and their usefulness is unknown.

An Exercise Designed to Help you Distinguish among Acquisition, Retention, and Transfer Failures

Directions: Indicate whether the learning problems described below are failures in acquisition, retention, or transfer.

_____ 1. On an exercise, a student fails to select the correct form to use for a loan guarantee. She makes the same mistake on a test.

_____ 2. On an exercise, a student selects the correct form to use for a loan guarantee, but misses the item on a test.

_____ 3. On an exercise, a student selects the correct form to use when the guarantor is a spouse. On the test, when asked to select a form to use when the guarantor is a corporation, the student selects the wrong form.

_____ 4. A student is learning to use a computerized program to calculate statistics. The student is learning to select the correct statistical procedure to use given a particular request for analysis. On an exercise, the student uses the correct procedure for entering the test score on a spelling test to obtain descriptive statistics. On a test, the student is given weather data for several cities and is asked what procedures to follow to obtain descriptive statistics. The student doesn't know the answer.

_____ 5. A student photographer is learning to develop black and white film. There are many steps in the procedure that must be performed exactly right. The instructor works with the student until he or she can do all of the steps correctly. The instructor schedules a test for the following week. On the test, the student mixes the chemicals incorrectly.

Probably the more comprehensive set of procedures for diagnosis and revision was developed by Gropper (1975). The key feature of his revision model is that it looks for retention, transfer, and acquisition failures in the same skills that task analysis had identified earlier. Analysis of student and program failures serves as the basis for prescriptions for systematic revision strategies. The model's major drawback is its complexity; in order to apply it, experienced designers must spend considerable time learning to use it.

In light of this complexity, Dupont and Stolovich (1983) developed their own revision model based on Gropper's work. Their purpose was to develop a model that incorporates Gropper's theory of revision, but assists designers in revision tasks without increasing the complexity of the tasks and the time required to do them. They tested the revision model on a manipulative test and a written test that measured students' ability to use an SLR 35mm camera.

Although the model did not produce superior student attainment of objectives compared to materials revised without its application, it should be noted that when the instructional materials were tried out initially, they produced relatively high results. Thus there was little room for improvement due to revision. Also, the learning task was relatively simple; when failures occurred they may have been easy to diagnose and fix. Whether the model would have produced different results with more complex learning tasks is unknown.

An interesting result of the study was that designers with different amounts of experience in formative evaluation produced revisions of about equal effectiveness. Users of the model reported they found it quicker for locating weaknesses in the original material and presenting relevant revisions to improve its effectiveness. Thus, even though there were no significant differences among any of the revisions, the results suggest that the model may have positive benefits for less experienced designers.

Small-group Tryout

Small-group tryout provides an opportunity to obtain feedback about how well the course achieves the learning objectives as well as duration of the instruction and instructor preparation requirements. The same issues applicable to tutorial tryouts are applicable to small-group tryouts.

Duration. Each learning situation fits into a larger context with schedules. By their nature, individual tryouts will not give you good estimates on the time to complete the program. Small-group tryouts consisting of eight to ten students are useful for estimating the duration of the instruction. For individualized instruction, the median completion time is usually calculated for each unit of instruction. In group-paced instruction, everyone moves at the same pace; therefore the instructor's task during the tryout is to determine whether the lessons can be contained within the time limits needed to meet the learning requirements of most members of the group and the practical time constraints of the organization offering the instruction.

Instructor Preparation. If instructional designers conduct the instruction themselves, they will learn a great deal from the instructor's point of view about problems with using the materials. Lessons learned from the tryout will have implications for the instructor's guides, lesson plans, and other materials and equipment used to prepare for and conduct the instruction. Findings will also influence the degree and scope of formal training necessary to prepare instructors to conduct the training.

A designer who lacks subject matter expertise required by instructor tasks should work closely with the instructor, collecting information to detect strengths and weaknesses in the materials and procedures required of the instructor.

An Exercise Designed to Help you Understand the Small-Group Tryout Process

Directions: Following are descriptions of how instructional designers approach the same problem in a small-group tryout. Select the one who is likely to obtain information from the tryout. Explain your choice.

1. Tryout of self-instructional text materials.

    _____ Designer A. The designer collected time data at the start and end of each day. At the end of the tryout, the designer calculated the range and median completion time for the course.

_____ Designer B. The designer collected time data for each module for each student, then calculated the range and median completion time for each module.

Explain your answer.

2. Tryout of instructor-led materials of a three-day workshop requiring the instructor to lead discussion groups on highly technical matters. The instructor for the small group tryout is the SME who has been working with the designer all along.

_____ Designer A. The designer constructs a checklist of issues he wants feedback on. At lunch and at the close of the business day, the designer and the SME/instructor review the events of the day against the checklist.

_____ Designer B. The designer constructs a checklist of issues that require feedback and asks the SME/instructor to complete it for each course segment. Because of the working relationship established during the course's development, the SME and the designer schedule a debriefing at the end of the course.

Explain your answer.

OPERATIONAL TRYOUT

In operational tryouts, the instruction is evaluated as an integral part of the environment where it will eventually reside, and it is delivered by the instructors and administrators who ultimately will be responsible for it. In addition to providing an opportunity to work out administrative, equipment, facility, or any other implementation problems, the operational tryout ascertains students's attitudes toward the course.

Satisfaction with the training is important. Although there is not always a direct connection between high satisfaction and learning effectiveness, as a rule satisfied participants will help ensure the success of a program. Some activities essential to learning may be difficult or tedious and therefore distasteful to the students. But a program that does not satisfy its students will probably not continue in business for long.

A standard approach to assess student satisfaction calls for having students use questionnaires to evaluate the environment, presenters, materials, length, and organization of the program. The survey may be done at the end of training or after some time has elapsed. These indices are disparagingly referred to as "smile" or "happiness" scales because of their dubious value.

Schwier (1982) discusses the design and development of student evaluation instruments and issues and variables surrounding them. He cites four uses in a developmental context: (1) As a placebo when student data are gathered but ignored, (2) as an ice breaker where the designer collects satisfaction data in response to client's concerns, (3) as a product appraisal where information about the difficulty, sequence, entertainment value, and instructional approach are used to provide insights to problems overlooked by designers, and (4) as an instructional appraisal where evaluations are used to identify perceived weaknesses and strengths of the instructional staff.

A number of important issues affect student evaluation outcomes. They include the reliability and validity of the instruments and intervening variables that influence students' acceptance of the course. Variables include class size, whether the instruction is compulsory or not, personality of the presenter, and the students's actual or anticipated grade. Although Schwier points out the difficulties of developing effective scales as well as the pitfalls of using them, Schwier concludes that student evaluations judiciously used and carefully constructed can contribute to assessing an instructional package.

Debriefing is another way to assess student satisfaction. A debriefing is a discussion—sometimes with an individual but usually with a group—about the activities just experienced. A debriefing session provides an opportunity to talk about emotions, such as frustration. A discussion or debriefing leader asks questions about emotions and about what happened, what was learned, and the relevancy of what was learned. Notes are taken on participants's responses. The debriefing approach is always used with simulation/gaming activities) (Heinich, Molenda, & Russell, 1982, 304–305).

Another approach to improving instruction on the basis of student comments is the evaluation interview, which is a form of debriefing. The U.S. Department of Labor's Employment Standard Administration (ESA) has pioneered a mechanism for gathering formative evaluation data through group interviews. The mechanism allows the instructor to improve an ongoing course and collect data for future revisions. The approach employs evaluation meetings and works best for workshops and training sessions that last longer than two days. Although no formal evaluation of the approach is known, it has been used by ESA trainers for more than ten years and by other organizations in modified forms (Stevenson, 1980; Pearlstein, 1988).

Meetings generally last thirty minutes and are attended by the instructor and representatives selected by the course participants. Evaluation meetings are held daily to determine how the course is going and to air issues that if allowed to go unvented might interfere with the course. Topics may include pace, problems with materials, problems with exercises or group activities, and problems with the instructors. If students are reluctant to reveal their real concerns, the instructor will have to probe—and be willing to accept and respond to negative comments.

Meetings are most effective if feedback will make a difference immediately. A meeting held at the end of the day should result in a change the next day. The instructor must be willing to follow through in the next session on any commitments, or students will feel that comments they make at the meetings are not taken seriously. On the other hand, changes that violate learning principles and harm the effectiveness of the course should not be made. A suggestion that cannot be acted upon can be handled by explaining that the basic course design is founded on principles of learning that are not subject to change. In other words, although learning is a cooperative venture, don't be coerced into altering the nature of the course.

An Exercise Designed to Help you Define and Sequence the Steps in Formative Evaluation

Directions: From your own experience, select an instructional design problem or materials used in a learning environment. Briefly describe them and prepare a plan for a formative evaluation. Your plan must include individual, small-group, and operational tryouts. For each tryout, specify the subjects, tryout environment, tryout procedures, and data collected.

An Exercise Designed to Help you Evaluate Plans for Formative Evaluation

Directions: Exchange evaluation plans from the previous exercise with another student and evaluate each other's plans. First construct a checklist against which you will evaluate the plan. Then hold a feedback meeting to discuss each other's evaluations.

FROM THE READING

Define the following terms.

Acquisition	Gatekeepers
Audience Specialists	Internal Review
Formative Evaluation	Operation Tryout

Retention   Summative Evaluation

Small-group Tryout   Transfer

ISSUES FOR DISCUSSION

1. Assume you have limited resources for developing instructional materials. Would you consider altering or eliminating any of the steps in the formative evaluation process discussed in this chapter? Defend your decision.

2. Once a course has been implemented it must be monitored continually to ensure that objectives are being achieved. Consider a course that you are familiar with. What factors affect how well it works on a continuing basis? How can changes that adversely affect the instruction be detected?

REFERENCES

Choi, S., Merrill, D. M., Callahan, E., Hawkins, R. T., & Norton, R. F. (1979). The relationship of test performance to ISDP rating in organic chemistry texts. *Journal of Instructional Development, 3*(1), 16–25.

Department of the Air Force. (1978). *Handbook for designers of instructional systems: Vol. IV, planning, developing, and validating instruction.* AFP 50-58.

Dick, W. (1977). Formative evaluation. In L. J. Briggs (Ed.), *Instructional design: Principles and applications.* Englewood Cliffs, NJ: Educational Technology Publications.

Dick, W. (1980). Formative evaluation in instructional development. *Journal of Instructional Development, 3*(3), 3–6.

Dupont, D., & Stolovitch, H. D. (1983). The effects of a systematic revision model on revisers in terms of student outcomes. *National Society for Performance and Instruction Journal, 22,* 33–37.

Geis, G. L. (1987). Formative evaluation: Developmental testing and expert review. *National Society for Performance and Instruction Journal, 26*(4), 1–8.

Glasgow, Z. (1974). Planning, developing and validating the instruction. In *Handbook for developing instructional systems: Vol. VI.* Contract No. F331615-72-C1363. USAF Human Resources Laboratory, Wright-Patterson AFB, Ohio. Butler, PA: Applied Science Associates.

Gropper, G. L. (1975). *Diagnosis and revision in the development of instructional materials.* Englewood Cliffs, NJ: Educational Technology Publications.

Heinich, R., Molenda, M., & Russell, J. D. (1982). *Instructional media and the new technologies of instruction.* NY: John Wiley & Sons.

Lowe, A. J., Thurston, W. I., & Brown, S. B. (1983). Clinical approach to formative evaluation. *National Society for Performance and Instruction Journal, 22*(5), 8–10.

Merrill, M. D., Reigeluth, C. M., & Faust, G. W. The instructional quality profile: A curriculum evaluation and design tool. In H. F. O'Neil, Jr. (Ed.), *Procedures for instructional system development.* NY: Academic Press.

Montague, W. E., Ellis, J. A., & Wulfeck, W. H. (1983). Instructional quality inventory. *National Society for Performance and Instruction Journal, 22*(5), 11–14.

Pearlstein, G. (1988). Gathering formative evaluation data daily. *National Society for Performance and Instruction Journal, 27,* 49–50.

Schwier, R. A. (1982). Design and use of student evaluation instruments in instructional development. *Journal of Instructional Development, 5*(4), 28–34.

Scriven, M. (1967). The methodology of evaluation (AERA Monograph series on curriculum evaluation, No. 1). Chicago IL: Rand McNally.

Stolovitch, H. D. (1982). Applications of the intermediate technology of learner verification and revision (LVR) for adapting international instructional resources to meet local needs. *National Society for Performance and Instruction Journal, 21,* 16–22.

Stevenson, G. (1980, May). Evaluating training daily. *Training and Development Journal,* pp. 120–22.

Thiagarajan, S. (1978). Instructional product verification and revision: 20 questions and 200 speculations. *Educational Communication and Technology Journal, 26,* 133–141.

Wager, J. C. (1983). One-to-one and small group formative evaluation: An examination of two basic formative evaluation procedures. *National Society for Performance and Instruction Journal, 22*(5), 5–7.

Chapter Eleven

The Team Approach

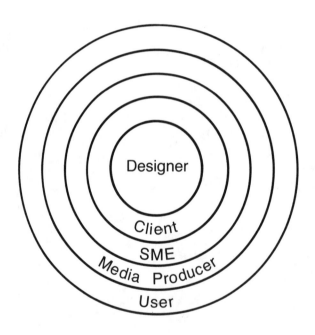

Objectives	■ Given task and maintenance functions, match phrases with the function they describe.

Objectives

- Given task and maintenance functions, match phrases with the function they describe.
- Given actions taken by an ID team and phrases describing leadership functions, match the action with the type of leadership it represents.
- Given a dyad, demonstrate listening skills through your verbal behavior.
- Given a listening skill technique, generate phrases to implement that technique.
- Given a small group and a task requiring discussion, demonstrate positive behavior as a team member.
- Given a group discussion, use consensus as a means of reaching agreement.
- Given tasks and dates, develop a Task Schedule.
- Given an ID team and a field setting, develop an instructional system that meets instructional design criteria.
- Given a completed ID project, write an ID project report that includes the ID model used, problem analysis, task and instructional analysis, objectives and tests, instructional strategies, method and media selection, and evaluation strategy.

Overview

The further one progresses in the ID process, the more likely it is that a team approach will be necessary. This is because the designer may involve others as the process moves beyond instructional strategies. The team approach often becomes more important at later stages in the ID process. When a project is large or complex, the team approach is used from the beginning, so that adequate resources and expertise are guaranteed. The advantage of using the team approach from the beginning is that all who participate become more deeply involved.

The team approach is successful when two conditions necessary for effective teamwork are present: skill in management and skill in interpersonal communications. It is essential to have clear delineation of roles to avoid conflict when using the team approach. Basic to the use of the team approach are leadership skills, interpersonal communication skills such as listening and discussion, and reporting skills such as editing and writing. Any team will function better if all members have both complementary expertise and a common base in interpersonal communication skills.

Study Questions

1. Why is the team approach used for ID projects?
2. How can the team approach be used effectively?
3. What are the criteria for an ID project?
4. How can an ID project be documented?

CIRCUMSTANCES FOR USING TEAM APPROACH

The designer may have sole responsibility for instructional design or work as a member of a design or production team. In either case, the designer's skill in relating to others can facilitate or hinder the design process.

Whether instructional design is carried out by one person or by a team will depend on a number of factors.

Size. Instructional design projects are often driven by deadlines. When a project is too big for one person to complete within schedule, the practical solution is to divide the work among two or more people.

Competencies. Some projects require more competencies than one person has. Then the designer must rely on someone else for subject matter expertise, or look "outside" the design department for special media production skills.

Acceptance. Politics or other circumstances make it important to gain acceptance of course content and goals from those who will use the materials. Users may be within the organization where the designer works or in a client's organization. In any case, acceptance of the product requires participation by others.

Summary of Task and Maintenance Functions

Most experts on group theory and skills stress that certain functions have to be filled if the group is to operate effectively. Functions are defined in terms of what actions are necessary for a group to achieve its goals. Task functions, for example, help the group to do the work. Maintenance functions are not directly related to achieving the group's goals; rather, they are directed toward group stability and making sure that individual members are satisfied. Johnson and Johnson (1987) summarized task and maintenance functions as follows:

Task Functions

1. Information and Opinion Giver: Offers facts, opinions, ideas, feelings, and information.
2. Information and Opinion Seeker: Asks for facts, opinions, ideas, feelings, and information.
3. Direction and Role Definer: Calls attention to tasks that need to be done and assigns responsibilities.
4. Summarizer: Pulls together related ideas or suggestions and restates them.
5. Energizer: Encourages group members to work hard to achieve goals.
6. Comprehension Checker: Asks others to summarize discussion to make sure they understand.

Maintenance Functions

7. Encourager of Participation: Lets members know their contributions are valued.
8. Communication Facilitator: Makes sure all group members understand what others say.
9. Tension Reliever: Tells jokes and increases group fun.
10. Process Observer: Uses observations of how the group is working to help discuss how the group can improve.
11. Interpersonal Problem Solver: Helps resolve and mediate conflicts.
12. Supporter and Praiser: Expresses acceptance and liking for group members.

Exercise to Recognize Task and Maintenance Behavior

Directions: Match the following phrases with the task or maintenance function they best fill.

Task Function

1. "Does everyone understand Dan's suggestion for data collection?"

2. "Dan wants to use the Delphi technique for our interviews. I believe Bob's suggestion is an approximation of the approach."

3. "Let me tell you our experience with this approach on another project."

4. "What type of data analysis is best for this approach on another project?"

5. "If we keep plugging away at this, we can finish by noon."

6. "We seem to be selecting the data collection method before we understand the nature of the problem."

7. "If each interview will last an hour, how can we finish all of them in the time allotted?"

Maintenance Functions

8. "Marty, tell us your understanding of the approach we've decided upon."

9. "Joe, what do you think of Dan's recommendation?"

10. "We have several issues to resolve this morning. Perhaps we are spending too much time on the early ones."

11. "There seems to be disagreement between Tom and Jack on how the tasks should be assigned. Let's discuss the viewpoints and resolve them."

12. "This group works well together. Virginia, your comments are always good."

13. "Did you hear the performance standard for God's job? CREATES THE WORLD IN SEVEN DAYS."

ID Activities That Require Team Skills

There are three activities where team skills are especially important.

1. Planning the tasks to be performed when you are a member of a design team. Working cooperatively and constructively with other team members will advance the work toward the agreed-upon goals.

2. Gathering information from content specialists to determine learning requirements. A designer often works with specialists who are experts in their field. The designer elicits information, clarifies ambiguity, and directs the discussion toward gathering precise information from people who are adept at performing their jobs but who may not be adept at describing what they do.

3. Gaining the client's commitment to the approach. Ultimately the instruction will be used by others. The user organization, whether an internal or external group, must be committed to the product if it is to be useful over the long run. Commitment will be easier to gain if the client is informed about the what, how, when, and why of design activities.

When Task and Maintenance Functions Are Most Effective

The effectiveness of task functions or maintenance functions will depend on the "maturity" of the group. Johnson and Johnson (1987), citing Hersey and Blanchard's (1977) theory of situational leadership, define maturity as a group's capacity to set high but attainable goals, willingness to take responsibility, and expertise (education and experience). Maturity is determined only in relation to a specific task to be performed. On one task a member may have high maturity, on another low maturity. The lower the group's maturity, the greater the need for task functions. The higher the group's maturity, the greater the need for maintenance functions. Ultimately, as maturity increases, the group comes to function autonomously. Table 11.1 shows maturity levels with the most effective type of leadership and behavior.

Exercise to Match Leadership Functions With Descriptions of ID Team Actions

Directions: Match the descriptions with one of the following categories:

a. High task/Low maintenance

b. High task/High maintenance

    c. Low task/High maintenance

    d. Low task/Low maintenance

_____ 1. Harry elicits different approaches and discusses pros and cons with group.

_____ 2. Betty assigns interview teams and conducts training on using data collection forms.

_____ 3. Don tells Jim that he will be responsible for working with a qualified SME. He discusses SME candidates with Jim. Then he and Jim talk about how the SME's can help Jim define training needs.

_____ 4. Rita asks someone to take on the data analysis task and listens to proposals for how to approach the problem.

_____ 5. At the ID team's meeting, the group delegates Tom the job of selecting an authoring system for computer-based training.

Interpersonal Communication Skills

The team approach's effectiveness depends on how well team members work together. Sometimes the team approach can take longer and result in a compromise that resolves conflict but pleases no one. When an integration of ideas occurs and new approaches evolve, however, the results will be better.

Interpersonal communication skills and management skills are essential to effective use of the team approach. Although these skills can overlap, as with leadership skills, generally they can be distinguished from one another. Interpersonal skills establish the conditions for successful communication with others. Management skills clarify the tasks and organization to be used.

The success of a task-oriented group depends on the interpersonal skills of its members. Bracey and Sanford (1977) have identified five interpersonal skill areas: self-concept, self-disclosure, clarity of expression, listening, and coping with emotions. Communication may be difficult for someone whose self-concept is poor. If your self-concept is good, you treat yourself with respect and you respond to others with respect; you are more accepting and understanding. Self-disclosure means you are willing to take a risk, to make an investment. Clarity of expression means you are sure of what you want to communicate and how to communicate it, and that you can discern when your explanation (or someone else's) isn't clear. When you practice listening skills, you actively respond to what is being communicated by asking for clarification or paraphrasing. Finally, team members must be able to cope with their emotions by admitting, investigating, and controlling them.

Table 11.1

Maturity Level	Leadership Functions	Behaviors
Low	High task Low maintenance	Define roles and use one-way communication to tell group how, when, and where to do task.
Moderate	High task High maintenance	Define roles, but lead through two-way communication and support to encourage group to accept decisions that have to be made.
Moderately High	Low task High maintenance	Members share decision making since all members have the ability and knowledge to complete task.
High	Low task Low maintenance	Decision making may be delegated to individuals. Considerable autonomy and trust exist among members.

Assertiveness training is helpful in coping with emotions. Language study improves clarity of expression. You'll learn what to disclose and when from experience. You will develop your self-concept and confidence from meeting challenges. Self-disclosure, self-concept, coping with emotions, and clarity of expression are too complex to consider at length in this chapter. Listening skills, however, will be introduced for practice.

Another area of interpersonal communication theory is non-verbal communication. What do your body language, facial expression, and voice tone convey? What can you learn from the nonverbal communication of others in the group?

Listening Skills. Listening skills include the ability to ask questions, perhaps for amplification or clarification, and to paraphrase or summarize. When you use these skills you force yourself to pay attention, to think, to be an active learner. Here is an example of each technique:

Summarize—(Repeat using speaker's words). E.g., You said that the X-Ray Department was understaffed and poorly managed.

Paraphrase—(Restate in own words). E.g., I think you are implying that the department is inefficient.

Clarification—(Ask for confirmation or information). E.g., Are you saying that the X-Ray Department is unlikely to meet the demand?

Amplification—(Request elaboration). E.g., Have you a plan to suggest?

When a group is discussing actions to take, using listening skills and the other interpersonal communication skills can help avoid breakdowns in communication.

An Exercise in Listening Skills

With a partner, conduct a conversation about one or more of these quotations. Decide who will choose the quotation(s) and initiate the conversation. During the conversation each of you should try to use the active listening skills of summarizing, paraphrasing, clarification, and amplification. Continue conversing for ten minutes. If an observer is available, have the observer note the number of times each partner correctly uses each technique.

All truly wise thoughts have been thought already thousands of times; but to make them truly ours, we must think them over again honestly, till they take root in our personal experience.
—Goethe.

If, instead of a gem or even a flower, we could cast the gift of a lovely thought into the heart of a friend, that would be giving as the angels give.
—George MacDonald.

In matters of conscience first thoughts are best; in matters of prudence last thoughts are best.
—Robert Hall.

The sober second thought of people is seldom wrong.
—Martin Van Buren.

The key to every man is his thought. Sturdy and defying though he look, he has a helm which he obeys, which is the idea after which all his facts are classified. He can only be reformed by showing him a new idea which commands his own.
—Ralph Waldo Emerson.

The greatest events of an age are its best thoughts. Thought finds its way into action.
—Christian Bovee.

There are very few original thinkers in the world, or ever have been; the greatest part of those who are called philosophers, have adopted the opinions of some who went before them, and so having chosen their respective guides, they maintain with zeal what they have thus imbibed.
—Dugald Stewart.

We may divide thinkers into those who think for themselves, and those who think through others.—The latter are the rule, and the former the exception.—The first are original thinkers in a double sense, and egotists in the noblest meaning of the word.—It is from them only that the world learns wisdom.—For only in the light which we have kindled in ourselves can we illuminate others.

—Arthur Schopenhauer.

A thought is often original, though you have uttered it a hundred times.—It has come to you over a new route, by a new and express train of association.

—Oliver Wendell Holmes.

(*The New Dictionary of Thoughts*, pp. 668–669)

An Exercise on Encouraging Phrases

Directions: Brainstorm lead-in phrases that could be used as listening skill techniques during a team meeting. For example, "Are you saying . . . ?" or "Is it your contention that . . . ?"

1. Phrases to encourage paraphrasing, e.g., "Is that what you said . . . ?"
2. Phrases to encourage summarizing, e.g., "How would you describe that idea?"
3. Phrases to encourage clarification, e.g., "Would you explain your point about . . . ?"
4. Phrases to encourage amplification, e.g., "Please elaborate on what you mean by . . . ?"

Team Behaviors. Edgar Dale (1967) says that communication is the sharing of information and feelings in a mode of mutuality. There are several barriers to communication, one of which is different knowledge bases or experiences. (Or as Dale puts it, "COIK—Clear Only If Known.") We must work hard at making sure we understand the other person's perspective and how it differs from ours.

A second major barrier to communication is the tendency to be prematurely judgmental. Suspend judgment until an idea is clear and concrete—and even at that point, value judgments will cause some team members to become defensive or to withdraw. A way to avoid this is to assume the devil's advocate role to help the group thinking process proceed.

It is important to be aware of your own behaviors and of how they affect the group. This self-analysis instrument will help you become aware of how constructively you behave as a group member.

A Self-Analysis Exercise on Team Behaviors

Directions: Describe a team or group situation in which intense discussion was held on a proposed course of action. It must be a situation in which you were part of the group. Recall the extent to which you engaged in the behaviors listed in the following self-analysis. Respond to each of the items on a scale of 0 to 3.

Circle the Number that Applies	Not at all	A Little	Some of the Time	All of the Time
1. *Stating a conclusion before a proposal was discussed.*	0	1	2	3
2. *Helping the team keep a pace slow enough to prevent premature conclusion and antagonism but fast enough to keep making progress.*	0	1	2	3
3. *Basing your conclusion on an emotional reaction.*	0	1	2	3

Circle the Number that Applies	Not at all	A Little	Some of the Time	All of the Time
4. *Withholding your conclusion until the leader called for it.*	0	1	2	3
5. *Requiring that the criteria of interest be met by an emotional rather than professional interest.*	0	1	2	3
6. *Contributing substantially to the discussion.*	0	1	2	3
7. *Waiting until consensus had been reached before objecting.*	0	1	2	3
8. *Examining rationally, not emotionally.*	0	1	2	3
9. *Stating that a compromise position was unacceptable without garnering adequate support for your position.*	0	1	2	3
10. *Trying to keep your comments pertinent, not pursuing tangents too far.*	0	1	2	3
11. *Not requesting clarification of meaning when an argument developed.*	0	1	2	3
12. *Helping to offer new options and to keep options open.*	0	1	2	3
13. *Not supporting members whose positions should have been discussed more fully.*	0	1	2	3
14. *Trying to involve other team members.*	0	1	2	3
15. *Not clarifying your position by putting it in writing when requested.*	0	1	2	3
16. *Setting criteria, directions, and goals for the discussion.*	0	1	2	3
17. *Not graciously allowing a matter to be tabled so that progress could be made.*	0	1	2	3
18. *Listening to everyone respectfully.*	0	1	2	3
19. *Not suggesting a consultant be called in to help.*	0	1	2	3
20. *Using the problem-solving, systems approach.*	0	1	2	3
21. *Always speaking first.*	0	1	2	3
22. *Calling for the question when discussion was no longer productive.*	0	1	2	3

Total the number of points for the even-numbered questions.

EVEN TOTAL _____

Total the number of points for the odd-numbered questions.

ODD TOTAL _____

If your "odd" score is higher than your "even" score, you need to work on your discussion skills.

Group Decision Making

In any group work there must be ways to reach agreement. Johnson and Johnson (1987, pp. 104–105) suggest seven ways to reach agreement during group work:

- decision by authority without discussion
- decision by expert member
- decision by average of members' opinions

- decision by authority after discussion
- decision by majority control [vote]
- decision by minority control [committee]
- decision by consensus

Although each method has its advantages and disadvantages, one generally effective method is to reach consensus by discussion until all ideas are accepted, rejected, or revised by the group as a whole. According to Johnson and Johnson, even though the consensus method takes the most time, it often reduces implementation time. When implementation is considered, consensus turns out to be the least time-consuming method.

Consensus is the way the League of Women Voters reaches its positions on national issues. The league holds study meetings in preparation for a meeting where consensus or agreement on a position must be reached and stated. Agreement cannot be reached by majority vote or minority committee, or expert opinion or authority; it must be achieved by action of the group as a whole. It is important that you experience consensus and understand how it works before undertaking the team approach. Although many decisions are of necessity resolved by authority or expert opinion, other decisions need the efforts of all to generate the best solution.

An Exercise in Reaching Consensus

These questions should be answered individually by each group member. Then the group member should summarize his or her position on the issue. Next the group should discuss the answers and reach agreement on an answer to each question. Finally, the group's answers should be used to write a recommendation that represents the thinking of the group as a whole.

One issue in higher education is whether there should be a core curriculum for undergraduates, and if so, what form it should take. Think about this issue as you answer yes or no (agree or disagree) to questions 1 through 8.

Statements	Individual Answer	Group Answer
1. There should be a core curriculum consisting of 15 great books representing western civilization.		
2. There should be no core curriculum.		
3. There should be a core curriculum of electives from required areas such as science, math, etc.		
4. The core curriculum needs only a required reading list representing all cultures, and seminars in which these readings are discussed.		
5. There should be a minimum of 12 required courses in areas essential to the literate individual, such as world culture and language.		
6. A core curriculum should be designed so there is flexibility to adapt to current issues.		
7. The core curriculum should reflect the diversity of our society.		
8. A core curriculum should be interdisciplinary in nature.		

Position Statement on Core Curriculum

Individual Opinion:

Group Consensus:

Figure 11.1   Task Schedule

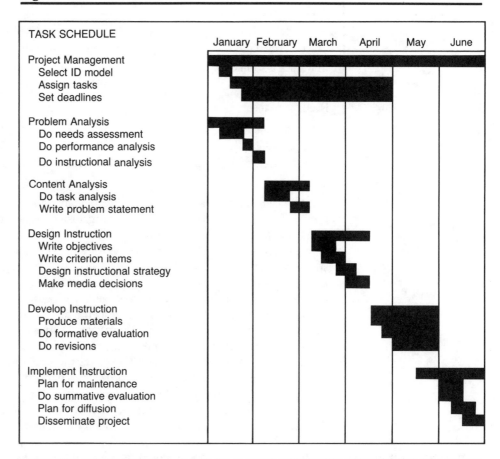

TASK SCHEDULE	January	February	March	April	May	June
Project Management						
Select ID model						
Assign tasks						
Set deadlines						
Problem Analysis						
Do needs assessment						
Do performance analysis						
Do instructional analysis						
Content Analysis						
Do task analysis						
Write problem statement						
Design Instruction						
Write objectives						
Write criterion items						
Design instructional strategy						
Make media decisions						
Develop Instruction						
Produce materials						
Do formative evaluation						
Do revisions						
Implement Instruction						
Plan for maintenance						
Do summative evaluation						
Plan for diffusion						
Disseminate project						

Management Skills

Management skills deal with clarifying tasks, procedures, and schedules. The team approach to instructional design requires clear specification of roles, tasks, objectives, and deadlines. There must be provision for someone to fulfill the leadership role of directing and coordinating communication. The leader is responsible for a plan that lets each group member know what is expected and when, but each group member needs to be familiar with the total plan as well. This plan can be developed through consensus or authority.

The plan should be shared in visual as well as verbal form. The schedule can show which tasks are undertaken at the same time and which tasks are dependent on other tasks being finished first. There are many different ways to show tasks and due dates. You can use flowcharts or PERT (Program Evaluation and Review Technique) diagrams. One way to represent scheduling visually is through a task schedule, as shown in Figure 11.1.

On a task schedule the tasks appear along one side and the dates along the top. Bars are used to show periods of activity. Sometimes the bars are color-coded, or initials or names are used to give further detail.

An Exercise in Developing a Task Schedule

Directions: Use the lists of dates and tasks to make a task schedule. Arrange the tasks in logical order and block out typical time periods for the tasks.

Tasks	Time	
Task Analysis	January	August
Criterion Reference Tests	February	September
Instructional Analysis	March	October
Media Selection	April	November
Needs Assessment	May	December
Implementation	June	January
Evaluation Strategy	July	February

Management is a way of planning, directing, monitoring, and controlling a group effort. How would you proceed if you were organizing the activities of an instructional design team? Members of an instructional design team need to fill several roles in order to be able to complete the ID project. These roles may include leader, designer, evaluation specialist, media specialist, writer, content specialist, producer, programmer, courseware developer, and information systems specialist. Not all these roles are essential; it depends on how the task is defined. In some cases there may be overlap in roles. When the project is small, it is not unusual for one team member to fill several roles. On a larger project, the team may simply subcontract some of these roles. Everyone on a team may decide to serve as a content expert or designer, providing all are qualified.

Time projections are important. They allow the leader to check progress and group members to monitor themselves. Time projections or deadlines remind team members of priorities and limitations. Most importantly, they allow team members or others to critique the phasing plan objectively. The task schedule is a way of graphing time projections so that everyone is aware of dependency relationships among the tasks.

Documenting an ID Project

An ID project may be documented by a record-keeping system, products, or reports. Sometimes a final report is not necessary. Other times it is required, especially with research contracts. Interim reports may also be used. Whatever form documentation takes, it is important to keep all design drafts, evaluation results, and materials in different stages, at least until this information has been summarized or recorded in some form. You need to be competent in writing interim or final reports on a design project.

The final report should explain why the project was done, how it was done, the results of the tryouts, and the recommendations for revision. If summative evaluation is done, that should be reported too. Although the outline for a final report can vary, one good general outline is the following:

1. The ID Process
2. The Problem
   a. Needs Assessment
   b. Performance Analysis
   c. Problem Statement
3. Task and Instructional Analysis
   a. Methods
   b. Results
4. Objectives and Tasks
   a. Objectives
   b. Criterion-referenced Tests
5. Instructional Strategy

6. Method and Media Selection

7. Evaluation Strategy

8. Recommendations for On-going Evaluation

9. Appendices (Documentation)

Under instructional strategy or method and media selection it is helpful to include a flow-chart showing the order of occurrence of activities. Under evaluation strategy it is helpful to refer to instruments used in the text and include them in the appendices. The appendices are often more useful if documentation is grouped by category, such as evaluation instruments.

Criteria for Evaluating an ID Project

Now that you are familiar with the steps in the ID process and with the team approach, you are ready to undertake an ID project in a field setting. Before you proceed, though, you should review the criteria for an ID project. Table 11.2 gives criteria used in evaluating an ID project.

Table 11.2 Criteria for Evaluation of an ID Process

Evaluation Criteria	Yes	No
1. ID Process		
a. Thorough use of ID model	___	___
b. Effective use of team approach	___	___
2. Problem Analysis		
a. Needs assessment supports problem identified	___	___
b. Performance analysis documents instructional nature of problem	___	___
3. Task/Instructional Analysis		
a. Skills, knowledge, attitudes identified	___	___
b. Type of learning identified	___	___
c. Prerequisites identified	___	___
4. Objectives and Tests		
a. Correctly follows chosen format for objectives	___	___
b. Criterion items		
(1) consistent with tasks and objectives	___	___
(2) consistent with item construction rules	___	___
5. Instructional Strategy		
a. Groups on logical basis	___	___
b. Adheres to sequencing guidelines	___	___
c. Principles of learning applied	___	___
6. Method and Media Selection		
a. Based on a selection model	___	___
b. Based on review of resources and strategies	___	___
7. Evaluation Strategy		
a. Includes internal review	___	___
b. Includes tutorial tryout	___	___
c. Includes small-group try-out	___	___
d. Includes operational try-out	___	___
8. Summary of the Process		
a. Adequate documentation	___	___
b. Coherent report on ID process and products	___	___
c. Adequate report of findings	___	___
d. Adequate recommendations for ongoing revision and evaluation	___	___

Comments:

This concludes the theoretical and practical background necessary to begin instructional design. You are on your own. Happy designing.

An Exercise in Developing an Instructional System as Part of a Team

Directions: Make an equal contribution with your team members to the design, development, implementation, and evaluation of an instructional system that meets the criteria set forth in Table 11.2. Establish the conditions for effective teamwork, then start by identifying a need at a field site. Conclude with a report that summarizes the group's work and includes the results of formative evaluation and recommendations for revision. Append to the report all design documentation and sample materials. Finally, use a group contribution form to report the group's management plan and accomplishments to the instructor.

FROM THE READING

Define the following terms.

Task Functions

Maintenance Functions

Interpersonal Communication Skills

Listening Skills

Consensus

Management Skills

Task Schedule

Group Contribution Form

Turn in individually at the last class.

Name _____

Date _____

Group Work Report

Project Description:

Your Contributions:

    Major:

    Minor:

Contribution of Other Group Members:

Name	Contributions
1.	
2.	
3.	
4.	
5.	

ISSUES FOR DISCUSSION

1. Should an instructional design plan have to meet all the evaluation criteria for an instructional design?

2. What would you do if you found you were part of an ID team that did not function effectively?

3. What are the relative merits of interim or final reports on ID projects as compared with no reports?

4. What leadership skills do you think are necessary to fulfill the leadership function on an ID team?

REFERENCES

Bracey, H. J., & Sandford, A. (1977). *Basic management: An experienced-based approach*. Dallas, TX: Business Publications.

Dale, E. (1967). *Can you give the people what they want?* NY: Cowles Education Corporation.

Edwards, T. (1963). *The new dictionary of thoughts*. Standard Book Co.

Hersey, P., & Blanchard, K. (1977). *Management of organizational behavior: Utilizing human resources*. (3rd ed.). Englewood Cliffs, NJ: Prentice-Hall.

Johnson, D. W., & Johnson, F. P. (1987). *Joining together: Group theory and group skills*. Englewood Cliffs, NJ: Prentice-Hall.

Epilogue

There are four components of the Seels and Glasgow ID approach remaining: Implementation and Maintenance, Summative Evaluation, Dissemination and Diffusion, and Project Management. This book isn't long enough to develop competencies in these areas through exercises; indeed, these topics require advanced courses. To help you proceed on your own, however, we will introduce you to a few basic topics and references.

Implementation and Maintenance

The implementation and maintenance requirements of a self-paced course differ from those of a group-paced course, although the categories of concern are similar. Any course or program must have a plan for administration and for staff development before implementation. Administration plans typically include registration, scheduling, record-keeping, personnel assignment, reporting, and material distribution. Staff development plans include instructor training, administrative staff training, and acquisition or allotment of equipment and facilities.

Once implemented, a maintenance plan maintains quality through staff competencies, equipment, and materials. A plan for updating content as changes occur in the field will also maintain quality. A maintenance plan requires on-going evaluation mechanisms, including summative evaluation that will make it possible to identify staff and support needs. This on-going evaluation can be both internal and external. A control group may be involved for summative evaluation, but not necessarily. A good beginning reference on implementation is "Planning for Instructional Systems" by Robert Morgan (1987).

Summative Evaluation

Summative Evaluation is for the consumer. Whereas formative evaluation gathers information that the developer will use in revising the system, summative evaluation gathers information that will help potential users of the system decide whether to adopt it. Summative evaluation yields norms, descriptive reports, and conclusions about effectiveness. It differs from formative in that it must meet higher standards for educational research. You can pursue the topic of summative evaluation by reading Chapter 12 in *The Systematic Design of Instruction* by Walter Dick and Lou Carey.

Dissemination and Diffusion

Dissemination means informing others of your research results. Diffusion means others adopt your ID project. There are few federally funded ID projects that do not have a dissemination component. The research on diffusion of innovations is extensive because it is a communication process that is important to most fields.

Because you have to use networks and different audiences use different networks, when you develop a dissemination plan you need to identify your audience carefully. Another concern is making printed materials readable and interesting.

When you develop a diffusion plan you have to be concerned primarily about what strategies to use. The choice of strategies, however, depends on the stage in adoption and the personalities of the people selected to diffuse the innovation. A diffusion plan must also take into account the channels and gatekeepers, so the process becomes complicated.

Begin diffusion planning by identifying whom you want to communicate with and why. Research suggests you will have more success influencing others if you start with opinion leaders who have an early adopter personality profile. Innovators may be too unlike their audience to be influential. The next step is to select communication strategies for each of the stages in diffusion: knowledge, persuasion, decision, implementation, and confirmation (Rogers, 1983, p. 164). At the initial stage, printed materials or merely talking to someone can be effective, but such measures will be less effective at later stages. To move people to adoption, you need to offer a strategy, such as a site visit, demonstration, or workshop, that involves them in creating an application.

Finally, consider who talks to whom, especially through informal channels, and who controls access and resources; you must have their support for some of the strategies.

If you want to learn more about dissemination and diffusion, try reading *Diffusion of Innovations* by Rogers or "Factors Affecting Utilization" by Ernest Burkman (1987).

Project Management

Project management is a component that affects every step in the ID process. The project manager is a team leader who must supervise and direct a large, complex project involving many resources. The project manager is responsible for scheduling project activities, staffing the project, allocating resources, budgeting, cost-benefit analysis, and maintaining the professional standards of instructional design. The project manager will be responsible for developing a management plan that specifies tasks, activities, events and products. The management plan will include timelines, organizational relationships, resources, budget, and reporting and evaluation due dates. To implement the plan the manager will have to develop a team, facilitate good work practices, and control and monitor project activities. Critical tasks of the project manager will be estimating time and resource requirements and predicting factors that will affect the project and its resources. The manager may also be called on to negotiate with contracting agencies to ensure that objectives are realistic. Baker's "Managing the Development of Comprehensive Instructional Systems" and Brown's "Management Checklists for Instructional Designers" may be helpful for project management. Romiszowski's *Designing Instructional Systems* includes a chapter on "Why Projects Fail."

REFERENCES

Baker, R. L., & Elam, R. J. (1978). Managing the development of comprehensive instructional systems. *National Society for Performance and Instruction Journal, 17,* 6–11.

Brown, J. L. (1978). Management checklists for instructional designers. *National Society for Performance and Instruction Journal, 17,* 3–5.

Burkman, E. (1987). Factors affecting utilization. In R. M. Gagné (Ed.), *Instructional technology: Foundations* (pp. 429–455). Hillsdale, NJ: Lawrence Erlbaum Associates.

Dick, W., & Carey, L. (1985). *The systematic design of instruction.* Glenview, IL: Scott, Foresman.

Gagné, R. M. (Ed.). (1987). *Instructional technology: Foundations.* Hillsdale, NJ: Lawrence Erlbaum Associates.

Morgan, R. M. (1987). Planning for instructional systems. In R. M. Gagné (Ed.), *Instructional technology: Foundations* (pp. 379–396). Hillsdale, NJ: Lawrence Erlbaum Associates.

Rogers, E. M. (1983). *Diffusion of innovations.* NY: Free Press.

Romiszowski, A. J. (1981). *Designing instructional systems.* NY: Nicols Publishing.

Name Index

Subject Index

WE VALUE YOUR OPINION—PLEASE SHARE IT WITH US

Merrill Publishing and our authors are most interested in your reactions to this textbook. Did it serve you well in the course? If it did, what aspects of the text were most helpful? If not, what didn't you like about it? Your comments will help us to write and develop better textbooks. We value your opinions and thank you for your help.

Text Title _____ Edition _____

Author(s) _____

Your Name (optional) _____

Address _____

City _____ State _____ Zip _____

School _____

Course Title _____

Instructor's Name _____

Your Major _____

Your Class Rank _____ Freshman _____ Sophomore _____ Junior _____ Senior

_____ Graduate Student

Were you required to take this course? _____ Required _____ Elective

Length of Course? _____ Quarter _____ Semester

1. Overall, how does this text compare to other texts you've used?

_____ Superior _____ Better Than Most _____ Average _____ Poor

2. Please rate the text in the following areas:

	Superior	Better Than Most	Average	Poor
Author's Writing Style	_____	_____	_____	_____
Readability	_____	_____	_____	_____
Organization	_____	_____	_____	_____
Accuracy	_____	_____	_____	_____
Layout and Design	_____	_____	_____	_____
Illustrations/Photos/Tables	_____	_____	_____	_____
Examples	_____	_____	_____	_____
Problems/Exercises	_____	_____	_____	_____
Topic Selection	_____	_____	_____	_____
Currentness of Coverage	_____	_____	_____	_____
Explanation of Difficult Concepts	_____	_____	_____	_____
Match-up with Course Coverage	_____	_____	_____	_____
Applications to Real Life	_____	_____	_____	_____

3. Circle those chapters you especially liked:
   1   2   3   4   5   6   7   8   9   10   11   12   13   14   15   16   17   18   19   20
   What was your favorite chapter? _____
   Comments:

4. Circle those chapters you liked least:
   1   2   3   4   5   6   7   8   9   10   11   12   13   14   15   16   17   18   19   20
   What was your least favorite chapter? _____
   Comments:

5. List any chapters your instructor did not assign. _____

6. What topics did your instructor discuss that were not covered in the text?_____

   _____

7. Were you required to buy this book? _____ Yes _____ No

   Did you buy this book new or used? _____ New _____ Used

   If used, how much did you pay? _____

   Do you plan to keep or sell this book? _____ Keep _____ Sell

   If you plan to sell the book, how much do you expect to receive? _____

   Should the instructor continue to assign this book? _____ Yes _____ No

8. Please list any other learning materials you purchased to help you in this course (e.g., study guide, lab manual).

   _____

9. What did you like most about this text? _____

   _____

10. What did you like least about this text? _____

    _____

11. General comments:

    May we quote you in our advertising? _____ Yes _____ No

    Please mail to: Boyd Lane
                      College Division Research Department
                      P. O. Box 508
                      Columbus, Ohio 43216-0508

    Thank you!